OLD LONDON BRIDGE

Also by Patricia Pierce

Canada: The Missing Years, The Lost Images of our
Heritage 1895–1924

London's Royal Parks

The Beauty of Canada

Great Cities of America

Old London Bridge

The Story of the Longest Inhabited Bridge in Europe

Patricia Pierce

HEADLINE

Copyright © 2001 by Patricia Pierce

The right of Patricia Pierce to be identified as the Author of
the Work has been asserted by her in accordance with the
Copyright, Designs and Patents Act 1988.

First published in 2001
by HEADLINE BOOK PUBLISHING

10 9 8 7 6 5 4 3 2 1

Every effort has been made to fulfil requirements with regard
to producing copyright material. The author and publisher
will be glad to rectify any omissions at the earliest opportunity.

British Library Cataloguing in Publication Data
Pierce, Patricia
Old London bridge
1. London (England) – Social life and customs
2. London Bridge (London, England) – History
I. Title
942.1'2

ISBN 0 7472 3484 1

Typeset by Palimpsest Book Production Limited,
Polmont, Stirlingshire
Printed and bound in Great Britain by
Mackays of Chatham plc, Chatham, Kent

HEADLINE BOOK PUBLISHING
A division of Hodder Headline
338 Euston Road
London NW1 3BH

www.headline.co.uk
www.hodderheadline.com

Contents

To Gordon Home (1878–1969) author, artist and illustrator.

If a person can love a structure, Gordon Home loved Old London Bridge, the idea of it and the fabric of it. He was there in 1921, after the second land arch from the City end was unexpectedly uncovered during construction work. Efforts by himself and others failed to save the narrow gothic arch built by Peter de Colechurch 700 years earlier. He wrote: 'The unique chance given by Time was thus ignored and *an historical monument of first-class importance was swept away as though it possessed no more interest than a disused railway arch.*'

List of illustrations

Endpapers: The Seven Stages of Old London Bridge. From a set of drawings by Gordon Home, from his book *Old London Bridge*, the Bodley Head, London, 1930, as are the line drawings credited to him below. Used by permission of his son, Gospatric Home.

What came before: *Page 14* Roman London *c.* AD 200, showing the two hills, the Walbrook Stream, the Fleet River and the main Roman features (Museum of London Archaeology Service); *Page 31* A water joust on the Thames based on a manuscript drawing (Sir John Soane's Museum/Guildhall)

Chapter One: *Page 33* Detail of Claes Jansz Visscher's *Long Prospect of London*, from the south-west, 1616. Before the fire of 1633, both medieval and Tudor houses can be seen over the length of the Bridge (Guildhall); *Page 35* Drawing by Antony van den Wyngaerde, from the south-east, part of a large view of London, *c.* 1550. This is the earliest known drawing showing the whole length of the Bridge (Ashmolean Museum); *Page 38* Two views of a Bridge pier drawn by William Knight, the resident engineer at London Bridge Works when Old London Bridge was being deconstructed (Sir John Soane's Museum/Guildhall); *Page 55* The Southwark approach to Old London Bridge. For centuries Southwark market was held in Long Southwark, now Borough High Street, leading to the Bridge and the City (Sir John Soane's Museum/Guildhall)

Chapter Two: *Page 69* An example of the elaborate initial letters found in the Register of Deeds, Bridge House Estates (Corporation of London, Guildhall); *Page 71* The Bridge in cross section as it probably was from the later Middle Ages until the mid-seventeenth century, drawn to scale by Gordon Home (British Library); *Page 77* Engravings depict jousting figures from Joseph Strutt's *The Sports and Pastimes of England*, 1831.

Chapter Three: *Page 97* The Chapel of St Thomas à Becket on the Bridge, built 1384–96, drawn by Gordon Home based on the illustration in the Duke of Orlean's MS and Van den Wyngaerde's drawing (British Library); *Page 98* Interior view of the upper chapel (Guildhall)

Chapter Four: *Page 133* The Chapel after its conversion to a house and shop from an engraving in the *Gentleman's Magazine*, 1753 (Sir John Soane's Museum/Guildhall); *Page 139* The exact position of the cage and stocks on the Bridge is unknown, but they were probably just inside the Great Stone Gate. Based on an engraving in Reverend John Fox's *New and Complete Book of Martyrs*, revised by Paul Wright (Sir John Soane's Museum/Guildhall)

Chapter Five: *Page 159* Nonesuch House from the most impressive south-west, or Southwark, side (The Mansell Collection); *Page 160* Nonesuch House from the much narrower west or upstream side (The Mansell Collection)

Chapter Six: *Page 175* James I in procession on the Thames (Guildhall); *Page 186* This detail from Wenceslaus Hollar's *Panorama of London*, published in 1647, shows the City, river and Bridge after the 1633 fire and before the 1666 fire. The palisaded gap at the north, or City, end of the Bridge marks where buildings were consumed in the 1633 fire; this gap created an essential fire break in the 1666 fire (Guildhall); *Page 201* Peter Morris's Waterworks at the north, or City, end of the Bridge (Mary Evans Picture Library)

Chapter Seven: *Page 213* The extraordinarily detailed trade card of Christopher Stedman, a mathematical instrument maker on the Bridge. It bears his shop sign (British Museum); *Page 217* The engraved trade card of Walter Watkins, a breeches maker, leather seller and glover, whose shop was at the bridgefoot at the Southwark end, conveniently near the slaughterhouses (British Museum); *Page 224* This souvenir of the frost fair on the Thames in January 1716 was 'Printed on the Ice' by an enterprising printer who had set up his press on the frozen river (Guildhall)

Chapter Eight: *Page 236* Detail of William Hogarth's *The Death of the Countess*, plate VI in his *Mariage à la mode* series (1743–5), showing a glimpse of the leaning houses on the Bridge when the old structure was in a period of decrepitude (National Gallery); *Page 238* The Great Stone Gate at the Southwark end, rebuilt in 1727–8, was the last gateway to remain on the Bridge. When it was demolished in 1760 the coat of arms was preserved on the front of a tavern in Southwark, where it remains (Guildhall); *Page 254* The burning of the temporary wooden bridge, 11 April 1758. Based on an engraving in *Chamberlain's History of London* (Sir John Soane's Museum/Guildhall)

Chapter Nine: *Page 262* The northern arches of the Bridge in its seventh and final stage, and the Church of St Magnus the Martyr. From a drawing by Edward W. Cooke, 1831 (Guildhall); *Page 263* One of the stone alcoves, erected 1758–62, drawn by Gordon Home from one removed to the courtyard of Guy's Hospital, not far from where Old London Bridge once stood (British Library); *Page 277* Two boys and a dog are rescued at the Bridge during the frost of 1814 after their boat has been wrecked on a pier. Drawn and etched by J.T. Smith (Guildhall)

What came after: *Page 288* A plan showing the relation of Old London Bridge to Rennie's bridge, drawn by Gordon Home (British Library); *Page 290* A view from the south-west of the demolition in progress, January 1832. Rennie's bridge can be seen in use next to it. Drawn and engraved by Edward W. Cooke (Guildhall)

Introduction

There never was another bridge like it. Old London Bridge summed up all the symbolism of a structure built over the physical and psychological barrier of water. Defensive, ceremonial, religious and a place of romance, it bridged the boundary of a north–south divide and linked moral and immoral London. This gateway to London Town, in its powerful setting over the 'liquid history' of the Thames, made it a prime commercial site, and it was habitable. At times a place of splendour, at other times of decrepitude, the Bridge pulsated with life, from the imploring cries of traders, the watermen's shouts and the hoofbeats of jousting knights' horses to the 'frequent shrieks of drowning wretches'. It magnified everyday life, national ceremony and turmoil. Until 1750 this was the only bridge in London over the River Thames, and from its completion in 1209 it was famed throughout Europe.

The idea of Old London Bridge took hold of me early on. I remember singing the nursery rhyme with my mother sitting on the chunky green-upholstered 1950s rocking chair, my older brother on one broad chair-arm, me on the other and baby brother on her lap. And on a rainy Canadian Saturday, with my brothers I sometimes built a 'bridge' of sturdy kitchen chairs to climb over. When it, of course, 'fell' and we had driven our mother to distraction, she might dive for the yardstick which hung beside the back door. Our usual exit blocked, we ran upstairs, scrambled down the cat-slide roof and went next door to our Culp grandparents' veranda-ed Victorian farmhouse. Grandpa Joe Ed was a local historian. One bedroom, with a bookcase to the ceiling and an old desk, he called 'the library', and from his own bedroom stairs led to the attic. In this cosy place, rain striking the roof, we would look through his boxes of books, dozens of scrapbooks full of clippings of facts, pictures and stories, and the forty or so Pennsylvania-Dutch family trees he had compiled from scratch. Somewhere among his belongings I saw a picture of a toylike hotchpotch of little houses on a bridge.

It was impossible to put aside the memory of the 'town on a bridge' so thrillingly sited above fast-flowing, dangerous water. Years later I began to search for references to its compelling history. I always first looked in a book's index to see if Old London Bridge was mentioned. Surprisingly often it was. And I knew there could only be disappointment when, in 1973, I first saw today's London Bridge. The bridge of three spans appeared to be eminently functional – with not the slightest nod to history or to romance. The 1973 bridge of pre-stressed concrete with low parapets of polished granite is topped by foot-wide stainless-steel handrails enclosing generous ten-foot-wide walkways, and space on six lanes for 40,000 cars a day.

From the east side of today's bridge I can see the green of the riverside garden of the Church of St Magnus the Martyr, only 100 feet away on the City (north) side of the Thames, beyond the regrettable obstruction of the neo-Egyptian Adelaide House, the tallest office building in London when it was built in 1926. Virtually part of Old London Bridge, churches on this site have been a sanctuary of peace and prayer for almost a thousand years, usually surviving the fires and battles that assailed the Bridge.

From another angle, standing beside the Monument to the Great Fire of London in Fish Street Hill – the road that led on to the Bridge in the City – and looking towards the river and the church with its great clock projecting out over what had been the bridge street, one can see how improbably narrow the road on the Bridge really was: only twelve feet across. Sitting within the church's opulent interior I puzzle: did Wren's post-Fire walls of Portland stone prevent the travellers' shouts and drovers' curses from being heard within? Were there fruit- and flower-sellers in the lobby where the shelves for the 'poor loaves' remain today? Did shawled women huddle laughing quietly and gossiping at the back, stepping over each other's purchases on the rush-strewn floor: a songbird on a string, vegetables from the country, a fresh loaf, a fish for dinner? At the least, it must have been a cool and comparatively calm place to rest from the turbulence only feet away, for the very footway on to the bridge street passed through the church's stately portico.

Begun in 1176 in the reign of Henry II, the first Plantagenet king of England, the Bridge was finished thirty-three years later in the reign of King John of Magna Carta fame. The constricting bulk of its weir-like structure often dictated events. It was massively defensive in its stone construction, in the formidable gateways built upon it, and because it physically prevented ships, including those of invaders, from passing upriver. This was the site of the Roman bridge or bridges (built of wood between about AD 80 and 300), which meant that the Roman wharves, customs and trade, and later Billingsgate fish market and the Custom House, were concentrated immediately downstream in what would become known as the Pool of London; the Bridge had a drawbridge, and until about 1450 the main landing place was above the Bridge at the Saxon port of Queenhithe.

The Bridge's very bulk inflicted immense and never-ending strains upon itself: no other bridge has been known to survive such forces of water and ice. During severe winters jolly frost fairs were held on the frozen river, and when the floes broke up, the ice trapped above the Bridge tore at it, sometimes pulling down an arch or two. And at all times it suddenly compressed the incessant tides into about one-third of the river's width. The nineteen massive boat-shaped piers required constant repair, and so grew in size, making the Bridge a kind of weir that restricted the narrow waterways and increased the turbulence of the fast-running tides as the years – and the centuries – passed.

'Shooting the bridge' was an irresistible challenge to the often fatally reckless, when at ebb tide the drop of the rapids could be as much as six feet. Occasionally, even the ceremonial water procession of an ambassador 'shott the bridge', presumably at 'still water' – even then a feat considered worth recording. Thousands died at this place, among them those whose boats were inadvertently caught in the currents, or reckless thrill-seekers pursuing the lure of the furious water.

Why was Old London Bridge famed throughout Europe? There were other habitable bridges (thirty-five in France alone) – remarkable bridges of complex history and timeless beauty, such as the Ponte Vecchio in Florence, 1345 (three arches, three floors), the Ponte di Rialto in Venice, 1588 (one arch, one floor), the Pont au Change in Paris, 1639 (five arches, six floors the entire length of the bridge), the Old Tyne Bridge in Newcastle (ten arches, three to four floors) or the Pulteney Bridge in Bath, 1770 (three arches, two floors). But none could compare with Old London Bridge of 1209 (twenty arches, three to six floors).

It was without rival for several reasons. There was its great length: 905 feet 10 inches, making it the longest inhabited bridge ever built in Europe, taking thirty-three years to construct and at an early date. Yet another was the exceptional length of time it was in use: 622 years.

Then there was the charming assemblage of its superstructure. Homes were sited above functional shops, as many as 138 shops at one time. A variety of striking and sumptuous features came, and went: two menacing gateways, as well as several other gateways; the Drawbridge; almost mid-stream the slender Gothic two-storeyed Chapel of St Thomas à Becket; colourful, spectacular Nonesuch House; and the unnamed gateway 'house with many windows'. The Bridge provided anchorage for waterwheels and corn mills making use of the force of the water; and it was also convenient for warehouses. An abundance of commercial activity, such as that of the man who invented the cork life-jacket, was attracted to and around the Bridge. Multi-functional and multi-layered, the Bridge was an organic thing, the structures on it evolving in response to the people, the times, the disasters, and so it adapted and changed over the centuries. But it always remained a focal point for commerce and, ultimately, control.

Only adding to its fame were the traitors' heads set upon a gateway at the Southwark end of the Bridge, where, to those arriving in London, the authority of the City began. This hideous sight, at once totally repellent and totally mesmerizing, was never forgotten either by the citizens or by foreigners approaching London; visitors recorded seeing as many as thirty-four heads at one time – there may have been more – and these highly visible and gruesome warnings were usually included in depictions of the Bridge. This unusual role required of the Bridge provided work for a Keeper of the Heads, who placed each new arrival impaled on its long wooden pole among the rotting heads, quarters and skulls already there. To make more space, what was food for seagulls became food for fishes: he simply tossed superfluous heads into the river below.

The Bridge survived attacks by nature and by people because for centuries it had its own administrative organisation, the Bridge House, to protect and care for it. Two Bridge Masters or Bridge Wardens led a permanent but varying work force of a Master Carpenter, a Tide Carpenter, who managed the tidemen who were paid by the tide, stone masons, cart-men, clerks, gate-keepers, rent and toll collectors, 'a cook and a boy', among others. They were based at the Bridge House on the river close by the Bridge in Southwark, with wharves and a yard that also served as a storage depot for quantities of stone and other repair materials. The Bridge was vigilantly examined on a daily basis, particular attention being paid to the piers. So essential was the Bridge to the City that workers at the Bridge House were exempt from impressment into the navy. And if funds for repairs to their Bridge were withheld, as they were for a considerable time by Queen Eleanor in the mid-thirteenth century, the ordinary people – the commons – reacted with fury.

Extraordinarily, Old London Bridge left a vital and ongoing legacy to London, for the Bridge accumulated its own inheritance, which remains to this day. The little-known Bridge House Estates is a registered charity, the Trustee of which is the Corporation of London. The Corporation is the local authority for the 'Square Mile', which it governs through the Court of Common Council. This governing body is older than Parliament. The charity can trace its origins back to 1097, for from the earliest times bequests, sums both minute and immense – from a widow's gold wedding ring, worn thin, to numerous valuable revenue-producing properties – were given 'to God and the Bridge'. A significant amount built up, to be managed by the Bridge House, where careful accounts were kept, and the books balanced each year.

These funds, increased by the numerous tolls and rents, have been skilfully administered over hundreds of years by the Trustee. Today, the Bridge House Fund has ever-growing assets, including a portfolio of commercial property, of more than £500 million. Monies from the Fund were used to build some of, and still entirely maintain and manage, the four bridges that cross the Thames into the City: London, Tower, Southwark and Blackfriars, this work being the prime objective of the Fund. There is more: millions of pounds in surplus funds are given to charities each year. The *Trustee's Annual Report* outlines gifts of more than £50 million between 1995 and 2000, focusing on five areas of importance to those living in Greater London: transport and access for older and disabled persons, the largest programme; environmental conservation; programmes for children and young people; the provision of technical assistance to voluntary organisations; and assistance enabling older people to remain within the community.

Occasionally, the Trustee makes an exceptional grant: £4.5 million was given to the London Millennium Bridge Trust to assist in the construction of the footbridge sited upstream from today's London Bridge. The sleek blade visually links the dome of Wren's St Paul's Cathedral on the north bank to the South Bank's Tate Modern, a gallery of modern art within a behemoth of a former power station. This first new bridge over the Thames in central London for over a century opens up views of city and river, while helping to regenerate Southwark.

Is it not remarkable that a bridge demolished 170 years ago can claim this tangible and positive influence on the lives of millions of ordinary people?

To us, the work of the medieval builders had a pleasing lack of symmetry, later making the Bridge a magnet for artists, such as Canaletto and Turner. Holbein and Hogarth reputedly lived on the Bridge itself, as did marine artist Peter Monamy. From all these images Gordon Home, illustrator and author in the 1920–30s, selected the most reliable and drew the sequential development of the Bridge in seven stages (see endpapers), stages that I have chosen as the inspiration for the chapters in this book. For the earliest years he used written descriptions by Stow, then illustrations by Van den Wyngaerde, Agas, Visscher, Norden, Hollar, Charles Labelye and others, but most essentially those by George Dance the Younger, the first person to accurately measure the elevations of the Bridge, as late as 1799.

The image of Old London Bridge is lodged in the consciousness of the English-speaking world, largely through the nursery rhyme 'London Bridge is Falling Down'. It never fell. But the time comes for every thing to have a rest, and for the Bridge it was an unusually clean-cut historical ending. Having been in exceptionally demanding use for more than six hundred years the Bridge began to be deconstructed in 1831, after its replacement (Rennie's bridge) had been built alongside it. Londoners lined the east side of the new construction each day to watch the death throes of the Bridge that had been there for a biblical twenty generations. Simon Schama, in *Landscape and Memory*, notes that Turner, the master of watercolour, 'to whom the Thames was truly home', and who painted the Thames and Old London Bridge many times, always striving to embellish their ancient myths, was '. . . not drawn to paint the *new* London Bridge'.

As well as the Church of St Magnus the Martyr in the City, some relics of the Bridge survive. In Southwark, the admirably carved stone royal arms of George II (later altered to George III), which once had pride of place over the entrance to the Great Stone Gateway at the Southwark end, is now hidden away not far from where the Bridge once stood, in narrow Newcomen Street, on the front of the King's Arms. This very South London pub is in an area of Southwark where traces of a much earlier London can still be sensed.

And Old London Bridge lives on in affectionate folk memory and, as long as children recite nursery rhymes, in the reality that is a child's imagination.

On Millennium Eve a thousand years ago a London bridge of wood was no doubt one of the sites where people anxiously sought clues to the future in the phase of the moon and the tides at the bridge. On 31 December 1999 the Thames and London Bridge took their centuries-old place at the centre of national celebration. As the twelfth chime of Big Ben resonated along the river, the fizzing anticipation became a continuous roar, a Concorde fly-past unheard, and fireworks erupted from Tower Bridge to London Bridge, and beyond. Fire once again flashed across the clear oval clerestory windows of St Magnus the Martyr, and in the rich interior of this great church splinters of noise and light and colour ricocheted off the 'inexplicable splendour of Ionian white and gold. . .'*

---

*T.S. Eliot, *The Waste Land*.

What came before

... Roman London was ideally situated as an administrative centre, lying at the junction of several tribal boundaries on a navigable waterway crossed by a bridge from which roads radiated out to the capitals of the [tribes] to the south ... the west and ... the north and east. The importance of the bridge to this network cannot be stressed too highly.

Gustav Milne, 1985

Buttercups and marsh marigolds once bloomed on the spot the Romans would choose as their site for a bridge over the Thames, a place that would gather around it a great city. Just where the north abutment of Old London Bridge was to stand, in a slight depression a few yards wide, willows shaded the wildflowers dotted among sedges and grasses.

It was geography and geology that determined the site of London and its Bridge. The Thames drains a large part of southern-eastern England, and the Thames estuary lies almost directly across the North Sea from the mouth of western Europe's mighty Rhine, still the lifeblood of the Continent. England's greatest waterway enabled native peoples to trade with each other and with the mainland of Europe, and it was an irresistible pathway inland for would-be invaders seeking the hinterland of the island.

Entering the Thames estuary, a small trading vessel moving upstream used the incoming tide to overcome the prevailing westerlies and the flow of the strong river currents seeking the sea. The river cut through the expansive alluvial plain of the Thames basin, in places two to three miles wide, in alternate straight stretches and large loops. The underlying clay hindered drainage, thus the land on each side of the river comprised extensive tidal mud flats and marshes. There were islands in the river and mud banks on which boats might easily become stuck at low tide. From both north and south shores, numerous streams and tributaries flowed into a river that was much shallower than today. At high tide the water rushing upstream was not contained by the ill-defined, shifting banks, but spent itself over the low-lying marshes etched with muddy rivulets and channels that were dangerous to the unwary. In the hazy distance on each side, early traders eventually saw the defining ridges of the basin.

There were few distinguishing features on either shore for the first thirty miles inland from the North Sea, until they saw today's Shooter's Hill at Greenwich on the south shore. Ten miles further along was the first obvious high ground on the north side: two squat gravel hills each about forty feet high. A wide stream ran down between these hills, and a substantial river flowed to the Thames beyond the furthest one. This would one day be the future site of London.

Opposite, on the marshy Southwark side of the thousand-foot-wide river — three to five times the width of today — the clay was overlaid by hard gravel and sand, which made a good, firm surface for beaching boats.

In the thousands of years before the Romans invaded in 54 BC, countless generations of Bronze Age and Iron Age people, broadly described as Celtic, lived in small family groups that were scattered along and near the river where they could fish and trade. But there was no pre-Roman settlement at London. Trade with the Celts across the water in Gaul had existed for thousands of years. One main route was from Brittany and Lower Normandy to the port at Hengistbury Head in east Dorset, and another was from the continental lands further north between the Seine and the Rhine to southern and eastern England. Proof of their cross-Channel trading is seen in their gifts to the river: a ceremonial jadeite axe head (dated to about 3900–2500 BC) from the western Alps, found at Mortlake, and stone axes from Germany. Other artefacts discovered in the Thames include a marvellous 'horned' bronze helmet near Waterloo

Bridge; the only known all-metal Celtic shield, dating from 400–250 BC, at Battersea; and a large number of bronze swords, many unused and probably intended as votive offerings to a powerful river that was also the principal trading route.

The head of the Thames estuary was the most logical spot for crossing the river, as well as for trade and for defence. This point was dramatically, and unexpectedly, illustrated by the discovery in 1999 of the remnants of a massive oak bridge built 3,500 years ago. During a Thames Archaeological Survey the remains of this Celtic bridge were discovered on the south foreshore of the Thames at Vauxhall, near where the River Effra entered the Thames. This bridge dates from the Bronze Age, a time of intensive trading, and it too left traces of the trade with the Continent, for a number of important artefacts, including a bronze dagger and two bronze spearheads, were found alongside the wooden piles. The wood of the paired oak posts, carbon-dated to 1500 BC, supported a platform fifteen feet wide – enough for two carts to pass, and a substantial confirmation of the organizational skills of the local people. The Celtic bridge was about two miles upstream from the Roman bridge, and had been constructed a millennium and a half before the bridge of the Romans. The latter until 1999 was believed to have been the first bridge over the Thames at London.

Caesar led the Roman invasion in 54 BC, landing on the south coast of England near Deal, with five legions and 2,000 cavalry. Meeting fierce resistance from a local Celtic tribe, the Catuvellauni, whose chief was Cassivellaunus, Caesar crossed the Thames about eighty miles from the east Kent coast, in the region of what is now London. *Caesar's Gallic War* records that the river 'can be forded only in one place and that with difficulty'. The Catuvellauni controlled the area north of the Thames and west of the River Lea (a large river that flows into the Thames about three miles downstream from the Tower of London on the north shore of a big loop in the river). Ignoring the threats, Caesar sent first the cavalry then the infantry into the water, and the tribesmen fled.

He recorded only one 'town' – possibly Wheathampstead in Hertfordshire – that was more like a central rallying-point with a high rampart and ditch within which cattle and men gathered when under threat, and which he captured. There is no mention of any settlement around what is now London.

But in the London area, it is possible that Caesar left behind at least a temporary floating pontoon bridge over the Thames, for the Roman military were unrivalled experts at technical warfare, and this included bridge-building. A year earlier, in 55 BC, at the end of Caesar's successful punitive German campaign, he initiated a still-remembered act that would symbolize Roman strength and ability to the tribes on the opposite side of the Rhine, which was the limit of the Romans' northern frontier. The General ordered his troops to build a bridge to take his army across – at a spot where the Rhine is deeper and wider than the Thames at London. Within ten days a pile bridge over the Rhine was constructed, and the army across it.

After Caesar's invasion, trade between Britain and the empire – particularly the Roman armies along the Rhine – greatly increased, so much so that the British were now obliged to pay the Romans duties on both imports and exports, as noted by the Greek geographer Strabo. In came luxuries from olive oil to ivory. Out went both goods and people, for slaves were a valuable commodity. Even over two thousand years ago, wool was important. British wool helped clothe the legions along the Rhine, and British grain helped feed them. Hides and cattle were also exported, as were the prized oysters, hunting dogs, leather, and minerals such as lead, silver and gold. With this increase in trade, the coastal harbours of Britain were eclipsed by those of the Thames estuary.

The Claudian invasion of Britain, in AD 43, almost a hundred years after Caesar's, was described by the historian Dio Cassius. Aulus Plautius, the commander of the Roman army, advanced from the Chichester–Portsmouth area, his 40,000 troops following the retreating local tribesmen. They came to a waterway, probably the Medway, across which some units swam in full armour – a feat for which they were specially trained – and so gained an advantage. They then reached the Thames '. . . at a point where it empties into the ocean and at flood-tide forms a lake'. The anti-Roman tribesmen crossed easily, because they could find firm ground and easy passages, but the Romans encountered difficulties. Some of the troops swam across, while others used a bridge a little way upstream. The site of this first written reference to a bridge in the London area is not known. It may have been a floating pontoon bridge the Romans built themselves, or an earlier timber bridge constructed by the Celts.

Plautius and his troops now paused to wait for Emperor Claudius to come from Rome, and probably spent the time consolidating their position, most likely at the ancient non-tidal Westminster–Lambeth ford. Claudius had acceded to the throne following the murder of his unstable nephew Caligula, and needed the prestige of a military victory to establish his authority with his own army. He duly arrived for his sixteen-day stay in a manner befitting an emperor: with war elephants to terrify the barbarians living at the edge of the civilized world. And on his return to Rome he erected a triumphal arch in AD 51 to commemorate the submission of no less than eleven kings in his conquest of Britain.

It was the Romans who founded London. Coming up the Thames in the flat landscape, they must have been relieved when they spotted the two squat gravel hills, today's Cornhill and Ludgate Hill. They would have appreciated the defensive benefits of this combination of the river-road, the hills and the fresh water flowing close by in the Walbrook stream (in places a hundred yards wide and just to the west of the 'bridge' spot) running down between the hills and the substantial Fleet River beyond the second hill. Would we recognize the place? Probably not.

Why is the Roman settlement important in the story of Old London Bridge? The site that they selected with great care – the only time they did so where no settlement had previously existed – established the location of Old London Bridge and of today's London Bridge.

By about AD 50 Londinium had been established, initially as a supply depot and staging post for the Roman troops as they penetrated the island. It usefully had access to the sea, but this also meant it could be invaded, so it grew around its defensive position

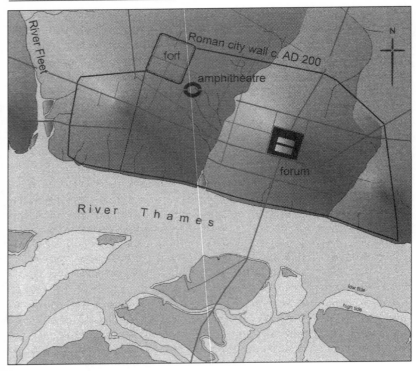

Roman London *c.* AD 200, showing the hills and waterways.

on the two hills on the north side, which would eventually have a fort and be walled.

For the first ten years the southern branch of Roman Watling Street (leading to Londinium from the Roman Channel port of Richborough in Kent) and the northern branch (leading from Londinium to Verulamium/St Albans) converged on the Westminster–Lambeth ford, on the north side of the river located between the two branches of the Tyburn stream. Most significantly, ten years later changes in the layout of the roads then aimed for a different spot – a place about twenty yards downstream from the present London Bridge – to what must have been a bridgehead near where the main road from the south coast and the Continent (today's Borough High Street) met the Thames, at the head of the estuary.

Why was this new river crossing point created in AD 60? Francis Sheppard, in *London, A History*, notes several reasons. The further downstream the crossing was located, the shorter would be the overland journey for the military going north-east of Londinium to Camulodunum (Colchester), at that time the Roman capital. Also, the bridge spot was usefully tidal, unlike Westminster, and this was of benefit to sailing vessels, which could move upstream to the wharves on an incoming tide against both the flow of the river and the prevailing west wind. Additionally, the land opposite Westminster was very marshy, whereas the terrain in Southwark was slightly more favourable, because small areas of firmer soil indicated the way across the river to the twin hills opposite, and there was a spit of gravel to support the end of a bridge on each bank. Finally, it was sensible to be near the defensive position of the two hills where the nucleus of the settlement stood, with the fresh water of the Fleet and the Walbrook nearby. And the river – even though it was a thousand feet wide at Londinium – was just slightly narrower at this very spot than elsewhere in the immediate vicinity.

All of this careful planning helped to make Londinium the most important trading centre in the British Isles. It was first mentioned ten years after its founding, by Tacitus, who described it as 'a place filled with traders and a celebrated centre of commerce'.

At this flourishing time there was a shattering catastrophe for the inhabitants of Camulodunum (Colchester), Verulamium (St Albans) and ascendant Londinium. Boudicca, Queen of the East Anglian Iceni, was enraged by the Romans' harsh and cruel treatment of her tribe after the death of her husband, the King. When she protested, she was flogged and her daughters raped. She led her followers and others in a massive revolt. Thousands died, for the inhabitants who did not flee were 'butchered' according to Tacitus. There were no survivors. All three settlements were burned to the ground. North of today's London Bridge, about thirteen feet below street level, is a bright red layer of soil, roughly eighteen inches thick, from the iron in the clay oxidized two thousand years ago by the intense heat as Londinium burned. Southwark too was sacked, and if a timber bridge existed, it is impossible to believe that a structure so closely identified with the Romans would have been spared in what was an overwhelming onslaught.

However, a positive decision to rebuild devastated Londinium was made about AD 80, with all the features of a principal Roman city: a forum and a basilica – indicating that it was self-governing – on the eastern hill where the law courts, civic administration and market were located; an amphitheatre on the western hill for spectacles, animal hunts and gladiatorial combat; near the amphitheatre a fort for the garrison that guarded the governor, and which was unusually made into a permanent structure by the time of Hadrian's visit; public bath houses for relaxation and social life; temples for the worship of a variety of deities; a governor's palace on the south side of today's Cannon Street laid out in terraces down to the Thames – and a bridge.

The existence of a Roman bridge is now accepted, and supported by archaeological evidence. Although the presence of such a bridge was questioned by experts for many years, the evidence began to mount in 1832 when Old London Bridge was being deconstructed. After the piers were removed, the bed of the river was dredged to deepen the channel, and Roman timbers and oak piles were revealed. And in the riverbed an extraordinary range of coins were found, following along near the line of Old London Bridge from the Church of St Magnus on the north side to what is now Hay's Wharf on the south. There were many thousands of Roman coins and medallions from the consular period and Pompey (106–48 BC) to Honorius (AD 384–423), the western Roman emperor. Antiquarian Charles Roach Smith, whose collection is now in the British Museum, was there to record the items as they came up. He noted that the gravel and silt contained these coins to a considerable depth, from which they were frequently dredged up in chronological series, as if they had been deposited at intervals.

The evidence was also noted by another antiquarian, H. Syer Cuming. The coins were 'slightly to the east of the site of Peter of Colechurch's erection', along the line of which 'there have been traced the remains of stout oaken piles with iron shoes, and huge conglomerates composed of ferruginous matter; the numerous

Roman coins [are] chiefly first and second brass of the higher empire'. He added that 'the presence of the iron shoes of piling' were a strong indication of the Roman bridge here; the iron was of 'the hard, tough, solid metal in the production of which the Roman *ferraria* stood pre-eminent'.

Work by the Department of Urban Archaeology and the later Museum of London Archaeology Service (MoLAS) has revealed a number of important Roman structures and artefacts round about the bridge area. Their ongoing investigations have shown that the Roman bridge was built, almost certainly by the military, from tall, straight-grained 200- to 300-year-old British oaks; the baulks were from thirteen to thirty feet in length. It was probably constructed of both piles and piers, with the sections on and near the foreshore built at low tide, the centre supported by piled trestles. To be practical on such a wide single-channel river, the structure must have had a central drawbridge.

The culmination of all this planning and effort was that by AD 100 Londinium, with a population of around 30,000, had become pre-eminent and replaced Colchester as the capital of the Roman province of Britannia, a position never seriously challenged over the next two thousand years. The very rivers and hills that had led to its founding now strongly influenced the course of the Roman landward city wall (AD 190–225), and that wall defined what is today's 'Square Mile': the City of London.

The first wooden bridge – dendrochronology has dated the wood to between about AD 80 and 90 – would have been an enormous stimulus to the Romans and to the native peoples living on each side of the river, Londinium on the north and what would become Southwark on the south. Historian R.E.M. Wheeler described London as a parasite of the bridge.

The construction of the Roman roads, famously straight, and the layout of the settlement was accomplished with all the precision of the Roman military. At least a dozen major routes radiated out from London, many centring specifically on the bridge, thereby reinforcing the bridge site for the centuries ahead. The road from the south end of the bridge aimed towards the south coast and the

Continent. From the north end, in an almost straight line, the bridge led on to what is now Fish Street Hill, then to today's Gracechurch Street on the eastern hill, a spot then straddled by the forum. In the forum's square layout, the basilica stood at the centre of the top side; it eventually became the largest basilica north of the Alps. And Roman Ermine Street ran north from the forum, also in an almost direct line with the bridge.

The western hill was the site selected for the amphitheatre. This spot has been located, and it is almost exactly where the Guildhall and Yard are sited today, remarkably still largely an important open public space two thousand years later. These substantial structures were surrounded by grid-pattern streets lined with red-tiled roofed houses of mud and wattle-and-daub, which were inhabited by the ordinary people. Most overlooked the river and the bridge.

Trade increased, mainly to supply the military but also because prominent Britons had joined their conquerors in a taste for Roman food and luxuries. Mediterranean food and goods were unloaded on the wharves, where initially imports exceeded exports. In addition to olives and olive oil there was wine, grape juice, dates and figs, fish and fish paste, red Samian pottery, glassware and bronze tableware, even emeralds. Wool remained a main export, along with minerals.

At the extensive harbour works near the bridge, trading vessels loaded and unloaded and visiting Roman warships were sometimes seen. Essential grain was stored in warehouses on both sides of the river and at the four Roman London ports: Billingsgate, Queenhithe, Dowgate (the mouth of the Walbrook) and Bridewell (the mouth of the Fleet).

When the empire was at its height, in AD 122, Emperor Hadrian visited the administrative centre of Britannia, his most northerly province and by now decidedly Roman. Near the Southwark end of the bridge, in 1832 dredgers brought up the bronze head of Hadrian, once part of a statue that may have stood on the bridge, and which probably dates from the time of his visit. Now in the British Museum, this rare survival is a little larger than life-size, depicting him with curls, a moustache and a short beard. A bronze hand on a matching scale was found nearby in Lower Thames Street.

942.12

The Roman bridge, or sequence of bridges, was in use and maintained until the early fourth century, according to archaeologist Gustav Milne. The Romans departed around 407 to consolidate their forces when Rome itself was threatened by Germanic peoples, as was Britain. The Romans, the first conquerors, who had become defenders and builders, left after almost four hundred years of occupation.

Even as the end of the Roman occupation approached, long-distance trade was decreasing and industries were becoming more localized. The dramatic decline of the city after the Romans withdrew meant there was little trade. Londinium lacked administration, an economy based on money, and defence, and so was increasingly attacked. It is doubtful that the civic organization remained to maintain a bridge, and the capital may have been abandoned.

But the auspicious qualities of the strategic site meant that people and commerce would always be drawn back to it, if they ever actually completely left in the centuries of anarchy following the Roman withdrawal.

The Anglo-Saxon period (about 490–1066) began with the invasion by West German Saxon and Danish tribes. It was a time of turbulence, with native Celtic peoples being pushed inland by the advancing invaders, a period marked by rebellious mercenaries, tyrants ruling small kingdoms and inconclusive fighting. There are very few sources to which we can refer, because the invaders – mainly from the tribes of the Angles, Saxons and Jutes – were illiterate for the first two centuries after their arrival in Britain. What did unite them was the bond of kinship and loyalty to a lord, and by the year 600 there are believed to have been dozens of kings.

But by 811 London was referred to as a famous royal city. From 842 the settlement was known as the Anglo-Saxon Lundenwic (London-port), and was located just west of the walled city along what is now the Strand. By 1000 it had become a powerful city of the Anglo-Saxons, the second conquerors.

The Anglo-Saxons worshipped the gods of later Norse mythology, and pagan cults that would be banned by the Christian

Church. Christianity had been introduced in 597 with a superficial impact at first, but with the building of churches urban life was reawakened. Interestingly, by 749 a charter records the duty of landowners to help in building bridges and fortifications. By the tenth century there was efficient local government, and the English counties were divided into 'hundreds' for administrative and legal purposes. By now the Church was strong enough to have acquired lands and privileges, and so was firmly established.

No mention had been made of a bridge between the seventh and ninth centuries, but in the tenth century, when Aethelwold was Bishop of Winchester, a bridge at London surfaced in a reference to witchcraft. In about 963, a widow and her son were found guilty of making a small wax effigy of a nobleman they wanted to harm, and stuck iron pins into it wherever there was to be an injury. For this criminal offence, their land was forfeited. The son escaped, but the woman was seized, bound and thrown into the Thames from 'London Bridge'.

Bede reported that by about 730 London had become 'a mart of many peoples coming by land and sea', almost an echo of what Tacitus had said 650 years earlier. In the reign of powerful Offa, King of Mercia (757–96) native coinage appeared, and in this century trading centres were being established in northern Europe.

The bridge remained a great attraction for trade. A mid-Saxon clay bank has been found at Billingsgate, and the medieval trading place and port of Queenhithe, upstream from the bridge, was originally Saxon. The exports gathered together on the nearby wharves included wool, wheat, tin, animal skins and honey, while among the imports were wine and fish from Rouen, timber and pitch from Scandinavia, walrus ivory from Greenland and elephant ivory from Africa.

That duties had already been established is illustrated in a list of tolls taken at Billingsgate below London Bridge during the reign of the Saxon king Aethelred II (978–1016). In this law, passed in 979, there are references only to ships laden with wood and to the ever-important cargoes of fish: 'Whosoever shall come to the Bridge [probably referring to the wharves adjoining the bridge] in a boat in which there are fish, that Mango [monger or fishmonger] shall give in tax one half-penny; if it be a larger vessel, one penny.'

Such a rich and easy source for plunder as Britain could never be left in peace for long, and the Anglo-Saxon kingdoms were forced to turn their attention to fighting off Viking attacks. The Vikings had burst upon an unsuspecting Europe with a shocking ferocity. The attack on the unprotected monastery at Lindisfarne in 793 marked the beginning of the Viking Age, which would last until 1042 in England. The Danes were the most numerous and prosperous of the Norsemen. Their fleets regularly caught the prevailing east to north-east winds in the spring to trade and plunder, returning home on the autumn westerlies.

The Norsemen reached the Thames in 842. London with her port was an obvious target, and the bridge at London soon emerged as a vital defence in frequent raids. But it was a confused scene of ever-shifting allegiances among leaders and men, when as well as fighting the Anglo-Saxons one group of Danes might fight another, or armies from the other Scandinavian countries.

The marauders were increasingly opposed by the strong Anglo-Saxon kings, notably Alfred, King of Wessex. In 886 Alfred recaptured London from the Danes, rebuilt it and became the first king of all England. But after Alfred's death in 899 the attacks resumed and were escalated by the ruthless and formidable Svein I Haraldsson 'Fork-Beard', who became King of Denmark in 985.

A London bridge was standing in 994, seemingly untouched by the serious fires in London of 961 and 982, for in that year a Viking battle was recorded at the bridge for the first time. The Danish king, Svein 'Fork-Beard', and Olaf Tryggvason (*c.* 965–1000), who would accede to the throne of Norway the following year, had followed the 'sea-road' to England, creating one powerful (but not powerful enough) fleet of ninety-four vessels. On 8 September they sailed up the Thames to London, the bridge featuring in the ensuing battle. The Norsemen first attempted to set fire to the city, but failed in a stubbornly contested fight in which they 'sustained more harm and evil than they weened that any townsman could do them'.

The defenders apparently repelled the attack with no assistance from the 'redeless' or ill-advised King Aethelred 'the Unready'. The Norsemen withdrew, turning their fury on defenceless places along the Thames estuary in Essex and Kent, desisting only when they received 16,000 pounds of silver, along with provisions and winter quarters at Southampton.

In 1008 Aethelred imposed a tax specifically to build a fleet of ships to ward off the almost annual attacks. In 1009, for the first time in fifteen years, the city was referred to in *The Anglo-Saxon Chronicle*, for this was a year in which 'they [the Norsemen] often fought against the town of London, but to God the praise that it yet stands sound, and they there ever fared ill'. The bridge is not mentioned, but that it was there is clear from the events that followed.

In 1013 Svein 'Fork-Beard' sailed for England, determined to conquer. A description of his fleet setting sail from Denmark was recorded by a monk at St Omer who in 1040 wrote the *Encomium Emmae Reginae*, perhaps with poetic licence, but projecting a blood-stirring image:

> . . . they went on board the towered ships, having picked out by observation each man his own leader on the brazen prows. On one side lions moulded in gold were to be seen on the ships, on the other birds on the tops of the masts indicated by their movements the winds as they blew, or dragons of various kinds poured fire from their nostrils. Here there were glittering men of solid gold or silver nearly comparable to live ones, there bulls with necks raised high and legs outstretched were fashioned leaping and roaring like live ones . . . When the signal was suddenly given, they set out gladly, and . . . placed themselves round about the royal vessel with level prows . . . The blue water, smitten by many oars, might be seen foaming far and wide, and the sunlight, cast back in the gleam of metal, spread a double radiance in the air . . .

Svein 'Fork-Beard' and his son, the exceptionally tall, blond Cnut

(Canute), approached London with their men from Winchester. Many of their people were lost on the march to London because at that time they apparently 'kept no bridge', which may have been destroyed by fire or storm. The account proceeds: 'When they came to the city the townsmen would not submit, but withstood with full war against him, because King Aethelred was therein, and Thorkell [a powerful Viking leader] with him.' With various leaders vying for power and changing sides whenever it suited them or they were given enough silver, the sequence of events is often confused.

All the kingdoms submitted to King Svein of Denmark, and Aethelred fled to Normandy. But Svein died five weeks later, early in 1014, and the Danish army elected nineteen-year-old Cnut to succeed his father. The English called for Aethelred to return, which he did in the same year, now aided by his former bitter enemy Olaf II Haraldsson (*c.* 995–1030), who became King of Norway in 1014, with many of his Norsemen, in an all-out attempt by Aethelred to regain his own capital from the Danes.

Worthy of the Saga Age are the vivid and immediate accounts of the Viking battles at London Bridge. Snorri Sturluson's *Olaf Sagas* records the desperate encounter at the bridge, when the Norwegian king, Olaf Haraldsson, led his men in attack. Of great interest in the story of a bridge at London, it is worth quoting at length.

> They steered first to London, and sailed into the Thames with their fleet; but the Danes had a castle within [on the site of the Tower of London]. On the other side of the river is a great trading place, which is called *Suthvirki* [Southwark]. There the Danes had raised a great work, dug large ditches, and within had built a bulwark of stone, timber and turf, where they had stationed a strong army. King Aethelred ordered a great assault; but the Danes defended themselves bravely, and King Aethelred could make nothing of it. Between the castle and *Suthvirki* there was a bridge so broad that two waggons could pass each other upon it. On the bridge were raised barricades, both towers and wooden parapets in the direction of the river, which were nearly

breast high; and under the bridge were piles driven into the bottom of the river. Now when the attack was made the troops stood on the bridge everywhere, and defended themselves. King Aethelred was very anxious to get possession of the bridge, and he called together all the chiefs to consult how they should get the bridge broken down. Then said King Olaf he would attempt to lay his fleet alongside of it, if the other ships would do the same. It was then determined in this council that they should lay their war forces under the bridge; and each made himself ready with ships and men. King Olaf ordered great platforms of floating wood to be tied together with hazel bands, and for this he took down old houses; and with these, as a roof, he covered over his ships' sides. Under this screen he set pillars so high and stout, that there was both room for swinging their swords, and the roofs were strong enough to withstand the stones cast down upon them. Now when the fleet and men were ready, they rowed up along the river; but when they came near the bridge, there were cast down upon them so many stones and missile weapons, such as arrows and spears, that neither helmet nor shield could hold against it; and the ships themselves were so greatly damaged that many retreated out of it. But King Olaf, and the Northmen's fleet with him, rowed quite up under the bridge, laid their cables around the piles which supported it, and then rowed off with all the ships as hard as they could down the stream. The piles were thus shaken in the bottom, and were loosened under the bridge. Now as the armed troops stood thick upon the bridge, and there were likewise many heaps of stones and other weapons upon it being loosened and broken, the bridge gave way; and a great part of the men upon it fell into the river, and all the others fled, some into the castle, some into Southwark.

Next, Southwark was stormed and taken, and when those in the castle 'saw that the Thames was mastered and that they could not hinder the passage of ships up into the country, surrendered the tower and took Aethelred to be their king'.

At the end of the description of the great fight at the bridge is a marvellous poem by the skald or poet Ottar Svarte. He includes homage to Odin, god of power and wisdom, battle and poetry, who resided in Valhalla where the Norse warriors knew they would join him one day:

> London Bridge is broken down,
> Gold is won, and bright renown.
> Shields resounding,
> War-horns sounding,
> Hildur shouting in the din!
> Arrows singing,
> Mailcoats ringing –
> Odin makes our Olaf win!
>
> King Aethelred has found a friend
> Brave Olaf will his throne defend –
> In bloody fight
> Maintain his right
> Win back his land
> With blood-red hand,
> And Edmund's son upon his throne replace –
> Edmund, the star of every royal race!

The same great fight inspired another memorable and vivid poem, this time by Sigvat:

> At London Bridge stout Olaf gave
> Odin's law to his war-men brave –
> 'To win or die!'
> And their foemen fly.
> Some by the dyke-side refuge gain –
> Some in their tents on Southwark plain!
> This sixth attack
> Brought victory back.

When Aethelred died, only two years later, in 1016, rival kingships emerged. His son Edmund Ironside was chosen by the southern Anglo-Saxon nobles to be king – but the Danes chose Cnut.

In the conflict that followed in 1016, Cnut resolved to find a way around the timber bridge, which was a total obstacle to the movement of his fleet on the river and even hindered ships fighting advantageously below the bridge. On the south side of the bridge, in the marshes of Bermondsey and Lambeth, he 'dug a great ditch', and his men dragged his vessels through it. This is not as far-fetched as it sounds, for the area of Southwark was swamp-like, with islands, rivulets and the River Effra. The ships were small, and in the low-lying marshy land there may have been drainage channels or water-ways which the Norsemen could have widened or connected. Whichever the way through, attempting such a formidable task indicates Cnut's mammoth determination.

Cnut defeated Edmund, and they agreed to divide the kingdom in two: Cnut ruled the north, Edmund the south. Edmund died soon after, and in 1016 Great Cnut became King of England (1016–35), making the Danes the third conquerors of Britain.

Events large and small were drawn to the only bridge. In 1023 it emerges in a story about Cnut. Cnut had converted to Christianity, aware of its benefits to a ruler. He decided to make amends for the brutal murder of Alphege, Archbishop of Canterbury, twelve years earlier. The Danes had captured the Archbishop at Canterbury with a view to ransoming him for silver, but the Archbishop refused to be ransomed. Held captive at a drunken feast at Greenwich, he was pelted with bones and the heads of cattle, then killed with the blow of an axe.

To atone for this gruesome death, Cnut decided to return the Archbishop's body to Canterbury, which meant crossing the river. Anticipating trouble on reawakening the memory of the murder, Cnut gave his men instructions to distract the populace by stirring up agitation at the furthest gates. From St Paul's a humble Cnut preceded the coffin-bearers on foot as far as the bridge, from which lines of armed men watched for trouble while the provoked rioting could be heard in the distance. The King carried the body of the martyr on board a waiting vessel and on the opposite shore reverentially placed it on a carriage to send it on its way home to Canterbury.

The bridge's role as a barrier to riverborne traffic and to invaders was dramatically highlighted when Anglo-Saxon England was nominally under the rule of pro-Norman Edward the Confessor (1042–66), who had long lived in Normandy, and retained foreign favourites. Edward was dominated by his overweening father-in-law Godwin, Earl of Wessex, who had helped place him on the throne, and had then married the King to his daughter, Edith. In 1051, after repeated confrontations, King Edward banished Godwin and his sons. But Earl Godwin was not a man to let the situation rest, and returned from exile in Flanders in 1052 as the leader of the anti-Norman party. With his powerful fleet he sailed on the incoming tide up the Thames to Southwark, where they anchored. As Earl Godwin, Lord of Southwark, waited for the tide to turn, he successfully persuaded those in Southwark to allow him to pass through the bridge. The fleet then 'steered through the Bridge by the south shore'. On the north shore they surrounded the King's small fleet of fifty ships, manned by men who did not want to fight their own kinsmen. After threatening moves and counter-moves, all parties conferred. So many of the commons, even the royal troops and the navy, had gone over to Godwin's side that the King had no choice but to meet Godwin's demands. He reinstated his father-in-law's family, and Godwin reassumed his position of great power until his death the following year.

But it was not long before the bridge in its strategic location witnessed happenings surrounding one of the great events in English history: the Battle of Hastings in 1066 and the Norman Conquest. Edward the Confessor on his deathbed named Godwin's son, Harold Godwinsson, to succeed him. But he had already promised the throne to William, Duke of Normandy, who was furious at being denied his inheritance. Duke William sailed with an armada of several hundred ships, war horses, stores and even pre-constructed forts to land unopposed at Pevensey Bay. At Hastings they awaited King Harold II – Harold Godwinsson – and his army, who were in Yorkshire, out of which they had just driven the army of Harald III Sigundsson Hardraade. Hardraade ('hard ruler'), King of Norway and himself a strong contender for the throne of England, died there at the Battle of Stamford Bridge, near York.

Harold Godwinsson and his depleted army, exhausted by battle and the long walk from York, paused in London. Then they must have walked out over London's bridge on a forced march to Senlac Hill at Hastings. On 14 October 1066, only nineteen days after the death of his Norwegian rival, the last Anglo-Saxon king was himself slain. Back across the bridge, a few days later, trudged the survivors with tales of disaster and defeat.

In anxious, fearful London news came of the approach of Duke William's victorious army. A force of citizen militia was organized to repel the victors at Blackheath, but on the way there they were met by a squadron of 500 well-armed Norman horsemen, who inflicted heavy casualties, driving them back into the shelter of the city walls. From Southwark Duke William of Normandy viewed London's bridge and walled London. He did not storm the bridge, but burned Southwark. He then swept west, out and around fortified London, causing devastation along the way, and isolated the city before entering it. The Normans, the fourth and last conquerors, were soon accepted and firmly in charge. The building of intimidating stone castles began at once, many of which remain today, including the White Tower in the Tower of London.

A bridge of timber was advantageous to the people living nearby on both sides of the river, for they were the ones mainly responsible for repairing and rebuilding it, which could be done fairly quickly. But even this did not compensate for the fact that wooden bridges were highly vulnerable to attacks by nature and by man, and the sequence of seemingly never-ending disasters must have made the population receptive to the idea of a stone bridge.

The first recorded natural disaster occurred on 16 November 1091 when a south-easterly gale 'coming from Africa' made the Thames burst its banks for some distance; the water came down so forcefully that it entirely swept away London bridge. The church of St Mary Overie, just upstream of the bridge in Southwark, was destroyed, and not rebuilt for some time. At the Tower of London, the stone White Tower, begun in 1078 and still unfinished, was 'sore shaken by tempest'. Over six hundred houses were wrecked, and several other churches destroyed. The wind unroofed St Mary-le-Bow (still standing in Cheapside, having been rebuilt several times): 'The roof was carried to a considerable distance, and fell with such force, that several of the rafters being about twenty-eight feet long, pierced upwards of twenty feet into the ground, and remained in the same position as they stood in the chapel.'

More frequent references to a London bridge of wood now occur, although still teasingly slight. London was always in danger of fire with the concentration of so much wood and thatch, for the use of bricks and tiles had ceased with the Romans almost five centuries earlier. There were at least seven great burnings between 1018 and 1132, and a calamitous fire in 1135, the year Henry I died, may have rivalled the Great Fire of 1666 in destructiveness. The fire of 1135 started the day after the Christmas festival in the house of a certain Ailward, who lived near London Stone – this stone, perhaps a Roman milestone, had become a symbol of civic authority and was so ancient it had taken on sanctity; the stone remains in Cannon Street. The fire spread eastwards to Aldgate, also sweeping in the opposite direction to St Paul's, and on its way 'the bridge of timber over the river of Thames was also burnt, but afterwards again repaired'.

Fiery-complexioned William II, Rufus (1087–1100), who succeeded his father, 'the Conqueror', is credited with rebuilding the wooden London bridge at this time, work probably financed by levies on land in Surrey and Middlesex. There is an early reference to the bridge in a charter of his brother and successor, Henry I (1100–1135), exempting a manor belonging to the monks of Battle Abbey from 'shires and hundreds and all other customs of earthly servitude, and namely, from the work of London Bridge . . .' Back in the reign of Offa, King of Mercia (757–96) each person had had a threefold obligation: service in the field, maintaining fortifications and maintaining bridges.

It was clear that the authorities had to keep the bridge functioning, for by 1097 districts near London were required to provide forced labour for London Bridge, no doubt weakened by severe storms. In both Saxon and Norman times this service to the bridge, in money or labour, included not only those who lived around the bridge and in London, but also the inhabitants of the counties surrounding the city. The people who lived near the bridge were particularly 'oppressed' by its demands. In the reign of Henry I a charter imposed one tax to raise funds for repairing London Bridge, and another tax for repairs to Pevensey Castle.

There is a story – legend, part truth or truth – of the ferry of St Mary Overie ('St Mary over the water') that must be part of an account of this river crossing. In the twelfth century, maybe earlier, 'before there was a bridge', one boarding place, to take a ferry to cross the river or to pass through a bridge when there was one, was immediately to the west of the bridge: the stairs of St Mary Overie (after the Reformation St Saviour's, and since 1904 Southwark Cathedral). There may have been a ferry in addition to a bridge, or due to some disaster the ferry may have replaced a bridge. It seems there was only one ferry business operating at this spot, with 'divers boats' carrying people, horsemen and cattle, and it was a source of great wealth.

The ferryman, John Overs, was a rich but miserly widower with one daughter. He was covetous and possessed an estate equal to the richest alderman, wealth acquired by unceasing labour and money-lending, yet he dressed and lived like a pauper. He decided to save a day's upkeep of his household by faking his own death, for no food was consumed for the twenty-four hours while a 'corpse' was in the house. But his servants rejoiced around his coffin, singing and eating all the food they could find. When he suddenly sat up to end the charade, the happy throng were now terrified. Believing him to be a ghost, the servants beat him to death. His distraught only child, beautiful, pious and educated Marie, then sent for her betrothed – a relationship unknown to her father – who was most keen to be Overs' heir. On his way to comfort her he fell from his horse, broke his neck and died.

Overs was buried at Bermondsey Abbey in the prior's absence. When the prior returned he ordered that the ferryman – a usurer and an extortionist who had been excommunicated – be dug up and tied to a donkey. Where the donkey stopped was where he would be buried; the donkey stood still near one of the many gallows, and shook off the corpse, which was buried there. That's how the story goes.

With the immense profits from the ferry and all the other goods Marie had inherited, the daughter of the ferryman withdrew from life, partly to escape from fortune-hunters. She built a religious house of sisters, where the uppermost end of St Mary Overie was to stand, and where Marie herself was eventually buried. Afterwards it was converted into a 'Colledge of priests, who builded the Bridge of timber, and from time to time kept the same in reparations . . .' Today the retrochoir in today's Southwark Cathedral, the Anglican Cathedral and Collegiate Church of St Saviour and St Mary Overie, was once part of the Augustinian Priory of St Mary Overie.

As early as 1122 the London bridge of wood already possessed revenue-producing lands, necessary to meet the constant expense of repairing the bridge: '. . . the bridge was maintained partly by the proper lands thereof, partly by the liberality of divers persons,

A Thames boat-joust in progress.

and partly by taxations in divers shires'. A Thomas de Ardern and his son, also Thomas, gave the monks of Bermondsey Abbey the sum of five shillings per annum rent out of 'land belonging to the Bridge', recorded in the *Annals of Bermondsey Abbey 1042–1432*. Such acts of generosity marked the beginnings of the extensive portfolio of properties belonging to the Bridge House Estates today.

In 1131 comes the first mention of an individual associated with working on the wooden bridge. A man named 'Geoffrey, Ingeniator' was paid £25 for rebuilding two arches. By 1179–80 five craft guilds of the Bridge had been recorded.

The last wooden bridge at this site, dating from around 1163, had been built of elm under the direction of Bridge Master Peter de Colechurch, Chaplain of St Mary Colechurch, at the corner of Poultry and Old Jewry in Cheapside, the wide main street of medieval London.

Whether or not a timber bridge was still in existence, the architect-priest must have realized that the time was long overdue for London to have a bridge of stone over the River Thames, and set about the great task which was to consume the last twenty-nine years of his life – and continue for four years beyond.

The river crossing at London, already deeply impressed with history, was about to move on to its most renowned stage: the construction and 622-year life of the medieval Bridge.

CHAPTER ONE

'to the Queen ... the custody of the Bridge'

London Bridge was built upon woolpacks.   Proverb

I N 1176, BEFORE THERE WAS A LORD MAYOR OF
L O N D O N , before the first English parliament was summoned,
the construction of Old London Bridge began. The site of the
first stone bridge over the Thames at London was exactly where
the wooden London bridges and the Roman bridge had stood.

The fact that the London of the early Middle Ages was able to
begin the first bridge of stone in the country since the Roman

Visscher's London Bridge and the City sky-line beyond, 1616.

occupation had ended about eight hundred years earlier – and over a powerful tidal river almost a thousand feet wide – testifies to the confidence and energy of a population heading for 30,000 to 40,000. At a time of growth and prosperity in what was almost a city-state, there existed the will and the organization to plan and carry out this immensely challenging project.

Priest-architect Peter de Colechurch, already an experienced bridge-builder, now undertook the great work of his life. The involvement of a priest was not unusual. Londoners needed the help of God in appeasing and combating the malevolent forces that superstitious minds believed were attracted to river crossings, places where the dangerous currents, fierce rapids and flooding were thought to be manifestations of the devil. The Church itself encouraged bridge-building, promoting this work as an act of piety, and chapels were frequently built on or near them. At Abingdon, an ancient market town set on a sharp bend in the Thames, a fifteenth-century poem from a Christ's Hospital manuscript commemorated the building of a new bridge at Culham Hythe: 'Of alle werkys in this world', after church-building, 'Another blessed besines is bridges to make.' Assisting wayfarers – especially giving them safe passage over rivers – was a benevolent act. And a completed bridge was itself due reverence and respect for boldly resisting the force of the water. A bridge at London required care, and Peter may have been head of a guild or fraternity of the Bridge, which built it, governed it and repaired it.

In France the link between bridge-building and religious orders was even stronger. Long-established guilds such as the Frères Pontifes or Pontist Brothers in the twelfth century were responsible for bridges over the Rhone, like the Pont d'Avignon and Pont Saint-Esprit. The Brothers' role was clear: on the front of their white robes were depicted a bridge and a cross. Indeed, bridges were considered cursed if the Brothers were not involved, and the technology of bridge-building advanced through their work.

Against this background, the foundations for the first pier of Old London Bridge were begun in 1176, according to the Annals of

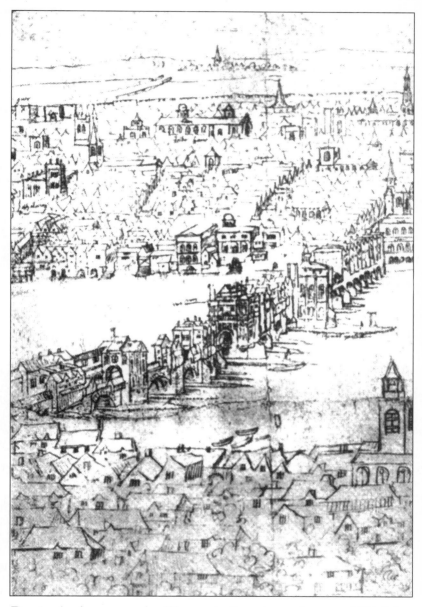

Drawing by Antony van den Wyngaerde, from the south-east, *c.* 1550. It is the earliest complete view.

Waverley Abbey of 1291, an abbey which was located near Farnham, Surrey. The king was Henry II (1154–89), the first and probably the greatest Plantagenet king of England. He was tough physically and superior intellectually. As well as initiating the construction of London's bridge of stone, he reformed the Church and established the right to trial by jury. England was but one part of his vast Angevin empire (Henry was Count of Anjou, the region of north-west France at the centre of the empire) that stretched from the Scottish borders to the Pyrenees. Henry's territories in France exceeded those of the French king himself, and he would have been familiar with the stone bridges on the Continent.

The 'Cittizens of London' and others assisted when 'they builded the same of stone . . .', but money was needed for this great enterprise, much more than had previously been available for the timber bridge. To accumulate funds for the Bridge, a wide-ranging tax was imposed: everyone was taxed on all wools, undressed sheepskins and leather, hence the proverb 'London Bridge was built upon wool-packs'. Wool was the basis of wealth in the kingdom, and it was England's chief export by far.

In a campaign to raise funds, one way the wealthy contributed was through endowments – that is, bequeathing a source of income. The first of many given to the Bridge was in 1303: the funds to pay for two priests and four clerks in the Chapel of St Thomas à Becket on the Bridge. Another kind of endowment was a chantry – receiving money in exchange for singing Masses for the good of a deceased person's soul. Over the years many chantries were added, some with a priest, some with a small chapel, and so the number of churchmen grew. One early chantry was that of Richard Cocus who in 1269 left his houses in Colcherche towards the maintenance of the Bridge.

Ordinary people contributed, as did great figures such as Richard, Archbishop of Canterbury (successor to Thomas Becket), and Cardinal Hugocio di Petraleone, who gave 1,000 marks. A mason who was the 'Maister Workeman of the Bridge' made a very individual and valuable contribution: he took on the heavy responsibility for the expense of the Chapel.

Money came from every level of society, but it seems that the King himself did not contribute.

The architect-priest knew that much would be asked of his stone structure. At every tide the energy of the water would challenge and threaten the emerging Bridge. As pier after pier was added, the water was increasingly and seriously restricted, and the work became more and more dangerous. The untamed river, furious at being ever more obstructed, all the while tried to claim whatever was placed within its domain. Even at still water under the illusion of calmness, the river unceasingly sought out weakness. And it would punish any mistake, probably fatally. Many lives must have been lost during the lengthy construction of the Bridge. Author Gordon Home estimated that as many as two hundred men may have died, calculated on the thirty-three years of construction and the number of deaths during the building of the replacement bridge more than six hundred years later.

How did they do it? How was a bridge of twenty arches constructed in the twelfth century across a very wide and fast-flowing tidal river? It would have been comparatively easy to build a bridge if the course of the dangerous waterway could have been diverted from the spot. Historian and chronicler John Stow thought that it had been. But the difficulties inherent in damming such a powerful river ruled this out, as did the problem of creating an essential diverting channel for the water. Interestingly, Sir Christopher Wren later considered the question, and concluded that the river had not been 'turned', 'but that every Pier was set upon Piles of Wood, which were drove as far as might be under low Watermark, on which were laid planks of Timber, and upon them the Foundation of the Stone Piers'.

This theory has been confirmed in the essentials through excavation, beginning when two piers were removed during alterations in 1826 and 1827, and through later research. William Knight, the Resident Engineer at London Bridge Works when Rennie's bridge was being built, recorded the materials comprising the foundations as they were removed, and made invaluable detailed drawings as Old London Bridge was being deconstructed. He concluded that

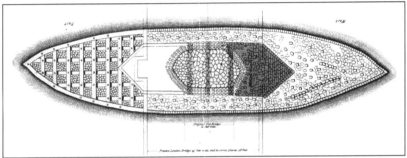

Two views of a Bridge pier by William Knight.

the foundations had been laid at low water 'as the heads of the small piles were a little above that level'. Men drove in the three rows of mainly elm piles all around the sides and the ends of each pier, about six or seven feet deep, and usually ten inches square. Loose rubble comprising stones, chalk and gravel was placed in the middle of these piles without cement.

Those idle passers-by who paused to watch the building of the Bridge saw the base of each pier being pounded into the mud and gravel. From barges tied alongside, tidemen operated pile-drivers: men pulled on ropes to raise a heavy weight to the top of a tall cone-shaped framework, then suddenly dropped it on the head of the pile to hammer down the material. At low tide work proceeded on the lowest course of masonry of the foundations; blocks of

Kentish ragstone were brought to the site by water, hoisted into position from barges, then hot pitch was poured in.

Three strong oak sleepers about twenty-one inches wide by nine inches thick were rammed in and embedded in the rubble. Straight-edged stone masonry was added to complete what was in effect a boat-shaped island, the points of a pier cutting through the water and forcing it to either side. As much work as possible would have been done on dry land, and transported by barge to the pier. The Bridge rose, and once the huge oak centring for an arch was in place, the stone wedge for the arch was placed on this temporary support, and the arch was built.

Following the discovery of late tenth- or early eleventh-century timbers on the Fennings Wharf site in Southwark, Tony Dyson and archaeologist Bruce Watson of MoLAS are re-assessing the evidence for the first medieval bridge.

The Bridge is notable for the great length of time that was taken over its construction: thirty-three years. From this overall time span we can estimate that one arch was built about every eighteen or nineteen months. We know that an arch at the City end was finished in 1192, because in 1730 a stone, a 'curious piece', bearing that date was found in the cellar of a house at the north end of the Bridge.

But delays would have occurred when funds ran out, or when there was some disaster. One kind of disaster for the Bridge – and for London and the country – happened only twelve years after the Bridge was begun: the accession of Richard I, 'the Lionheart' (1189–99). Richard took no interest in Bridge or country, making only two brief visits to England in ten years. He did find the time to deplete the nation's reserves of money and assets, as well as selling charters of self-government to the towns, and offered to sell London if anyone could find a buyer. All this to raise funds so that tall, athletic Richard could pursue his Crusades thousands of miles away. His incessant demands for enormous amounts of money could only have delayed the construction of the Bridge.

Although Richard I's successor, King John (1199–1216), spent a lot of time on the Continent battling unsuccessfully to prevent the break-up of the Angevin empire, he did make time to assist the emerging Bridge. He gave the City of London some 'void places' for 'building upon', the rents from which would help pay for the future never-ending repairs in the years after London's new bridge was completed. In 1209 John made further provision for its funding: the halfpence taken in duties from foreign merchants was given to the work of the Bridge.

It was not only the Bridge that required financing. So too did the King. A pattern was being established: when a king needed money, he went to the rich City merchants and tradesmen who had grouped themselves together by trade or craft in guilds. These guilds became the Livery Companies, sharing the aims of giving mutual help, protection and regulation to their own trade or craft and the practitioners of it. One of the first to regulate their trade were the fishmongers, whose Hall was built at the City end of London Bridge. The drapers were merchants in woollen cloth, the skinners controlled the fur trade, and so on. The result was the creation of a powerful elite merchant class, for these men became civic leaders who cannily used such situations to slowly wrench their liberties from the King and vigorously protect what they had already gained.

When King John borrowed money from them to pursue his wars, the City in return acquired vital rights of control over the Thames, rights extending from Staines to Yantlet Creek near the mouth of the river. Equally crucial was the right to 'choose to themselves every year a mayor'. The first Mayor (later Lord Mayor) of London was Henry Fitz-Ailwin, who served from 1192 until 1212, after which the Mayor was elected annually. The first three Mayors were Freemen (meaning free to trade) of the powerful Mercers Company (derived from the French for 'merchant'), and today it is still the premier Livery Company in order of precedence. The Mayor was supported by the aldermen, who were chosen from the Freemen of the Livery Companies. The City was well on its way to becoming a self-governing and self-elected city-state.

As one year of bridge construction passed into yet another, Peter de Colechurch grew older and more infirm. It was time for astute, energetic King John, who was a good administrator, to attempt to appoint a successor to Peter. Was there a note of impatience in the King's letter to the City officials, advising them to make use of 'our faithful, learned, and worthy Clerk, Isembert, Master of the Schools of Xainctes' (Saintes). Isembert had just built the Pont St Sauveur at La Rochelle, a port and ancient regional capital on the Bay of Biscay in Brittany, and a bridge at Saintes, both apparently completed quickly. Although the King 'entreated, admonished and . . . urged' Isembert to come to London, there is no other mention or record of his involvement, if it did happen.

Peter de Colechurch must have been a very old man when he died in 1205, having borne the responsibility of his pioneering bridge-building work for almost three decades. One hopes that the structure was sufficiently advanced while he was still well and fit enough to have been able to conduct the Holy Offices in the rush-strewn, candle-lit Chapel on the Bridge, which must have been the pride of every Londoner. Peter was buried on his Bridge. This was a fitting – and the only – internment within a unique memorial.

The custody and care of the Bridge had to be resolved on Peter's death. King John appointed 'Brother Wasce' and some others: 'The King to Geoffrey Fitz Peter [Chief Justice of England], & c. We will that Brother Wasce, our Almoner [who distributed alms], and some other lawful men of London, provided by you and the Mayor of London, be Attorney for the custody of London Bridge. And, therefore, we command you that they give the whole to these men, like as Peter, the Chaplain of Colechurch, possessed the same from them . . .'

History records that three men completed the Bridge in 1209, almost eight centuries ago. All later became Bridge Wardens, and one was three times Mayor. They were William de Alemannia (or Almaine), Warden in 1223 and 1233; Beneditwricte (Benedict Botewrite), Warden in 1232; and Serle le Mercer, Warden in 1233 and 1237 and Mayor in 1214, 1217 and 1222.

Control of river and Bridge evolved slowly. The river, and the Drawbridge over a thirty-foot opening near the Southwark end, were regarded by some as marking the boundary of the City's power on the Bridge. In 1258, during the hearing of pleas in Surrey, men of Southwark and Surrey claimed that the sheriffs and citizens of London unjustly collected customs beyond the Great Stone Gate, although their rights extended only to the Drawbridge Gate. The accused argued that it was lawful for them to collect customs outside the Great Stone Gate (the names of the two main gates varied confusingly over the centuries; this one at the Southwark end is referred to throughout as the Great Stone Gate) as far as the staples (the wooden posts, sometimes linked by a chain in place from at least 1258 marking the boundary of the City's jurisdiction) because the water of the Thames belonged to the City for some distance seawards. Twelve knights of Surrey agreed, giving the City rights over the whole length of the Bridge. Control of the Bridge by the City was established.

Old London Bridge was owned, carefully administered, robustly defended and its rights vigilantly protected by the City. The Bridge Masters or Bridge Wardens were in daily charge, and it was Edward I (1272–1307) who established the regular appointment of Wardens in 1282. He instructed the Mayor to appoint 'two or three of the more discreet and worthier citizens' in connection with collecting tolls on the Bridge 'because of the sudden ruin of the Bridge of London'. In 1282 a goldsmith, Gregory de Rokesle, who had already been twice Lord Mayor, in 1274 and 1280, became a Bridge Warden. In 1284, with the selection of Richard Knotte and Thomas Cross as Bridge Wardens, the appointments to these responsible positions became regular.

The two worthy men were required to be members of one of the leading Livery Companies, perhaps mercers, drapers, ironmongers, goldsmiths, grocers or fishmongers, from the dozens that existed. They served for two consecutive terms, and after a break in service could be re-elected. Some Bridge Wardens spent a measurable portion of their lives working for the Bridge, perhaps holding office for ten or twelve years, and one, exceptionally, for twenty-three years. When two Wardens formed an effective team, they might work together for long periods for the benefit of the Bridge.

They swore to serve the City of London; to repair and sustain the bridge, using its lands and rents for its best profit; never to be wasteful to the estate, but to increase it when possible; and to prepare honest accounts. They were urged to buy materials at the lowest prices (always considering the quality and nearness of source), and with no profit to themselves. Their annual salary was £30 with some expenses allowed, but it was not a way to get rich.

The Wardens elected on Midsummer's Day held in their 'warde' – were responsible for – all the goods of the Bridge. This considerable power was coupled with considerable responsibility: for the Bridge, for the residents who lived on it, for a huge range of goods and properties, and for large sums of money – £750 a year in the late fourteenth century, but double that by the mid-sixteenth century. The goods of the Bridge included rents from the buildings on the structure itself and elsewhere, commodities, tenements and lands – in 1358, the Bridge owned property in London, Southwark, Hatcham, Camberwell, Lewisham and Stratford. Managing, collecting rents and carrying out repairs meant considerable organization, work and effort.

Inevitably, at times there was mismanagement. When in 1390 rent-collector William Leddrede failed to account for £38 8s. 7½d., the Court of Common Council eventually made up the difference, but warned the Wardens that they were not setting a precedent, and that the Wardens alone were responsible for the servants of the Bridge. In the mid-1400s, Warden William Weyenhoe had been negligent, and so on leaving office was not given his 'reward', which could have been money or gifts.

From the earliest days there must have been an organized team to care for the Bridge, for it required vigilance from the very beginning. The Bridge House, the administrative centre for the Bridge, was first mentioned indirectly in 1243. At the beginning it was located in a house 'attached to the Chapel': the Bridge House, so called in a will of 1272 leaving property to the Bridge. The Bridge House – the same name was used for both the administrative organization and the building – had moved to Southwark by around 1350, 'the house belonging to the said bridge in Suthwerk', where it was close to the Bridge, on the river downstream. In a plan of

Southwark, about 1542, the 'brust house' is situated immediately east of St Olave's church on the river, and usefully gave the Bridge House workers a good overall view of the downstream side of the structure and of activity on the river. This was where the clerks worked, wages were paid, materials stored and meetings held. The bustle and comradeship of the workers in the buildings, yard and garden and on the wharves made the Bridge House a busy, highly organized and self-contained place.

The first of the seven stages of Old London Bridge covers the period from when it was completed in 1209 to about 1384. Unfortunately, no drawings of the Bridge from this period exist. What we do know is based on the detailed descriptions of John Stow, 'Citizen of London', in his endearing *Survey of London* (1598), the first attempt at a comprehensive history of the city (for which he was paid '£3 and 40 copies'). The historian and antiquarian was born in 1525, and lived through four reigns. Lean, tall John Stow used his 'small crystalline eyes', his intellect and his curiosity to research London's story. He wrote down the oral traditions, what he saw about him and what he knew. In so doing, 'the merry old man', by trade a tailor, was destined to live in poverty, even though the value of his work was recognized by James I, who granted the humble chronicler two effusively worded Letters Patent authorizing him to beg – but gave him no money.

Working backwards from later drawings, we can establish details of the buildings and of the appearance of the arches in the Bridge's first stage. That is more than enough to enable us to visualize a remarkable structure seen from the river by the watermen.

The young watermen on the Thames had observed the Bridge being built all of their lives. Now before them low over the water sat a street which visually joined up the reassuringly familiar St Magnus the Martyr on the City side and St Mary Overie on the Southwark side. The jumble of unevenly projecting timber buildings – the projections held up by wooden struts – sat on and linked the piers of grey Kentish ragstone.

As they lowered their masts to 'shoot the Bridge', where the drop of the swirling water was at times as much as a terrifying six feet, the nineteen piers alarmingly blocked almost half – 405 feet – of the width of the river. The massive piers themselves varied greatly in width from twenty-five feet (the norm) to thirty-four feet, adding to the unpredictable currents. Similarly, they warily noted the unequal dimensions of the broadly pointed arches over the twenty openings: twenty-eight feet in width was most usual, but it might be as little as fifteen feet – very narrow indeed. The highest part of an arch was thirty-one feet eight inches above low water at the neap (lowest) tides, which occurred twice a month. During the tides at the spring equinox, when the river was at its highest, the clearance between the boat and the underside of an arch might be only thirteen feet in the middle arch, and eight feet under the lowest arch at the northern or City end. Such variations probably occurred because the builders had to find the firmest places on the river bed. Knowing the characteristics of each arch and pier and always approaching them with respect could mean the difference between life and death. The death toll at the Bridge began to mount, and in the records of the neighbouring churchyards, 'drowned at the bridge' now became a frequent entry, as it would be for centuries. The Bridge soon inspired proverbs, and one refers to these numerous dangerous openings: 'If London Bridge had fewer eyes, it would see better'.

The watermen soon named most of the twenty openings under the arches according to their individual features: the most important at the Drawbridge was Draw Lock, the arch south of the Chapel was known as Long Entry or Narrow Passage Lock, the wider one on the City side north of the Chapel was Chapel Lock, and there were Rock Lock and Gut Lock among others, the latter name memorably reflecting the tortuous narrowness of the opening for boats. The watermen rapidly became familiar with – but never entirely certain of – the ever-varying dangers of the rapids at each of these openings.

Twice a day when the watermen grouped together waiting for the tide to turn, they gossiped, argued, made wagers and watched for people who had either fallen off the Bridge by accident or had suicidally thrown themselves into the rapids. Or if a frightened pig or a cow had slipped off as it was being driven across the bridge street, the young men rushed in their boats to herd the frantically swimming beast to shore. Those not in difficulty always helped those who were, for they knew the situation could very easily be reversed: 'One good turn will meet another, if it were at the Bridge of London'. As it got dark they also kept an eye out for any slops that were thrown from above into the river. Although there were strict, if difficult to enforce, laws about disposing of waste in the City, it was hard to see a stream of urine – or worse – caught in the wind and coming from somewhere above.

Then, when the tide was right, the watermen raced to be first through the Bridge, exhibiting a competitive, sometimes violent streak thought to be typical of Londoners. This frequently resulted in men being drowned, and boats being smashed, ground against the piers, or even left stranded on a pier that the high water dangerously hid from sight; in the latter case the boat remained sitting helplessly on the pier for six hours until the next high tide.

Although the Bridge was almost completely lined with buildings, when the watermen looked up they could still keep an eye on activity on the twenty-foot-wide platform of the bridge street, which was about thirty feet above them at low tide, because there were at least three open places (more after a fire or the collapse of a building): one was just inside the Great Stone Gate at the Southwark end, another at the Drawbridge and a third in the Square by the Chapel. The street over the water was itself only twelve feet wide.

The appealingly irregular overall appearance must, in part, reflect the long period of construction. Or it may have been the medieval way of building bridges. No two arches were alike on the twenty-four-arched bridge near the mouth of the Torridge at Bideford, Devon, built in the early fourteenth century. But who can deny that the resulting irregularities on London Bridge were pleasing to the eye? Encouraged by the example of London's bridge, more stone bridges were beginning to appear in England, one being Elvet Bridge in Durham. The fame of London was spread far and wide, and news of the new bridge would have reached the Continent quickly. In France in 1177 St Bénézet began the famous bridge of twenty-three arches that stretched over the Rhone at Avignon.

No one had ever seen anything like Old London Bridge, and spectacular as its rivals on the Continent were, they couldn't match it. This considerable achievement was rightly a source of great pride to the citizens, merchants, nobility and monarch. Visitors had heard about it and were eager to see it for themselves.

Imagine you are a visitor from the Continent approaching London via the muddy, rutted Dover Road and Southwark for the first time. As the City comes into sight, flat green and brown fields, vineyards and gardens retreat behind a line of taverns, shops and houses, buildings that crowd in on one another in a ribbon development. Having so far successfully avoided being fleeced by the many waiting beggars and opportunists jostling around you, you are thirsty and tired. Overtaking pack horses, mules and a herd of cattle heading for the Bridge, you see a horse-drawn cart pull into a balconied tavern courtyard, the driver knowing there is little stabling for the horses at the other end of the approaching Bridge. You follow it, and after a London beer or two (brewed from Thames water) – you will find no taverns on the Bridge itself due to lack of cellarage – curiosity and excitement make you forget that you are foot-weary. Back in the street you are surrounded and caught up in the dense throng of Southwark hawkers in the market being held in the middle of the street and the extraordinary array of people and animals going to the City.

After the quiet of the country, the increasing noise hits you. There are the teasing, angry, fearful noises made by people and animals being forced along a strange road, mingling with the cries of the street vendors – 'Pots and kettles to mend', 'Hot puddings', 'Wood to cleave?' – and the din of the workshops, from the tip-tap of the cobbler to the hammering of the blacksmith. The road itself is encroached on by those at work in front of their shops or sheds: tin-smiths, turkey-pluckers, tailors and carpenters. Your stout boots try to avoid the sticky drying puddles from the morning's rain, every kind of dung, and dogs fighting over bloody entrails they have dragged from a fleshmonger's near the Bridge. The contrasting smells from the properties of the bakers, the dyers and the glue-makers are almost overwhelming. As you near the Bridge, you pass a bruised, silent man in the pillory, whom boys are pelting with stones, then say a prayer at the comforting sight of the prominent churches at the southern end of the Bridge: to the left or upstream side St Mary Overie, to the right or downstream side St Olave's on Tooley Street – and the church bells peal, echoed by others across the river. You smile, eyes wide open, at this good omen as London Town greets you.

You look towards heaven, and see thin smoke from the many chimneys poking up from the uneven roof lines of the Bridge, caught by the wind and billowing along the river. There is only a moment's sad thought of a warm fire and your family at home before you fend off a tug at your side as someone's hands lightly but unsuccessfully search for your purse, then vanish. Ahead you see the formidable Great Stone Gate, with shops, taverns and houses packed all along the way right up to it. Now, just before the Bridge, you pass the chains hanging between the wooden posts – the 'staples' or 'stuples' – that mean you are about to come under the jurisdiction of a powerful merchant class led by a Lord Mayor: 'here the King ends and the Lord Mayor begins', as is written on an early map of the area.

The gate is right before you at the south end of the Bridge, and crammed between it and the staples are ten shops on each side. A group of men are betting on a vicious fist fight, blood is flowing, but you are are carried along by the crowd, and are now all tucked in behind a carriage that is clearing the way ahead for you. In the gateway, you see the wooden gates and the portcullis overhead, then comes an open space, then seven more shops on each side, all built of wood.

In sight is the timber Drawbridge, and you stumble on it for it is rough underfoot and in need of repair, and you can hardly see your feet in the crush. From here there are views of a lively river and your first glimpse of the City beyond, views somewhat obscured by the loungers, hawkers and villains looking for an easy victim among the country people and foreigners. The Drawbridge, first mentioned in 1257, is over the seventh arch from the Southwark end. This crucial opening is more than twenty-eight feet wide; the low tide exposes the muddy banks, and you hear the tidemen repairing the piers, the repairs that will make it even narrower for ships to pass through safely. Raised, the Drawbridge prevents a land attack, and allows trading vessels through to dock at the ancient upriver trading place of Queenhithe, described by Stow as 'a principal strand for landing and unloading against the middest and hart of the Citie'. Closed, it prevents raiders' vessels from passing upriver, instead leaving them within range of the nearby menacing bulk of the Tower of London. You hear the calls of the fisherwomen and jokes of the watermen on the river.

Your eyes are drawn to one of the sights of London, the famous heads on the Drawbridge Gate, also called Traitor's Gate, and now count five, each on a stave, some with a mocking coronet of ivy, each decaying and drooping, with hair bleached by the sun and standing on end in the wind. The timber gate – the third line of defence, set on the eighth pier – is painted, gilded and decorated with images of the saints and of the King.

Walking ahead and almost tripping over two furious geese that have become separated from a flock being driven in – soon snatched up by a thief – you see twenty shops on the left, seventeen on the right. The colourful shop signs, nine feet off the ground so horse and rider can pass safely underneath, are swaying in the breeze. Each shopkeeper must display a sign, and anyone who does not is prosecuted. The image on each sign represents a trade, and colourfully indicates to the illiterate the goods on sale: Adam and Eve for a fruiterer, a globe for a map-seller, a gold ring for a goldsmith.

Hours ago, at dawn, each shopkeeper had lowered his long wooden shutter on the front of his shop to make a narrow counter from which to sell goods. You can buy a hat – yours may have just been stolen or blown off on the Bridge – or spurs for those on horseback who may need a replacement after a long journey. There are ropes and haberdashery, fishing gear and toys. Eager shopkeepers, the story of their lives etched on their characterful, alert faces, try to catch your eye, and apprentices call out, 'What lack ye? What do ye lack?' with teasing, cruel comments about your foreign apparel. After you pass by, a rotten egg hits you in the back of the head – a perfect shot – with the jeers and laughter rippling along the street. Surrounded and threatened, you know enough not to look back.

You also feel trapped on the dark, narrow street because a number of the half-timbered shops have hautpas – that is, they are joined overhead, making an extra room over the street and strengthening the buildings on each side. This creates what is an overall dark, tunnel-like effect, with spots of blindingly hard sunshine where there are no hautpas. The smells on the bridge street, unable to escape, intensify as you walk along it, and noise reverberates.

And there is a lot of noise being made. A heavily laden wagon is wedged under a hautpas with all the ensuing cursing and shouting from the frustrated drayman looking around for someone to blame as schoolboys stop fighting to tease him, while the red-faced owner of the damaged building waves his arms wildly. Harnessed in single file, the eight plumed horses trying to pull the immovable wagon are frightened and impatient, wild-eyed and with foaming mouths, one trying to break from its traces. The people and animals coming from both directions are single-minded in their determination to move on, yet from the quick smiles you can see that there are some witty quips being made. A lumbering wagon coming out from the City foolishly tries to squeeze past, and is itself trapped against two shop fronts.

Following the other foot travellers, you scramble over and through this chaos, and come to the beautiful Chapel of St Thomas à Becket with its pointed Gothic arches perched on its large pier. Beyond the Chapel is the open Square. Upstream on the Southwark side, you can see low-lying meadows bordered by dykes stretching to Lambeth and beyond. On the City side, past Queenhithe, the water-fronts of palaces and great houses follow the curve of the river from Blackfriars to the hump-backed Westminster Abbey on the horizon. Downstream, on the City side, is the Tower, and ships at their anchors swing and creak with the tide in the Pool and at the numerous quays.

Now, thirty-two shops on the left or upstream side, thirty-five shops on the right or downstream side offer more luxurious goods, from fine gloves and fabrics to mathematical instruments. You pass a knight in chainmail using his helmet to carry home the ingredients for his dinner; a filthy child lying in a doorway, his leg visibly broken; a dark-haired woman in a voluminous long tunic, girdled at the waist, late for Mass and rushing towards the church of St Magnus the Martyr. One hour after you first stepped on to the Bridge, you reach the other end, and pass the church, from which chants and incense waft out. With a backward glance, then dodging a wine barrel naughty boys have let loose to roll down Fish Street Hill, you leave the world of Old London Bridge and enter the world of the City.

Old London Bridge was intended to be inhabited from the start, making it a vital, living structure, for in 1201 King John had decreed that 'the rents and profits of the several houses . . . to be erected upon the Bridge aforesaid, to be for ever appropriated to repair, maintain and uphold the same'. The site was commercially desirable, and the rents from the properties on it were a built-in guaranteed source of maintenance funds for the many years ahead.

In the double row of tall dark buildings, each individual structure comprised a tiny shop at street level – some shopkeepers sensibly had two shops, side by side, for more space, but others rented half a shop – with living quarters for the tradesman and his family above, making a unique community of work and life over the water.

To help visualize Old London Bridge, we can look at an existing habitable bridge: Wren's Pulteney Bridge over the Avon in Bath, built more than 550 years later. (A draper, Sir John Pulteney, who had been three times Lord Mayor of London, was an ancestor of the Earl of Bath, who built it.) This was one of the last habitable bridges to be constructed at a time when most others were being pulled down. There are eleven shops on each side, all with lofts, and those over the three arches have cellars; there were toll houses at each end. The rooms on the classically austere 'front' side of the three-arched bridge are flush with the face of the structure; even so they are about ten feet deep, creating a small, long, narrow, but usable room for today's shops. On the somewhat hidden 'back' of the bridge, various overhangs have been built higgledy-piggledy, a view somewhat like the exterior of London's bridge. With these extensions, some rooms are almost twice as deep.

At street level on Old London Bridge the typical shops and houses were about seven feet deep with no overhang, about double where there was a projection. Only four feet of each building rested on the stonework of the Bridge; the rest overhung the river on massive wooden struts. About a quarter of the houses had hautpas, mainly towards the northern end. Surprisingly, no thought seems to have been given to the outside appearance of such an important structure, unlike the considered architecture and display of its threatening gateways.

No views of the interiors exist, but they would have been much like any other shop/house of the period in which they were built, although smaller. The ground-floor room had a door, a small window, a hatch opening and a breakneck staircase or ladder to the rooms above. The tiny rush-strewn room with a doormat of rope was dark but candlelit, and the main rooms had a fire. Furniture was sparse, basic and sturdy – table and chairs, a bed, a chest for clothes, with curtains covering the windows and doors to keep out draughts. Weapons, cooking implements and clothes hung on the walls.

It is the overall scale of London's bridge that is hard to grasp. Pulteney Bridge Street in Bath looks small and picturesque, but London's bridge street was only one-third its width, yet three to six storeys high and more than ten times as long: Old London Bridge was diminutive but high, the street tunnel-like and dark, with some building fronts decorated, some perhaps gilded.

Of the surviving inhabited bridges in Europe, the three-arched Ponte Vecchio ('Old Bridge') over the Arno in Florence, completed in 1345, gives the closest idea today of what Old London Bridge once looked like. And it captures a little of the atmosphere, with its overhangings, shops, streams of people – and brio.

Of all the buildings on the Bridge, we know most about the Chapel of St Thomas à Becket. The Chapel stood on the downstream side of the eleventh pier from the Southwark end, the ninth from the City end, but visually appeared to be almost in the centre. Chapel Pier was noticeably wider and longer – thirty-five feet wide by 115 feet long – than the others, and projected out about sixty-five feet beyond the line of the Bridge. On it sat 'St Thomas of the Chapel' – as it was affectionately known – comprising an upper chapel and an undercroft or lower chapel. The building was sixty feet long and twenty feet wide, and a handsome forty feet high on the street front. The substantial size and length of the pier, noticeable in the later illustrations, must have helped to stabilize the entire structure. In the late 1600s architect Nicholas Hawksmoor thought the Chapel Pier 'to be a Steadying of the whole Machine . . . So this Fortress was placed in the Middle of the Bridge to stem the Violence of the Floods, Ice, and all other accidents that might be forced against it.'

The naming of the Chapel was significant, perfectly timed and a great impetus to keeping money flowing to the Bridge. Brilliant, challenging Becket had been martyred in 1170 by his former friend Henry II, and canonized only three years later, just before work on the Bridge began in 1176. The awkward 'turbulent priest', who had championed the rights of the Church over the King, was born a Londoner and christened in 1118 in St Mary Colechurch at the corner of Poultry and Old Jewry only a few doors from his home and near the Bridge. This was the church where Peter de Colechurch had been priest, and the men no doubt knew each other. Londoners regarded Becket as their very own saint and martyr, and he soon became the focus of a popular cult.

With this dedication the popularity of the Chapel was assured, and pilgrims setting out for Canterbury Cathedral, a long sixty miles away, turned inside to pray for the Blessed Martyr and for protection from the hazards on the road. While it was very much the wayfarers' chapel, it was equally important in the lives of the devout watermen and fishermen; when the tide was right, they tied up their boats on Chapel Pier and ascended to the undercroft through a door at river level.

The saint's standing was supreme; Becket's image appeared on the Common Seal of the City in the early thirteenth century, enthroned above the Bridge with a view of the City and the City Wall. On one of the ancient seals of London Bridge, he featured on both sides, the reverse side depicting his martyrdom, with one of two armoured knights striking him on the head.

At the City end still stands 'The Church of St Magnus the Martyr at the foot of London Bridge', so mentioned in the confirmation of a grant made by William the Conqueror in 1067 to Westminster Abbey. The church was there before Old London Bridge was built, and for 622 years was almost a part of it.

The Chapel came under the control of the parish priest of St Magnus, although the Chapel's chaplain and other members of the 'Brothers of the Bridge' enjoyed some freedom, which they and the Bridge Wardens fiercely protected. In 1413 the Wardens hired four horses for three days to visit the Archbishop of Canterbury, who was at Tonbridge, and to complain to him that the priest at St Magnus was claiming the money given at the Chapel. In 1483, after another disagreement, the chaplain of the Chapel was granted the right to keep the alms collected during services for himself and his community, provided he made a generous contribution to the finances of the parish. As the years passed, responsibility for the Chapel was shared with the Bridge House, and cooperation usually prevailed.

As for St Magnus and its parish, they needed all the money they could get. This church could not avoid being intimately involved with life on the Bridge, and with all the responsibilities that entailed. Serving the northern half of the structure, to them fell much more than the spiritual well-being of those who lived nearby or the thousands who crossed the bridge street. Many foot travellers were injured or killed by carts and cattle on the Bridge, and for centuries these unfortunates were the heavy and seemingly endless responsibility of the parish of St Magnus the Martyr.

Chaplains and clerks resided near the Chapel and the church, for people who worked on the Bridge usually lived on the Bridge, and not just the shopkeepers; the Bridge House accountant had rooms there and the gatekeepers inhabited the gateways. They were together, yet divided, at least during the day, by the traffic of people

The Southwark approach to Old London Bridge.

and of animals. At about nine p.m. in the summer, earlier in the winter, curfew was rung. The seven City gates, including those on the Bridge, were locked, and the bridge-dwellers retreated into their own world.

The Bridge, it has often been said, was a microcosm of the City. It was a slice of exuberant life, and the games on the river near the Bridge encapsulated the energy and vibrancy of the time and place. In the 1170s the monk William FitzStephen described one game: water quintain. At Easter, the watermen, whose livelihood depended on knowing the currents, made use of them for fun and thrills, perhaps a wager. A target was securely fastened to a mast or a tree trunk fixed in the middle of the river. Each young waterman in turn stood upright in the stern of a boat that was propelled quickly forward by the current and by two oarsmen. He had to strike the target with his lance, and won his point only if he hit the target, broke the lance – and remained in the boat. If his blow didn't break the lance, he was certain to be thrown into the water. Young men in two boats waited on either side of the target to rescue him from the fast flow, while 'Upon the bridge, wharfs and houses, by the river's side, stand great numbers to see and laugh thereat'.

After such energetic activity and thrills, they went to a nearby tavern to relive the day's fun and quite possibly tragedies. A place as central and as continuously busy as the Bridge would have seemed to be a natural place for taverns, but there were few if any inns or taverns right on the Bridge itself because there was no cellarage, yet in 1320 five retailers of ale on the Bridge – Robert de Amyas, Robert le Ceynturer (Girdler), Henry de Flete, Thomas ate Hide and Anslem de Latoner – were forbidden by the Mayor's court to sell ale there. There were, however, many inns to choose from at each end of the Bridge. We know that one was the Three Neats' Tongues at or near the City end and close to St Magnus, because the churchmen patronized it.

But it was the Bear at the Bridgefoot that came closest to being the Bridge's tavern, located as it was just off the Bridge at the Southwark end. It was probably on the west side of the street, the side nearest the Bear Gardens on Bankside. Before the tavern swung the sign of a chained and muzzled bear.

The Bear was first mentioned in 1319, the year it was probably built by taverner Thomas Drynkewatre – a name that surely evolved from the opposite meaning. He leased the inn for six years to a wine merchant, James Beauflur, from 'the Feast of Christmas in the eleventh year of the reign of Edward II'. It was a quid pro quo arrangement. A sum of money was paid by lessee vintner Beauflur for improvements to the Bear, and also to give landlord Drynkewatre's own business a financial boost. For his part, Drynkewatre agreed to sell Beauflur's wines and to provide Beauflur with an account of the sales and of the quantities of wine received. Drynkewatre also contributed handled mugs, some of silver, some of wood, the cloths to be placed on the tapped casks and other items that the tavern required. Centuries later a silver-rimmed tankard from the Bear was found nearby in the Thames. Importantly, the Bear was located by the landing stage for the tilt-boats, the large boats with great awnings to protect passengers from the elements, and propelled by oarsmen on the two-day journey to Greenwich and Gravesend. The tavern had yet another attraction – archery was practised in the grounds beside the Thames.

The Bear was the more famous, but the Tabard in Long Southwark (Borough High Street) was the 'most ancient' according to Stow, and may have dated back to 1304. This inn was the starting and finishing point for Chaucer's 1388 pilgrims in *The Canterbury Tales*. Henry Bailley was landlord of the inn – 'A seemly man oure host' – and himself one of the pilgrims; it was his idea for the pilgrims to tell stories along the way.

Old London Bridge was to witness uprisings and battles, and extravagant processions commemorating welcome, victory and death. One of the first of these spectacular occasions was the arrival of Louis, Dauphin of France, in May 1216.

In the events leading up to this occasion, King John was nicknamed 'Lackland' and 'Softsword' because he had lost almost all the English territories in France. This, along with heavy taxation and disputes between King and Church, created unrest among the nobility, and even the demands of bridge-building added to the burden. In June 1215 the King was forced to meet the barons at Runnymede where he signed the Magna Carta, which defined the rights and responsibilities of crown and subjects for the first time. The twenty-third clause stated that no village or individual should be compelled to build bridges at river banks, except those who were legally bound to do so in previous times: the Great Charter removed from freemen the obligation to build bridges and transferred this duty to districts.

King John willingly accepted the Pope's annulment of the Magna Carta two months later, and civil war broke out. The barons tried to depose John by seeking help from Louis, Dauphin of France, the eldest son of King John's enemy Philip II, who had reclaimed the extensive English dominions in France. Louis agreed to accept the crown of England, and landed at Sandwich with his army, then marched to Southwark. In 1216 the invited invader-saviour was received with enthusiasm by the commons as he and his men marched over the Bridge on their way to St Paul's Cathedral. Their allegiance soon shifted, however, and on King John's death only a few months later, the child-king Henry III was crowned immediately. But Louis – who had been so enthusiastically welcomed a short time before – was unwilling to give up half the shires of England. After battles and sieges, the City was relieved when the future Louis VIII of France, who had been paid 1,000 marks to come, was given ten times as much to go away.

The Bridge was susceptible to more than fires and natural disasters. Sometimes there was the flagrant abuse of royal privilege and responsibility. During most of the long reign of Henry III (1216–72), antagonism smouldered and flared between the King and the City. From 1258 the King's misgovernment caused agitation, and although he signed the Provisions of Oxford in 1258 limiting royal power, he repudiated the document in 1261. Three years later this launched a convoluted civil war known as the Barons' War.

To fund his wars, in 1249 Henry III claimed control and all the revenues from the Bridge. The King was to retain the power to appoint the Bridge Wardens up until 1281. The Brethren of London Bridge, as those in charge of its daily care were now called, neither had the money to pay the Bridge House staff nor to make the usual repairs to the Bridge, although they were instructed to care for it. Henry side-stepped his responsibility by giving a grant of protection to the Brethren in 1252: they were ordered 'to travel over England and collect alms for the Bridge' – that is, to beg for funds.

Henry was hated and his queen, Eleanor of Provence, even more so. This beautiful but excessively avaricious woman promoted her family at every opportunity. Immediately following the royal marriage, three of her French uncles became ministers of the Crown: the strong influence of foreigners was one of the triggers for the Barons' War.

Eleanor's lavish expenditure always exceeded her income, although a substantial part of her debt was incurred on the King's behalf. The tolls at Queenhithe had traditionally formed part of a queen's income. She now ensured that the most valuable cargoes were unloaded there. This meant that the vessels had to go through London Bridge, also paying tolls at the Drawbridge, which she received, and it would be reasonable to suppose that she would keep the Bridge and Drawbridge, so essential in every way, in good repair. She did not, and the Bridge, the great asset of London, was placed in great peril.

The Barons' War accelerated unrest and confusion in the country. Frightened by mob violence against the King, on 13 July 1263 Queen Eleanor decided to go by barge from the Tower, where she had been with the King, to join Henry's heir Edward at safer Windsor Castle. The news spread and the mob waited on the Bridge, noisy and armed with missiles. As the royal barge prepared to pass through the Bridge, the commons let fly with curses, eggs, stones, mud – always plentiful on the streets of London – and abuse. Eleanor was forced to return to the Tower, and then took refuge at St Paul's in the Bishop of London's palace. Wriothesley's *A Chronicle of London* tells of her narrow escape: 'Elianor the quene was foule repreved', adding 'and almost sclayn [slain] upon London Bridge'. This violence and public humiliation was as much against Henry as Eleanor, and neither the King nor his son, Edward, would ever forget it.

In 1264, word came that the leader of the barons, Simon de Montfort, Earl of Leicester, was marching towards London. De Montfort, 'the chief disturber of the realm', was the King's brother-in-law, having married Henry's sister in 1238, and – opposing foreigners in the court and government – was himself born a foreigner. He entered the City from the north and went over the Bridge into Southwark, where he set up headquarters. King Henry approached from the south, ordering the citizens to repel Earl Simon. The Earl was relying on sympathizers in London under the anti-royalist Mayor Thomas FitzThomas to admit him, but opinion in the City was divided, as was often the case.

Leading the opposition was John de Gisors, a mercer who had become rich by importing peppercorns from the East Indies, and had already been Mayor three times. He took control, ordered that the Drawbridge be raised, the gates closed and the keys thrown into the river. This was done on 11 December.

But the never-to-be-ignored commoners sided with de Montfort, the barons and FitzThomas. They flexed their considerable muscle by going on to the Bridge from the City end, forcing open the gates and lowering the Drawbridge. London was soon in the hands of de Montfort, and a new Mayor was illegally 'elected', although his name is unknown. The King meanwhile used the resources of the Cinque Ports to block the Thames and prevent supplies from reaching London.

In 1265, the year in which de Montfort summoned the first English parliament, he was killed at the Battle of Evesham, defeated by Edward, heir to the throne. But the war continued. By spring 1267 the barons were led by the Earl of Gloucester, who had been invited to London by a mediator, Cardinal Ottobuono, the papal legate. The unease at the approach of Gloucester's armed following meant that their entry was negotiated: a deputation rode out to meet them, and it was agreed that they be quartered in Southwark. They entered the City, probably at Ludgate – the main gateway of the City – and they too went over the Bridge to Southwark. The Earl was allowed back across the Bridge with some followers for a conference with the Cardinal. The bridge-dwellers were increasingly alarmed by the mounting tension.

At first the Earl of Gloucester was in control of his men, but a few days later, after John d'Eyvill, another baron, had arrived with his undisciplined following, looting began in Southwark. The commons, alarmed, raised the Drawbridge, leaving the Earl in the City. But the resourceful Earl regained control by somehow getting the keys to all the City gates, including those for the gates on the Bridge. Those living in Southwark were free to cross the Bridge, and, terrified, they took advantage of this to flee. The Earl's daily proclamations had little effect on the behaviour of his men, but punishment for the latter was immediate and final: all those rebels found guilty of misdeeds by their leaders were bound hand and foot and thrown into the Thames. For two months London was controlled by the rebels, but by summer King Henry had made peace, received the leaders of the barons and forgiven the City.

By 1265 the Bridge was being administered by 'the Brethren and Chaplains of the Chapel of St Thomas on London Bridge', for a document in the Calendar of Patent Rolls in the Public Record Office so addressed informed them that the custody of the structure and every single thing that belonged to it were now to be committed to 'the Master and the Brethren of the Hospital of St Catherine near to our Tower of London' for five years.

However, in 1269 the King again gave Queen Eleanor the custody of the Bridge for her personal use. The City-chosen Wardens were replaced by others of her choosing, who collected the rents and assets but spent nothing whatever on repairs to the Bridge. Within a year she was alarmed by a warning about its condition. Rather than risk being responsible, she resigned. The City elected two Wardens on 1 September 1270. The frustration of everyone who used the Bridge can be imagined when only two weeks later Eleanor reasserted her right to its revenues. Even her husband the King's death in 1272 did not stop this blatant abuse of privilege, perhaps because her son Edward was away on a Crusade when he inherited the throne. In the reign of Edward I, Eleanor remained in possession of custody of the Bridge, and by then more than rents and tolls were needed to repair it. At the regular investigations into why it was in such a state of decay, the same reason was always given: that it was in the hands of 'the Lady the Queen, Mother of the Lord the King', which was 'to the great detriment of the Bridge and the prejudice of all the people'. The citizens petitioned Edward I (crowned in 1274) for relief.

Finally, London Bridge reverted to its rightful owner, the City of London, and just in time, for it was 'greatly and perilously decayed'. In 1281 Edward I issued a royal patent 'Concerning the Relief and Reparation of the Bridge of London' in which he commanded that alms be collected throughout the country to raise money to restore the Bridge, which was in a 'ruinous condition' and unless repaired would fall, and kill the innumerable people dwelling on it.

In 1282 Edward I left off hammering the Welsh, the French and the Scots to issue the Mayor with what amounted to a charter for the Bridge – pontage or bridge tax: 'Know ye that in aid of restoring and sustaining of the Bridge of London, we grant that from this day and until the complete end of the three years next following, the underwritten customs shall, for that purpose, be taken of saleable goods over the Bridge aforesaid and of those which pass under the Bridge . . .' Little was left out of the long list of goods to which tolls applied, and the charter continued: 'For every man crossing from Southwark to London or vice versa – 1 farthing. For every horseman crossing from Southwark to London or vice versa – 1 penny. For every pack carried on a horse crossing either way – 1 halfpenny. And nothing should be taken onto the Bridge except for its repair.'

As well as the tolls, a further grant by the King authorized the Mayor to acquire for letting three portions of wasteland in different parts of London; the rents were to support the Bridge. And Edward gave the City the site of the Stocks Market, where the Mansion House now stands, the rents from there to be used to help maintain the much weakened Bridge. We don't know why the rent-collectors were given an extra allowance for drink when they made their weekly visit to the Stocks Market to collect the money from the butchers and fishmongers. Did they need to fortify themselves for the strain of dealing with the traders, or was the extra money for a convivial drink to ease from them the rent owing? The traders could be hard to handle, and when they fought among themselves, knives, swords and staves were the norm.

As for the tolls, the City was always reluctant to place them on crossing London Bridge, and whenever they were introduced they were removed as soon as possible. The tolls were abolished in 1315, but by 1356–7 there were again toll-collectors: a Thomas Gandre and a John Clerk, the latter's name perhaps reflecting that in the earliest days the toll-collectors were, oddly, the Chapel clerks. From 1490 to 1758 the collection of tolls was farmed or leased out; in the first nine years to a haberdasher who initially lost money because 'divers great persons' would not pay.

Long-term sources of money were always needed, and tolls were reintroduced when more extensive repairs were required. At any time the Bridge might suffer severely from rampaging high tides, fierce storms, snow and ice. The Bridge, in bad repair, had somehow survived an exceptionally high tide in January 1268. But by the end of 1281, the Wardens wrote to the Mayor to warn him about the ice building up above the Bridge. According to Stow, the Bridge was unable to resist the force of the ice, for 'through a great frost and deep snow, five arches of London Bridge were borne down and carried away'. The Thames was frozen from Lambeth to Westminster, and many bridges, including the timber bridge at Rochester, were destroyed.

With this destruction by ice of almost one-quarter of Old London Bridge, the song of the *Olaf Sagas* was easily adapted in the late thirteenth century – perhaps very much earlier – to become a popular nursery rhyme. Four of the many and variable verses from *Gammer Gurton's Garland; or the Nursery Parnassus* of about 1760 read:

> London Bridge is broken down,
> Dance o'er my lady lee;
> London Bridge is broken down,
> With a gay lady.

> How shall we build it up again,
> Dance o'er my lady lee;
> How shall we build it up again,
> With a gay lady?

> Silver and gold will be stole away,
> Dance o'er my lady lee;
> Silver and gold will be stole away,
> With a gay lady . . .

> Build it up with stone so strong,
> Dance o'er my lady lee;
> Huzza! 'twill last for ages long,
> With a gay lady.

The near-immortal nursery rhyme of London Bridge has for centuries been sung throughout the country and in much of the English-speaking world.

The Bridge had to be rebuilt, but since the foundations were in place the reconstruction may not have taken long. Stone bridges were more durable and thought to be more important, hence attracted more gifts than wooden ones, so money and property flowed to the Bridge House in a greater volume than ever before. As revenues grew the Wardens must have been relieved to have sufficient funds to make repairs comfortably. The many gifts, according to Stow, were recorded on the Chapel wall 'in a table fayre written for posterity'.

Where there were customs to be paid, as there were on the Bridge, the inevitable disputes followed. On 7 March 1299, John Le Leche, a miller with a horse laden with a quarter of wheat belonging to a baker named Henry le Cupere was stopped at the Southwark end by John le Wayer, the customs officer. He warned that the baker for whom Le Leche worked was in arrears with his duty, not having paid the duty owing on 'four quarters' of wheat; but the miller declared that only a halfpenny was outstanding. When the customs man grabbed the harness of his horse, Le Leche lost his temper, seized the officer by the throat, and pulled the tax-gatherer's hat down over his face – an attempt to blind him with it, the officer later claimed. The customs man struck the miller, and both drew their knives. While the men fought to an inconclusive end, the horse wandered back to its stable. The customs officer took the matter to the Mayor's Court, although the outcome is not known.

William FitzStephen had written in the 1170s of a London blessed in every way: 'Amid the noble cities of the world, the City of London . . . is one which has spread its fame far and wide, its wealth, and merchandise to great distances . . .' There were only two 'plagues': the immoderate drinking of fools and the frequent fires.

The timber London bridges had suffered from fire many times over the centuries. Only a few years after the stone Bridge was completed, the pride of every Londoner had experienced a fire of epic proportions. On 11 July 1212, a blaze started in Southwark. St Mary Overie burned down, then three separate columns of fire headed for the Bridge, soon engulfing the houses at the southern end. Then the north end was in flames. The great number of people on the Bridge were fatally trapped in the middle: '. . . an exceeding great multitude of people passing the Bridge, either to extinguish or quench it, or else to gaze at and behold it, suddenly the north part, by blowing of the south wind was also set on fire, and the people which were even now passing the Bridge, perceiving the same, would have returned, but were stopped by the fire'. Soon both ends were ablaze, the people in the middle running back and forth between the flames at each end.

A number of vessels came to their rescue 'into which the multitude so unadvisedly rushed, that the ships being drowned, they all perished. It is said that, through the fire and shipwreck, there were destroyed about three thousand persons, whose bodies were found in part, or half burnt, besides those that were wholly burnt to ashes, and could not be found . . .' The houses were gone, the Chapel almost a ruin. The number of deaths would have been great, although three thousand must have been an exaggeration. For years London Bridge remained a partial ruin, but partially usable.

There would be many more fires to come, including the two devastating fires of the 1660s, one of which was the Great Fire of London in 1666.

Coupled with fire, water was also a threat, whether from storms or flooding. Anyone who lived near the river would have kept an eye on it. In February 1238, thirteenth-century chronicler Matthew Paris recorded that the Thames flooded low-lying houses as well as the Palace of Westminster, where 'spreading itself, so covered the area that the middle of the hall might be passed in boats, and persons rode through it on horseback to their chambers'. In Southwark, the Augustinian Priory of St Mary Overie was frequently flooded; a monk wrote to the King: 'we are obliged to battle continuously against the violence of the river Thames, on whose banks our tiny house is situated'. Flooding would remain a problem until the Thames was fully embanked centuries later. Even

Bridge House in Southwark, with all its practical expertise, was not immune. In 1576 labourers were quickly sent for when the high tide 'did drowne all the neither [nether or lower] romes within the Bridge House'.

At a time when life was cheap, human tragedies on the Bridge were commonplace. In a cruel world the cause sometimes seemed almost frivolous. In May 1278 a Gilbert Clope, waiting for a boat to take him to Tower Wharf, fell asleep leaning against the low parapet, overbalanced, fell in and drowned. His body was seen floating in the river, and two watermen collected him up; the inquest declared that he must have been *non compos mentis*. In July 1301, eight-year-old schoolboy Richard le Mazon stopped to play on the Bridge on his way back to school after his midday meal. He climbed out on a beam, and hung from it. But his young arms were too weak, he fell into an incoming tide and his body was swept upstream to Queenhithe.

Southwark had always been free of the strict jurisdiction of the City, and was a haven – a sanctuary – for villains fleeing the City, where numerous laws regulated every activity. To stop criminals escaping to Southwark, in 1327 Edward III granted the Manor of Southwark to the City of London. A bailiff was appointed with the right to pursue criminals over the Bridge; however, this edict was hard to enforce until as late as 1550, when Southwark was sold to the City for £642 2s. 1d. but it continued to attract the unsavoury.

There were the usual crimes to contend with on the Bridge, as elsewhere in rough and violent London, where the most minor dispute could end in death. On 18 May 1339 Elena Sharp had quarrelled with Roger de Ingleby, and later on that evening, just after the bells had stopped tolling for Vespers, this woman, together with her brother and two other men, knifed him to death near the Chapel of St Thomas à Becket, according to the *Calendar of the Coroners' Rolls of the City of London*. The brother and sister fled, as did one of the other men. The fourth, Roger le Brewer, was arrested and sent to Newgate prison.

The head of betrayed Scottish patriot William Wallace launched a gruesome tradition forever linked with the Bridge when it was placed on the Drawbridge Gate in 1305. Wallace had been sent to London fettered and heavily guarded. He was dragged by a horse from Westminster Hall to the Tower, then taken to Smithfield and hanged. Taken down half dead, he was disembowelled, his intestines burned and his head cut off. It was impaled on the gate in sight of both land and water travellers to become a kind of fourteenth-century tourist attraction, the citizens having being told that Wallace was exceptionally evil. This macabre sight began a custom that was to last for the next 350 years. Within twelve months it was joined by the head of Sir Simon Fraser, dealt with equally barbarously. Both had been tried and executed for treason: not agreeing to Edward I's claim to the Scottish throne.

Treasonable heads faded somewhat into the background as foreign enemies were confronted. During the first phase of the Hundred Years War (1337–60) England prospered. But in November 1348 the Black Death reached the City of London. As the river became silent, the bridge-dwellers saw an increasing stream of people laden with their goods as they fled across Old London Bridge on their way to the Channel. But for around 50,000 people in London – forty per cent of Londoners – and one-third of the population of Europe there would be no escape.

Still, the citizens could revel in Edward III's victories over the French at Crécy and Poitiers. At the latter battle, the success of his warrior son, the Black Prince, created the occasion for another unforgettable scene on Old London Bridge.

CHAPTER TWO

'with speares sharpe groond for life and death'

London Bridge stands like a link of stone and wood, no ordinary construction, but having several gates with portcullises and dwelling houses owned by divers sorts of craftsmen built above the workshops.
Jean Froissart, *c.* 1360

I N THE ONGOING HUNDRED YEARS WAR, THE VICTORY over the French at Poitiers led to the greatest occasion on the Bridge to date. On 24 May 1357, the son of Edward III, Edward, the Black Prince – so called because of his black armour – returned with a most important prisoner: the King of France.

An initial letter from the Register of Deeds, Bridge House Estates.

In the City, excited crowds made it impossible to move in the streets. Waiting to greet the royal procession in Southwark were the Lord Mayor, sheriffs, aldermen, representatives of the twelve great Livery Companies of the City of London and a thousand citizens. Everyone thrilled at the sight of the Black Prince on his small black horse, followed by his captive, King John II of France, the 'noble prey', who rode on a richly caparisoned white horse.

At centre stage in the victory celebrations, the London Bridge that the royal captive saw was already almost 150 years old. By now the consequences of the devastating fire of 1212 had disappeared, and the structure had been slowly rebuilt. On the bridge street itself, the bridge-dwellers set before the French king what was intended to be their own proud and intimidating display. Jean Froissart, French chronicler and poet, recorded that they hung out their own tapestries, carpets and weaponry from windows and balconies, in a tradition that would endure for centuries. There was an '. . . amazing quantity of bows, arrows, shields, helmets, croslets, breast and back pieces, coats of mail, gauntlets, vambraces, or armour for the arms, swords, spears, battle axes, harness for horses, and other armour offensive and defensive that the like had not been seen in the memory of man'.

The captive king was lodged beside the Thames in the Savoy Palace, and was – as sometimes happened with a valued royal captive – treated royally. He was given a certain amount of freedom, including visits to the City of London.

Edward III expected money, and a great deal of it, in exchange for the release of his important prisoner. A peace treaty of 1360 set out what was truly a king's ransom – a massive three million gold crowns. To try to raise it, King John was allowed to return to France, leaving his second son, Louis, Duke of Anjou, in his place. But the enormous sum was impossible to meet. After Louis escaped in 1363, John returned to captivity, believing that his honour had been damaged by his son's abrupt departure. He surrendered himself with the words, 'If good faith were to disappear from the rest of the earth, it should still be found in the hearts and mouths of kings', so on his return in January 1364 the bridge-dwellers saw the splendid scene of 1357 repeated.

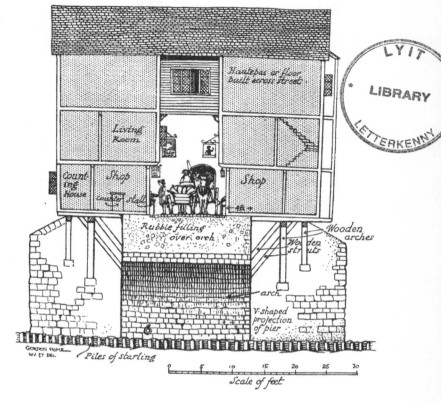

The Bridge drawn in cross section.

John the Good's surprising and noble act ensured that he received even more respect and magnanimity from his captors. Soon he was the guest of a rich City merchant, Sir Henry Picard, when this former Mayor entertained no fewer than five kings to dinner. Edward III of England and John II of France were joined by David II of Scotland, Pierre de Lusignan, King of Cyprus, and David, King of Denmark. Today at their banquets the Vintners drink a toast, 'Prosperity to the Vintners' Company', accompanied by five cheers for the five kings. But shortly after the celebratory dinner, King John died and his remains were taken with great ceremony back over the Bridge on their way home to France.

After the English defeat off La Rochelle in 1372, the French and their Spanish allies controlled the seas, and between 1377 and 1380 there were devastating attacks on Dartmouth, Plymouth and Gravesend. With a threat of attack, everyone rallied. To protect London, the quays between London Bridge and the Tower were defended with wooden palisading that was crenellated and covered with protective roofs.

One important duty of each City alderman was to lead and organize defensive measures in his ward when an emergency arose, and each man in his ward had to swear to be ready with his weapons. The aldermen of Walbrook were responsible for defending the river front between Billingsgate and the Bridge. The Bridge itself and the wharves as far as Ebbgate were to be defended under the aldermen of Bridge Ward; they were ordered to have good ordnance on the Bridge and the necessary supply of stone balls and 'shot' for their still primitive guns. Extra guards were put at the City gates, and the City hired arbalesters (men with large, powerful crossbows) who were to remain on the ships at anchor in the river between the mariners' village of Ratcliffe downstream and the Bridge. After all this preparation, the French made no attempt on London.

Henry Yevele was an eminent stonemason and architect who became the King's Mason. He was elected a Bridge Warden in 1368, an inspired choice, for his specialist knowledge was invaluable. An individual of great ability and character, much of his energy was directed towards the Bridge, and he was a Warden for an exceptionally long period (1368–78, 1381–7, 1388–92 and 1399). And all the while he carried on with his regular work, including the immense commission by Richard II to build Westminster Hall, between 1394 and 1400; its 660-ton hammer-beam oak roof was the greatest achievement of medieval carpentry in Europe.

Henry Yevele's second and third terms as a Warden covered a period of increased activity on the Bridge – probably because he was the driving force. Between 1384 and 1397, a time when the population of London exceeded 50,000, the entire structure of London Bridge was rebuilt, presumably as it looked in about 1500, when the first illustrations appeared. And the stonemason-architect would have had a hand in the preparations for the new Drawbridge built in 1388. The Drawbridge Gate was larger, more elaborate and more important than the Great Stone Gate at the Southwark end. On the tower, by 1393, stone images of Richard II and Queen Anne were set within 'tabernacles', with shields of the King, Queen and St Edward, all brilliantly coloured against a white plaster background to make the figures stand out to those passing underneath on the Bridge.

Richard II had become king at the age of ten in 1377, because the expected heir, his father, the Black Prince, had died the year before. The country was always weakened when the monarch was under-aged, for without fear of a strong ruler, those with grievances were quick to assert them and opportunists took advantage. Even though labour was scarce following the Black Death of 1348–9, wages remained low, and feudal laws still bound man to master. The people flared up at the news of wars, knowing that rising taxes to pay for them would soon follow.

Between 1377 and 1380 a series of poll taxes were imposed both to finance the war with France and to compensate for government mismanagement. The tax on a graduated scale included the poorest peasant, for whom it was quickly increased several times over. The 1379 tax was higher than ever, and the result was evasion, violence and the poll tax riots of 1381 known as the Peasants' Revolt, led by Wat Tyler.

The King was only fourteen when angry, discontented men began to gather in threateningly large numbers. Wat Tyler led his Kentish men towards London, meeting up with others from East Anglia. A force, some say 100,000 strong, reached Blackheath and marched to Southwark where they burned two prisons and broke into the Bishop of Winchester's palace. Lord Mayor William Walworth ordered the drawbridge to be raised against them and secured with a chain. On 13 June 1381 the rioters, unable to enter the City, wrecked the Bankside brothels, some of which Walworth owned, although this highly profitable enterprise was mainly controlled by the Bishop of Winchester.

Londoners robustly supported the insurgents, and the developing events were noted gravely by Wardens John Hoo and Henry Yevele, for the Bridge was literally in the firing line. Walter Sybyle, the alderman in charge of the Bridge on the morning of 13 June, held it with such a weak detachment of armed citizens that defence was impossible, and he inexplicably refused the help of additional armed citizens who volunteered to assist. Later that day he offered no resistance when Wat Tyler appeared at the end of the Bridge and threatened to burn down the houses on the first six arches if the Drawbridge was not lowered immediately: it was lowered. The terror of those living on the Bridge can be imagined, having seen and heard the destruction at the bridgefoot, and now the insurgents were only an arm's length away, rushing past their shops and homes. As the mob passed the Chapel they heard the priests inside earnestly praying for peace.

The City always carefully considered its options before deciding which way to jump, and at first the rebels were seemingly welcomed by aldermen John Horne and William Tonge. Once Tyler's men were over the Bridge, the City was soon in their hands, for he had wide support in London, reinforced by thousands of discontented peasants from Surrey, as well as Jack Straw's men from Essex.

The peasants took out their fury on any foreigners they met, killing them in considerable numbers, then carrying their heads on staves as they ran through the City. They burned down the Palace of the Savoy, and gained control of the Tower, where they seized the person who was the focus of their hatred, Simon of Sudbury (Archbishop of Canterbury and Chancellor), along with Sir Robert Hailles (Treasurer). Both were executed on Tower Hill. The Archbishop's scarlet cap was nailed to his skull, and his head was paraded through the City and finally positioned just above the eight others that soon adorned the Bridge.

Meanwhile, at Smithfield, young King Richard agreed to meet an insolent Tyler and his men, but almost before negotiations had begun, Lord Mayor Walworth dishonourably struck a blow against the rebel leader. History has it that young Richard took control of the rest of the mob, and promised concessions. The force of the uprising was defused when the Kentish men saw Tyler decapitated. As they streamed across the Bridge on their way home, above them on the Drawbridge Gate now sat the heads of Wat Tyler and Jack Straw, replacing those of the Archbishop and others that had been placed there only a few hours earlier.

Sir William Walworth had been a Bridge Warden of Old London Bridge and Prime Warden of the Fishmongers Company, and when Lord Mayor of London had killed Wat Tyler. When he died in 1385, he was was buried at St Magnus the Martyr – directly opposite Fishmongers' Hall – 'in a fair tomb with images of him and his wife in alabaster'. His epitaph read:

> Hereunder lyeth a man of Fame,
> William Walworth called by name;
> Fishmonger he was in life-time here,
> And Twice Lord Mayor, as in Books appere
> With courage stout, and manly might
> Slew Wat Tyler, in King Richard's sight.

When Henry Yevele later died in 1400, he too would be buried in St Magnus, hard by the structure that had been a part of his remarkable life. Indeed, his own house was at the north end of the Bridge, opposite this church.

In 1387 the Chapel on the Bridge still stood, but more than 175 years had passed since the original building by Peter de Colechurch had been repaired, and probably rebuilt in part, after the fire of 1212. Now a new Chapel was designed and constructed under the supervision of Henry Yevele, between 1384 and 1396. The style was Perpendicular Gothic, notable for its pointed arches, vertical tracery work and fan vaulting.

The Bridge House accounts show that the Wardens purchased and assembled stone for the Chapel between 1384 and 1396. One of the later entries was for forty-three cartloads of Reigate stone 'for the upper vault', the battlements and the spiral staircase, costing £14 3s. 6d. For the spiral staircase, 'twenty great pieces of hard stone from Kent called noweles' were ordered. Most of the stone was probably worked in the Bridge House yard, for an entry in 1392 in the Bridge House Records notes twenty-one cartloads of Reigate stone being delivered there.

In the next year glazing of the Perpendicular windows began. The stained glass was sold by the foot: 150 feet were ordered, glass in which heraldic shields and images of the saints were already set, at a cost of £6 17s. 6d. At the same time 116 ½ feet of 'white glass' was ordered.

The slender, elegant Chapel was two storeys high. The upper chapel had a groined roof springing from beautiful clustered columns, while the undercroft was vaulted, with a number of Gothic windows. This revered place, which was also a well-loved decoration sitting upon the Bridge, was served by four chaplains and a clerk. When in the early 1400s for some unknown reason the priests were 'unjustly and maliciously suspended' by the Church, to keep the Chapel functioning, the Bridge Wardens' many responsibilities extended to purchasing an absolution for them.

Other insights into small events around the Chapel are found in the *Calendar of Letter Books*. In 1441, John Seynjohn, a clerk of the Chapel, had been injured and incapacitated elsewhere in the service of the City; the Lord Mayor and Corporation granted to him – with the assent of 'the Masters of the work of London Bridge for the time being' – a weekly pension of twelve pence 'so that he might pray for the City's welfare and laudable prosperity of the Bridge'.

In 1443 a William Cheyne had been appointed one of the four chaplains at a salary of ten marks per annum; additionally he received bread, wine, candles and surplices. He was also to have one of the chambers in the Bridge House reserved for laundering, as well as, interestingly, 'shredes' from the waste products produced from the carpenters employed on Bridge repairs, presumably to light his fire.

The Chapel formed a backdrop for what may have been the most extraordinary event ever to take place on the structure: the joust on Old London Bridge in 1390.

One way of releasing tension between England and Scotland was

through 'jousts of war', usually held in the Scottish Borders. The idea of the match was first raised at a banquet in Scotland, when convivial dinner conversation turned to the subject of courage and valour. Writer Raphael Holinshed's *Chronicles* records the challenging question that was asked: Are the Scottish or the English more courageous? Lord John Welles, the English Ambassador to Scotland and a man of action, impetuously challenged a Scotsman present to meet him in the lists 'with speares sharpe groond for life and death'. Representing Scotland, Sir David de Lindesay immediately responded in the affirmative.

The joust was to be between the Champion of England, Lord John Welles, and the Champion of Scotland, Sir David de Lindesay. The Englishman chose the place, London Bridge, and the Scotsman choose the day, 23 April, St George's Day, popular for tournaments because St George was the patron saint of soldiers.

The King, a lavish patron of chivalry, granted permission. He remembered the indoor jousts held by his grandfather Edward III in the Great Hall at Windsor when he was a child, in which he had been allowed a safely passive role.

A document dated 22 January 1390 granted 'Safe conduct for David de Lyndesey, Knight, for the duel to be fought with John de Welles'. It stated that Lindesay would be allowed to bring with him twenty-nine people of his company and retinue in armour, the knight himself to be included in this number, 'and twelve other knights with their Esquires, Varlets [attendants], and Pages also accounted, and with thirty horses'. The safe conduct was valid from 1 April for two months.

When it was initially agreed that the joust be held outside Scotland, London Bridge seemed an inspired and symbolic choice, but it was still a surprising one because of the lack of space. Fighting over a famous, wide and fast-flowing river, gave a thrilling edge to a spectacle that drew together chivalry and romance on the Bridge that was regarded as a Wonder of the World. The Bridge was a uniquely fitting location in a period that positively revelled in excess and the unusual, expressed in tournaments, elaborate pageants, ridiculously excessive clothing and lavish feasts.

The youthful King enjoyed the tournaments traditionally held in the vast space of Smithfield ('smooth field'), less than a mile north-west of the Bridge, where another joust was held that same year. On that occasion, in a scene that may have been repeated for the joust on the Bridge, a spectacular cavalcade rode out of the Tower of London at a gentle trot to the cheers of the tumultuous commons. At the head of the brilliant procession, sixty knights sat on sturdy wooden saddles, the horses caparisoned in matching colours, and on the noble heads of the beasts were masks of cloth with cut-outs for eyes, ears and nostrils. Next came sixty ladies riding side-saddle on fine horses, all richly apparelled, and each fine lady led with a chain of silver a knight on horseback – the knights who were to joust on that day. Under their glamorous outer robes these knights wore thin chain-mail armour. Trumpets and music accompanied them through the streets to Smithfield, where the King and Queen waited in a richly adorned viewing stand.

It was a short move to having a tournament on the Bridge. Henry Yevele, along with fellow Warden William Waddesworth, prepared for an occasion in extreme contrast to the events surrounding Wat Tyler's uprising witnessed by the Bridge only nine years earlier. The highest-ranking heraldic officer, the king-of-arms, was in charge of the detailed planning for the joust itself, while the Wardens were responsible for the safety and readiness of the structure. Yevele remembered the story of one of Edward III's jousts at Cheapside, about sixty years earlier, when the frame of a wooden tower-like grandstand from which Queen Philippa and her ladies were watching collapsed, and some knights standing underneath were injured. The vengeful King and council intended to punish the carpenters, but they were spared due to the Queen's pleading.

Old London Bridge was prepared for the joust. No expense was spared, even though there was a deficit in the Bridge House accounts at that time, which the wardens would try to balance the following year, and expensive fabrics and materials would be saved and re-used. To prepare for the event, additional workers were taken on by the Bridge House, including three masons, and the Tide Carpenter hired ten extra tidemen. The bridge street and the approach roads were cleaned, freshly gravelled and water carriers were employed to keep the dust down. The essential refuges for first aid were set up.

In a brilliantly colourful event the like of which had never happened before and would never happen again, blue and red predominated, banners and flags flapped in the breeze, shopkeepers and residents rented out every space, including the rooftops, the shores were lined with people and revellers stood in the garden of the Bear on the Southwark side to take in the view. Boats of every description were tied up as near as possible to the scene, some inevitably becoming caught up in the currents and forced to 'shoot the bridge'. As the vast, excited crowd strained for a better view, at least one man tumbled off the Bridge and into the rapids.

All the places with the best views on the Bridge were claimed by the nobility. The ladies wore tight-fitting tunics in the richest of fabrics, with high collars, long sleeves trailing on the ground and trains. On their heads box-like understructures held up fluted veils, setting off a small 'horn' of hair on each side of the temple. Over short, tight padded tunics the men wore capacious cloaks, which had huge funnel-shaped sleeves. The men's long-toed shoes at their most outrageous length were chained to each knee so they could walk. Richard was an arbitrary young king to whose vanity the richness of the exaggerated dress appealed. Such luxurious apparel reinforced the class system and vividly communicated the pleasure of indulgence in absurd extravagance.

On 23 April 'both parties . . . were most honourably conducted to the Bridge', probably having formed up at the Tower or after attending Mass with the King at St Paul's. The four Scottish knights led by Sir David de Lindesay wore the blue and white colours of Scotland and blue-grey armour. The four Englishmen led by Lord John Welles wore the King's device of the white hart, or hind.

The structures on the Bridge were being rebuilt at this time, probably allowing for the space to be temporarily adapted for the joust, and the open area in front of the Chapel was the most likely location for the event. The King, wearing a plain gold coronet, took his prominent place on his dais under a panoply of cloth of gold on a grandstand. Still only twenty-two, Richard's cheeks were flushed with excitement. This was the kind of bold venture he enjoyed. The physical vigour of the joust appealed to the frail-looking young man. It was a fitting symbol for the ruler in his first year of full kingship, and would convey the message that he was confident, manly and warlike. It was also sure to appeal to both the nobility and the commons, all of whom relished these spectacles.

The knights were to fight single battles, first with lances of war and then on foot with daggers. Attendants held each of the brilliantly caparisoned and armoured warhorses. The heralds made the customary cries in the four corners of the lists or the field of combat. The crowd roared, thrilled by the fame of the knights and the unique tilt-yard, as the immensely strong and fast heavy horses pranced nervously. The judge waved his white baton to signal the start.

As the sun caught the armour, the two knights spurred on their horses, charging full at one another. On this first charge, the twelve-foot-long 'square-ground spears' were broken, but both men remained seated, although Lord Welles's lance broke on Sir David's helmet and visor. Seeing this, the commons yearned for an instant and different outcome: 'The people beholding how stiffelie earle David sat without moving, cried that the Scottisman was locked in his saddle.' On hearing this, the fully armoured Sir David leaped down beside his horse, and very nimbly mounted his horse again 'to the great wonder of the beholders'.

Each man was ready with a fresh lance, a second course was taken, and once more the weapons were broken 'and yet without anie great hurt on either part'. The great warhorses were wild-eyed at the noise and excitement.

For the third time Sir David and Lord Welles charged one another. But this time Lord Welles was unhorsed, and falling heavily to the ground was 'sore hurt', while the commons cried out that he had been killed. The judge quickly signalled the end of the joust. The Champion of Scotland, Sir David de Lindesay, had scored the highest points by unhorsing his opponent.

To the pleasure of all, Lindesay responded like Chaucer's 'parfit, gentil knight': he was quickly off his horse, knelt by Welles's side, and tenderly held his opponent. The doctors viewed the patient, then Welles's men took their lord home, while the people rushed to collect up the shattered lances and any other souvenirs left on the tilt-yard on a bridge.

In the days following the joust, Sir David visited Lord Welles's bedside every day until he recovered. The King gave the victor valuable gifts, and Richard and his court became so fond of the Scotsman – whose fine qualities were apparent to everyone – that, at the King's request, Sir David twice prolonged his stay in London. When the warrant was finally issued for the knight's departure on board the Scottish vessel the *Seinte Marie* of Dundee, it specifically noted that the mariners 'were not to carry with them any property or goods whatsoever, not any illicit goods, or prohibited merchandise out of the kingdom . . . excepting only one complete Armour of War for the body of David Lyndesey of Scotland, Knight . . .' Sixteen years later, Lindesay became the Scottish Ambassador to England.

There were many other spectacular jousts throughout the country, including water jousts, but none to equal the one held that day on Old London Bridge.

But by 1392 King Richard, aged twenty-five, was becoming increasingly reckless with money. Over and over the young King went to the City to replenish his coffers. He made various money-raising suggestions, but the Londoners always refused to cooperate.

Undeterred, the King approached a Lombard, who agreed to arrange a loan. But when the King heard that this rich Italian banker had himself turned for financial support to those wealthy citizens who had refused their sovereign's own request, he was furious, and imprisoned the Lord Mayor, John Hende, and the sheriffs. On 1 July the appointment of a new Lord Mayor and two new sheriffs was announced. There was more: the Courts of King's Bench and Exchequer were transferred to York, and a huge fine of £100,000 was inflicted on the City. In this impossible situation the citizens were forced to look for ways to appease Richard.

In August the King announced that he would leave his palace at Sheen (Richmond), Surrey, and go to London by road. Chronicler Robert Fabyan recounted how the citizens sent a deputation to Richard, humbly asking for his pardon. Queen Anne and others worked to resolve the situation and the King accepted the invitation 'to ryde throughe his chaumber of London', encouraged by a gift of £10,000.

For such a crucial occasion, one of the most magnificent receptions ever seen at the Bridge was organized. Four hundred important Londoners, all dressed in livery, met the royal pair at Wandsworth to escort them to London. In Southwark, at St George's Church, Richard and Anne were greeted by a great number of clergy and five hundred choristers. At the Great Stone Gate – freshly scrubbed – an assembly comprising almost every citizen arranged by age, rank and sex presented the King with gifts. Richard was pleased to receive the two carefully selected milk-white horses, the one for him sumptuously 'trappyd in ryche cloth of gold' with silver ornamented saddle, while the trappings of the Queen's horse were embroidered with red and white, her saddle ornamented in gold. As the steeds snorted and nodded, the silver bells on the musical harnesses tinkled.

The great reception had begun. The King was moved by the devotion and generosity he received, which also appealed to his vanity and calmed his insecurity. A month later he remitted the fine of £100,000 he had imposed, liberated the Lord Mayor and sheriffs and returned the liberties of the City. After his queen, Anne of Bohemia, died in 1394, his behaviour worsened, but he was soon to marry again.

In the autumn of 1395 Richard and Charles VI of France met

at Arls in Picardy. A peace treaty was drawn up to continue, optimistically, for 'thirty winters'. Fabyan notes that at the same time 'the Frenshe Kyng delivered unto kynge Rycharde dame Isabell his doughter', who was eight years old. The marriage was celebrated with great magnificence in November of 1396 at Calais. Richard typically squandered huge sums of money on entertainment, after which, in the same vein, he took his child-bride shopping.

London was soon alerted to the royal couple's arrival at Dover. Husband and young bride passed over the Bridge on their way to the royal apartments in the Tower. In the great crowd eight or nine persons were crushed to death on the Bridge. Among them was an unfortunate matron who lived at Cornhill, who had apparently felt it worthwhile to join the throng streaming towards the Bridge to see for herself the girl whose coronation would shortly take place. Also crushed was a prior of the Augustinian house of St Mary and St Nicholas at Tiptree in Essex, who was visiting London.

Tolerance of Richard's uncontrolled extravagance and tyrannical behaviour came to an abrupt end in 1397. Four knights, Richard's favourites, had crossed to Calais, where they murdered the King's uncle, the Duke of Gloucester. The deceased had robustly opposed Richard for some time, and it was believed that the King had ordered the murder. Richard and his court were imprisoned in the Tower, and the four knights were arrested by Henry Bolingbroke, who would later succeed Richard as king. They were accused of murder and handed over to the Lord Mayor, following which there was a memorable scene at the Guildhall, when the charges were read out against Richard II and the knights. The latter were sentenced, and paraded before the royal apartments of the Tower in view of King Richard. Then, '. . . Without saying a word, these four were dragged from the Tower, through the streets to Cheapside, and, on a fishmongers' stall, had their heads struck off, which were placed over the gate on London Bridge, and their bodies hung on a gibbet'. The excitement over, and justice seen to be done, Froissart concludes: 'After this execution every man returned to his home.' Richard was forced to abdicate in 1399, nine years after the great joust on London Bridge, and died in 1400.

On a day-to-day basis, it was the Bridge Wardens who were in charge of one of the City's greatest assets. The Bridge itself, with its nineteen piers and twenty arches, and the structures on it, almost 140 houses and gateways, formed one very large element under their care. But there was much more. A substantial portfolio of revenue-producing properties had been assembled by the mid-fourteenth century. Many were originally valuable gifts of property, some of which are recorded in the *Calendar of Wills proved and enrolled in the Court of Husting*. The Bridge's assets included more than a hundred shops and tenements in the streets to the north and east of St Paul's, some property elsewhere, farmland, the manor of Lewisham, two mills on the River Lea and thirty tenements in Southwark. Records from 1381 to 1382 note that monies came in from rents of tenements in London and Southwark; quit-rents (a small rent in lieu of services by the tenant) in London and Southwark; and farms (leases) of numerous lands and manors.

Then there were the rents paid by butchers and other tradesmen who had stalls in the Stocks Market. And tolls were collected from ships passing through the Drawbridge and from iron-shod carts going over it. The latter toll was first imposed in 1356, the earliest of many references to the damage caused to the bridge street by these carts; thereafter all carts were compelled to help pay for the repairs to the road surface through a toll, with new edicts reinforcing the previous ones in attempts to deal with a problem that plagued the Bridge for centuries.

But money went out as well as coming in. The Bridge sometimes could not avoid exceptional demands on its resources. By the end of the fourteenth century, civic government was slowly maturing, and the City was administered from the Guildhall. The construction of the stone Guildhall between 1411 and 1430 on what had once been the site of the Roman amphitheatre proved to be extremely costly. From 1413 the Bridge was required to contribute 100 marks sterling annually to 'the New Work' for six years. The

Common Council called on ten other sources for funds as well, but this still did not bring in enough money, so the financial support by the Bridge was extended for another three years.

The Bridge Wardens were based at the Bridge House in Southwark, where there was a house and garden for a Warden, among a variety of buildings. Most work on the Bridge was done in the long summer days when the water flow was less than in the winter months, and every March the Wardens began to assemble the materials required for both the planned work and the inevitable emergencies. This included stone for fine masonry, and soft rubble, chalk, pitch and tar for waterproofing; cement, iron pileshoes to tip the piles, elm for the piers and large pieces of timber. Goods for work on the Bridge could be delivered directly to the wharf at Bridge House yard. The Wardens were always on the look-out for anything that would be of use. A specific and highly desirable tree, a fine elm growing 'next Trillemyllebroke', near the Holborn house of the Bishop of Ely in Elizabethan times, did not escape their notice, and it was taken for the Bridge.

The number of staff based at the Bridge House varied but could be considerable. In 1381 to 1382, in addition to those at the Chapel, there was the important Clerk of the Drawbridge, who supervised the work, six carpenters, four masons, two sawyers, one mariner, a cook, and one or two rent-collectors and a rat-taker. Until 1462 the Bridge House owned a team of cart-horses and one or two carts, after which independent carriers were hired.

The confident carpenters were among the permanent workers and seemed to regard the Bridge House as a comfortable home from home, for they kept two cooks there just to buy, dress and roast the meat for their meals. In 1480 they were reprimanded for doing this without permission, and the cosy arrangement was forbidden; the order added that every one of them 'shalbe bothe by day and by night to help yf any jeparde and casuelte of hurt falle atte bridge . . .'

The 1405–6 records show that a legitimate cook and housekeeper of the Bridge House itself also cared for and fed the guard dogs: for over two hundred years there was a meat allowance for the hounds. But they could be expensive in another way. When someone was injured by 'the Bridghouse dogges', the Wardens were compelled to pay compensation.

This was but one of innumerable unexpected ways in which the Bridge Wardens were considered to be financially responsible. In 1426, when there was an undisclosed affray at the bridgefoot, a cartman was forced to wait at an inn in Southwark with his horse and cart until 'le fray' was subdued, and he later charged the Wardens for the feed his horse had eaten during the delay.

When a disaster suddenly occurred or the day of a royal spectacle neared, extra workers were brought in; they might range from wood-carvers, painters, gilders, tilers or plasterers to plumbers or smiths. And in an emergency they were paid extra to work through the night without food or sleep. The condition of the piers was the responsibility of the Tide Carpenter, who took on extra tidemen as necessary. On one occasion twenty-one tidemen – paid per tide – worked for six hours 'at the ram', pounding down fresh rubble into the damaged outworks of piles or 'starlings', as they were called, which surrounded each pier to protect it from the incessant currents and the debris in the river.

Workers' loyalty and hard work was rewarded with extra payments, and they were treated with consideration. A 'shuteman' was in charge of the 'shute' or barge belonging to the Bridge, which day and night carried the most frequently needed timber and building materials. But the bridge weir was so dangerous in the dark that the Wardens came to an agreement with the church of St Mary Overie, upstream of the Bridge in Southwark, permitting the shutemen to tie up at the church stairs to await the dawn. And a shelter with a fireplace was built in the Bridge House yard for the wet and tired shutemen, but they were warned not to take advantage, and that the shelter must not become a dwelling or be used to entertain their friends.

There was paid sick leave and even pensions for those too injured, too sick or too old to work. When in 1407 the shute required repairs at Deptford, the shuteman was also in need of repair: the wardens paid 2d. 'for his aid to cure his finger wounded and broken in the work of the bridge'. In 1547 two City surgeons were paid 'for healing a great wound in the head of John Alerton, the carpenter of the bridge by default of the old gin', or windlass. There may also have been a kind of clothing allowance: there is a notation nine pairs of shoes were purchased in 1441 for carpenters who were working in the water.

On the bridge street one busy man's job was to keep carts moving. In 1413 an officer must have been kept very active indeed, for he was required to both supervise the working of the bascule at the Drawbridge and manage the traffic.

Trading standards were maintained by the City and by the Livery Companies. In 1372 two pouchmakers who lived on the Bridge, John de Leye and Thomas Gandre – also a toll collector on the Bridge – were appointed by the Lord Mayor and aldermen to prevent the sale of counterfeit roe-leather (deer-skin). Any sheepskin or calf leather scraped and made to resemble roe-leather that they found was seized and burned. All trades were strictly watched, and the punishment was an example to all: when in 1319 a William Sperlying was accused of selling two putrid meat carcasses, he was put in the pillory and the meat burned beneath him, a not unusual punishment.

Clerks, sometimes the clerks of the Chapel, wrote up the accounts, and helped the Wardens with various duties seemingly unrelated to their calling. The earliest accounts, from 1381 to 1405, were written on parchment rolls, and from then on kept in leatherbound volumes. Until 1480 records were written in Latin, with beautifully elaborate initial letters and other ornamental features; seventeen of these early rolls survive at the Guildhall.

The carefully kept Bridge House accounts were supposed to be submitted annually, but this more usually happened when the Wardens finished their term. Then they were compelled to make an inventory of the extraordinary variety and number of goods the Bridge House had in hand to be passed on to the care of the new Wardens. This included all the items in the Chapel of St Thomas à Becket, recorded by H.T. Riley in *Memorials of London and London Life*, the numerous details of which reflect a thriving establishment.

Nothing was too small not to be noted: in 1392 three service books were bound, costing 8s.; a veil was purchased for covering the sacred vessels at Lent, and a cloth for covering the cross and the image of St Thomas; and in 1396 the purchase of two keys was noted, along with a 'havegooday' – perhaps a knocker – and two iron plates for the outer door.

One exact accounting in the Bridge House Records remains. It was prepared by outgoing Wardens Alan Gylle and John de Hardyngham for the period from Michaelmas (29 September, the feast of St Michael the Archangel) 1348 to 1 November 1350. All materials and goods possessed by the Bridge House at that time are listed in an impressive and lengthy testament to highly detailed organization. The list comprises quantities and values of building materials, implements and boats.

There was timber for fourteen 'pre-fab' shops, made and framed, ready to be erected, each year for several buildings on the Bridge or elsewhere under the care of the Wardens either became dilapidated or burned down and had to be rebuilt; 400 great pieces of oak; another pile of timber stacked in a garden by the river; 120 elm piles for strengthening the piers; 'two engines with three "rammes"' for driving in the piles; 57,000 'hertlathes' (made from the heart of the wood), among thousands of other pieces of various kinds of wood selected to be used for specific purposes.

As for the quantity of Portland stone held, they reckoned there were 1,734 pieces, both unwrought and wrought, including 690 feet handworked. The list goes on and on, including 'cement for the Bridge' at £3 and seven barrels of pitch at 4s. per barrel. Two boats were filled with ragstone and one with chalk, perhaps because work was underway on the Bridge. Unlike Rochester Bridge, London Bridge, surprisingly, did not own its own quarry.

In the 'werkhaus' were 7½ weys [a lead measurement] of old lead and vast numbers of nails, 400 large nails used for the heavy timbers of the Drawbridge and 23,000 roof nails among them. There was a presser, two cauldrons and five brass pots, but only three boats: a 'great boat', a small boat and a timber barge. When necessary, additional boats were hired.

From about the same time (1358), a list drawn up by the Wardens in the Bridge House Records has survived to give us a rare and more or less complete insight into who was on the Bridge at one particular time.

BETWEEN THE STAPLES OF THE BRIDGE AND THE STONE GATE [Great Stone Gate] ON THE EAST SIDE.
Ten shops.
In the aforesaid gate is a certain house which is delivered to John Bedell for keeping the gate.
Sum £11 9s. 4d.
ON THE WEST SIDE.
Ten shops and a mansion in the Stone Gate.
Sum £8 2s. 4d.
BETWEEN THE STONE GATE AND THE DRAWBRIDGE ON THE EAST SIDE.
Seven shops (three with *hautepas)*.
Sum £8 6s. 8d.
ON THE WEST SIDE.
Seven shops (three with *hautepas*).
Sum £8.
BETWEEN THE DRAWBRIDGE AND THE CHAPEL ON THE EAST SIDE.
Seventeen shops (five with *hautepas*).
Sum £14 6s. 8d.
ON THE WEST SIDE.
Twenty shops (four with *hautepas*).
Sum £16 2s. 8d.
BETWEEN THE CHAPEL AND THE STAPLES OF THE BRIDGE TOWARDS LONDON ON THE EAST SIDE.
Five shops (nine with *hautepas*).
Sum £50.
ON THE WEST SIDE. A NEW SHOP NEXT THE COUNTER [counting-house].
Thirty-two shops (10 with *hautepas*).
Sum £43 16s. 4d.

The rents totalled £160 4s. The rents were slightly higher as one neared the City end of the Bridge, where the shops tended to sell better quality goods, especially beyond the Chapel.

The community who lived on the Bridge usually worked there too. In 1351, in a very early reference to a trader living on the Bridge, Thomas de Gloucestre, a glover, was granted a life tenancy at an annual rent of 36s. 8d. by the Wardens for a shop situated between those of Thomas Ledred and John de Mucham. The gateway-keepers, the Keeper of the Heads, who was kept busy adding and replacing traitors' heads on the Drawbridge Gate, and perhaps others as well, were granted leases to live in the gateways, and in 1358 gateway-keeper John Bedell lived in part of the Great Stone Gate. In 1399 the gate was granted for life to William East, 'Serjeant and citizen', presumably as his residence. The Wardens had to sort out staff problems, and when in 1345 a John le Conduit was appointed gateway-keeper he was replaced for an unknown reason only nine months later by a cordwainer or shoemaker named Henry de Aumbresbury.

It was the fishmongers who were among those most closely connected with the Bridge, for it was central to their lives. The fishermen worked under and around it on a river teeming with fish, while at the City end of the Bridge Billingsgate fish market lay on one side and the Hall of the Fishmongers Company on the other. The Fishmongers Company, one of the twelve great Livery Companies of London with an unbroken existence of more than 700 years, were organized long before their first charter from Edward I (1272) gave them a monopoly on this essential food. No fish could be sold in London except by them, and it was their responsibility to check that the fish were 'sound'.

They contributed in a variety of ways to the funds for the Bridge. At this early date it seems that fishing was allowed under the Bridge itself, unlike later, for there was a leased 'farm' to control the fishing and payments; this meant that tolls or fines were leased out to a person or group, who 'farmed' the resource for a specified term with a fixed sum paid to the City. And fishmongers who had stalls under the wall of the Friars Minors in London paid rent to the Bridge House, as did those in the Stocks Market.

When it came to pageantry, the fishmongers boldly tried to outdo all the other Livery Companies. In a royal procession of 1298, their pageant included four gilded sturgeons carried on four horses, four silvered salmon on another four horses, followed by forty-six men on horseback and one representing St Magnus. In a 1313 pageant they constructed a ship in full sail that was emblazoned with the heraldic devices of the English and French royal houses. For the coronation of Richard II it was noted that they had again excelled themselves.

Those working or travelling on the river could hear the chanting of priests in the Chapel, a comforting spiritual strand among the danger, noise and confusion. Fishermen could enter the lower chapel from the pier, and it played a daily part in their lives. In the reign of Henry III (1216–72), services in the Chapel and at St Magnus had regulated the times fishermen could begin selling fish. Those from the south coast, going over the Bridge to sell their fish at Billingsgate, were regulated by the Statutes of the Fishmongers Company. The *Liber Albus* of 1419 by John Carpenter, in which the City's laws, customs, privileges and usages were recorded, notes that to prevent forestalling (buying up goods in advance), the sale of freshwater fish had to wait for the end of the Mass, and salt fish could not be sold until the Office (or service) of Prime (the bell rung at the first of the canonical hours, six to seven a.m.).

St Magnus at the City end may well have been something of a sinecure for the clergy. Arnold's Chronicle (*c.* 1502), quoted in James S. Ogilvy's *Relics and Memorials of London City*, recounts that when services were being held, '. . . dyvers of the priests and clarkes, in the time of divine service, be at taverns and ale-houses, at fyshing and other triflis . . .'

William Walworth wasn't the only fishmonger among the early Bridge Wardens. For several terms from 1355 to 1363 the Wardens were John de Hatfield senior, chandler or candle-maker; and Richard Bacoun, a stockfishmonger, who typically made a bequest of 100 marks to the Bridge. The companies of the rival saltfishmongers (wet-fish traders) and stockfishmongers (dried-fish traders) merged in 1536.

For two terms, from 1339 to 1342, the Bridge Wardens were Alan Gylle and John Lovekyn, who was a prominent fish merchant, and Lord Mayor in 1348 and 1366. Lovekyn lived in a house near the north end of the Bridge, and in 1349, when a Thomas de Kyngestone and an Edmund Ware were settling an argument in the 'High Street of London Bridge', the prosperous-looking Lovekyn intervened. Lucy Toulmin Smith's *Itinerary of John Leland* records that the two men immediately forgot their own fight and turned on him, beating and abusing him 'to the terror of passers by and in contempt of the King'. They had picked on the wrong man, for only the year before Lovekyn had been Lord Mayor. Both pleaded not guilty at their trial, but the records are silent as to the sentences passed.

The Thames presented an ever-changing scene, with smaller craft above the Bridge conveying passengers in wherries or water taxis, while below the Bridge larger trading vessels also served the warehouses and wharves. The river was 'full of swans white as snow', and the Bridge House had, for a time, a keeper of swans. The cygnets were marked with nicks in the beak indicating ownership at the summer swan-upping ceremony. And for centuries, from the reign of Richard II to that of James I, the Constable of the Tower of London was entitled to lay claim to all the swans that went through the Bridge towards the Tower. Surprisingly, swans must have nested under the quieter, less used arches of the old Bridge, for he claimed a payment of one cygnet from each swan's nest there. Oxen, pigs, cows and sheep being driven across the Bridge fell into the water frequently enough for the Constable to have a claim to them too if they swam through the middle arches to the Tower.

But who claimed the people who for one reason or another ended up in the water? By Dickens' time, and probably much earlier, the lowest of the low were the 'river-finders' or dredgers, like Lizzie Hexham's father in *Our Mutual Friend*. Henry Mayhew, a social historian and contemporary of Dickens, wrote: 'Dredgers are the men who found almost all the bodies of persons drowned. If there were a reward offered for the recovery of a body, numbers of dredgers will at once endeavour to obtain it . . . no body recovered by a dredgerman ever happens to have any money about it, when brought to shore.'

In 1403, during the turbulent reign of the strong Lancastrian Henry IV (1399–1413) who had replaced Richard II, Kent was once again the centre of spreading discontent. More than a hundred esquires and gentlemen threw in their lot with the rebels. The rising was led by a previously loyal supporter, Henry Percy, Earl of Northumberland, and his impetuous son, also Henry, known as 'Hotspur'.

Hotspur's death at Shrewsbury in 1403 ended the first Percy rebellion, and was immortalized by Shakespeare in *Henry IV, Part II*:

> The King is almost wounded to the death;
> And, in the fortune of my lord your son,
> Prince Harry [Hotspur] slain outright . . .

Hotspur's body was cut into quarters, and the sheriff of Shropshire was ordered to dispatch one quarter to London, where the Lord Mayor and sheriffs were told to place it on the Bridge, the quarter 'to remain there as long as it will last'. The old Earl, Hotspur's father, got off with a heavy fine, but two years later rebelled again and was captured; this time it was his head that ended up on Old London Bridge.

CHAPTER THREE

'Jack Cade hath gotten London Bridge'

Upon thy lusty bridge of pillars white
Been merchantes full royal to behold,
Upon thy streets goeth many a seemly knight
In velvet gownes and chaines of gold ...

London, thou art the flower of cities all.
William Dunbar, 1501–2

UNBELIEVABLY THE BRIDGE HAD NOT BEEN DEPICTED BY ARTISTS IN ITS FIRST THREE HUNDRED YEARS, or at least no drawing has survived. Finally, an illustration was about to appear, and as a direct result of the Battle of Agincourt in 1415.

Within months of his accession, Henry V (1413–22) had reopened the Hundred Years War in an attempt to regain lands in France. On 25 October at Agincourt the army he so boldly led was victorious over a French army three times larger. When the news reached London only two days later, all the church bells rang out to celebrate a victory that would never be forgotten. Among those captured was the French commander, Charles, Duke of Orléans.

This occasion remains an historical landmark for the country and for Old London Bridge. The French duke was to be a prisoner in the Tower of London for twenty-five years, well into the reign of

England's Henry VI, when he was finally ransomed. He spent his time composing ballads and poems, and this resulted in a priceless contribution to the story of the Bridge: the first known illustration. The Duke wrote a manuscript of romantic poems that was bound in a beautifully illuminated volume, now in the British Library, and in it is the earliest contemporary representation of the Bridge. Within one exquisite composite illustration the Duke, a nephew of Charles VI of France who had married the widow of Richard II of England, is depicted at various stages of his captivity at the Tower of London – palace and prison – and in sight of Old London Bridge. In the background a portion of the Bridge at the City end can be seen. The lovely Perpendicular Chapel of St Thomas à Becket is there with its battlemented parapets. The stones of the piers and arches are a soft grey, the roofs reddish-brown, against a dream-like sky of blue.

The appearance of Old London Bridge in the second of its seven stages at about 1500 is established by this illustration, the details confirmed by the others that began to appear shortly after. One of these is the charming bird's-eye view of London by Antony van den Wyngaerde. Wyngaerde was a Fleming, probably in England in the entourage of Philip II of Spain in 1558. His panoramic drawing of London Bridge from the south-east, about 1553, was the first time the whole length of it was depicted, reflecting the rebuilding carried out in the last half of the fifteenth century. (The view is ten feet long and one foot five inches deep. Once kept as a roll, it is now mounted on fourteen separate sheets in the Ashmolean Museum, Oxford.)

All the famous elements, as well as the details, are there. At the Southwark end boats rest on the large exposed bank at what must have been low tide. The Great Stone Gate, with its chimney for the fire of the gatekeeper, has a gabled roof, higher in the centre than at each side, where there are projecting three-storey hexagonal extensions built out over each end of the pier. Approaching enemies cannot hide in the open space before the thirty-foot gap of the drawbridge opening, and the Drawbridge Gate itself is much larger and more solid than the gate at the Southwark end. On four levels each corner of the Drawbridge Gate has defensive slits, there are

The Chapel of St Thomas à Becket on the Bridge.

two parapets, one halfway up, and heads are exposed above the top parapet. Other details of this gate have come down to us: the west wall of its tower was adorned with two statues; the one of St Thomas of 1492 had been joined by St Catherine. In 1552 more statues were added: Saints Peter, Paul, Michael and George, as well as two richly gilded lions. At the Chapel of St Thomas à Becket the Perpendicular columns elegantly stretch all the way from the water line to the roof line.

And there is Ralph Agas's less detailed, less sophisticated *Plan of London,* dating from about 1560–70, a bird's-eye view from the south. The view of the rooftops on the Bridge shows just how many hautpas there were. Very little light could have penetrated to the bridge street.

That day in late November 1415 when Henry V returned to London with his prisoners after the victory at Agincourt, the City's reception eclipsed anything previously seen.

Interior view of the upper chapel.

The King had landed at Dover in the first week of November. He first rested at Eltham Palace, and then on 23 November rode on to Blackheath, to be greeted in a stunning scene by the Mayor, representatives of the Livery Companies, and 10,000 nobles and citizens dressed in red cloaks with hoods of black and white.

About a mile from the City, King Henry was met by a great procession of clergy wearing rich copes and carrying censers. With the King in their midst, the cavalcade reached Southwark. For the first in the sequence of excessively elaborate pageants that day, the Chronicle of Adam of Usk 1377–1421 describes how outside the Great Stone Gate stood 'an armed giant . . . outtopping the walls in height, having a spear even like to the spear of Turnus, and a mighty axe . . . and by his side was his wife, so huge that not only was she fit in truth to give birth to giant devils . . .' This tradition of giant figures continues today in the huge carved figures of 'Gog' and 'Magog' in the Great Hall at the Guildhall, supposedly representing legendary pre-Christian conflict between ancient Britons and Trojan invaders.

John Lydgate, Benedictine monk and poet, who was employed to record the event in every detail, described how:

> Upon the gate they stode on hy,
> A gyant that was full grym of syght,
> To teche the Frensshmen [the Duke] courtesye.

When the procession reached the Drawbridge, 'there issued out empresses thre' representing the goddesses of Nature, Grace and Fortune, and wearing golden crowns studded with transparent stones. Seven attendant maidens wearing crowns were dressed in white with sapphire 'baldrics' (shoulder-to-waist belts for holding swords). There were trumpeters in the turrets, and a tower was built across the Bridge on which stood an effigy of St George, his head adorned with laurels interwoven with jewels. At the Drawbridge Gate were two 'outworks': on the right a lion holding a lance; on the left an antelope from whose neck hung a shield bearing the royal arms.

The chroniclers seem to have tired of describing these extraordinary spectacles by the time of another great royal reception almost five years later. In the Treaty of Troyes of May 1420, the French king, the demented Charles VI, was forced by Henry V's victories to acknowledge him as his regent and heir. The pact was sealed by the English king's betrothal to Charles's daughter, Catherine. They were married two weeks later, and the royal bride was brought to London for her coronation in February 1421. No details remain of the welcome pageant and formal procession. A weary Robert Fabyan wrote: 'I wyll passe over the great and curyous ordynaunce'. Historian and chronicler Edward Hall's only comment on the 'mervel' was '. . . which for tediousnesse I over passe'.

But the Wardens would remember the reception, for it had left them with the problem of a serious overspend of £35 for decorating the Bridge. The accounts for the formal welcome for the King and his new queen included a range of items, from a payment of 2s. 8d. to John Silkeston to cover the cook's stipend, the hounds' food and the ale, 'to 18d. to W. Goos for carving the head of the Giant for the Bridge against the King's coming'. The list went on and on. Two carpenters had been employed for the whole week before the great day. Also to be paid for were sixteen alder poles; thousands of different types of nails; gilding the image in the Great Stone Gate; nineteen garments of linen cloth for the virgins on the Bridge; wings for the angels. Then there was the cost of the bread, wine and ale for the Lord Mayor, sheriffs and aldermen when they came to the Bridge to check the arrangements before the reception, as was usual before such occasions.

Prince Henry was born in 1421, and Henry V returned to France. But the next procession into the City was unexpected, for it was that of the King's funeral cortège bringing him home.

Henry V had died of dysentery in 1422 at Vincennes Castle near Paris, leaving his ten-month-old son King of England. Two months later the infant became King of France as well. King Henry was embalmed and placed in a lead coffin borne on a carriage pulled by six richly trapped horses, the details of the procession recorded in *Hall's Chronicle*. The coffin was covered with gold brocade, upon which lay a wax effigy wearing royal robes, and a crown set with jewels, and holding the sceptre and orb. The cortège processed homeward from the Bois de Vincennes, through Paris, Rouen and Abbeville to Calais and the Channel.

In London the bridge-dwellers prepared to watch a spectacle celebrating death. After passing over the rough country roads, on 11 November 1422 the procession reached St George's Bar in Southwark, where the Mayor and others waited in white robes. On either side of the funeral carriage rode 'five hundred men of armes al in black harnes and their horses barded black', carrying spears reversed, while three hundred others held long torches. As the funeral carriage passed over the Bridge, fifteen splendidly attired bishops chanted the Office for the Dead.

Daily life continued. In the same month as the royal funeral, the wardens of Rochester Bridge consulted with Sir William Sevenoke, a notable figure in the Grocers Company who was a Warden of London Bridge in 1404, represented the City in Parliament in 1417 and was Lord Mayor in 1418. They asked him how to fix their bridge. Sevenoke went to Rochester to examine the cracks, and they gratefully accepted the advice he offered. Gifts were often presented to benefactors or would-be benefactors of a bridge, and in this ongoing relationship several years later Sir William received a boar as a present from the wardens of Rochester Bridge.

As already noted, Henry VI was an infant when he acceded to the throne, making unstable times even more volatile. Initially, the country was run by Humphrey, Duke of Gloucester, who was Regent of England. Struggles for power could erupt without warning, but there were some predictable trigger points, one being the election of a new Lord Mayor. A serious disturbance occurred at the bridge-foot on 29 October 1423, the day of the election, recorded in Gregory's Chronicle of 1428–9. The Regent sent for the chief magistrate, who was at the Lord Mayor's Guildhall banquet. The Lord Mayor and aldermen were warned to take special precautions for the safe-keeping of the City both that night and the next, so a watch was kept at the gates, especially at the Bridge. All this activity was the result of strained relations between the Regent and the Bishop of Winchester, whose palace was close to the Bridge in Southwark.

The next morning an attempt was made by some of the Bishop's retainers to remove the chains between the staples or wooden posts in Southwark that marked the boundary of the City at the Bridge. The force on the Bridge drove them off, and on hearing that the Bishop's men were preparing to attack, more armed citizens rushed to defend the Bridge. At this critical point the Lord Mayor and other peacemakers intervened, riding back and forth between the two parties until calm was restored. No harm done, the citizens went home and took off their armour, and the bridge-dwellers relaxed a little.

Among the tumult of people and animals crossing the bridge street were riders on horseback, while those among the rich who didn't ride were carried in litters. Sledges, carts shod with iron, and hand barrows came over the Bridge, as under it rubbish, dead cats, dogs and horses and entrails from the slaughterhouses were pulled by the tides. When one of the arches cracked in 1424, giving a frightening view of the river below and the unpleasant contents of the 'troubled' water, the driving of carts shod with iron was totally banned; the punishment for the cartman was 'imprisonment of hys body' and a fine, but even this did not work, and further orders were required over many years to come. And the vibrations from the wheels of iron-shod carts made the beer in the barrels on the carts work up so much that barrels which seemed to be full when purchased, when opened lacked as much as a gallon.

The crack that was blamed on the iron-shod carts may have forced the decision to build a new Drawbridge Gate, this time with a much stronger tower. But additional money was needed to launch into this endeavour. To discuss the finance required for a new Drawbridge Gate, a no doubt generous working breakfast was held at the Bridge House, where a well-appointed room was used by officials for meetings and for the meals held after the group had carried out one of the regular examinations.

The breakfast was attended by Bridge notables, who intended to seek help from the executors of the will of Richard Whittington.

Whittington was a wealthy mercer who imported silks and velvets, and was four times Lord Mayor of London. This philanthropist had died in 1423, leaving his fortune – equivalent to £5 million in today's money – to a trust which has been of great benefit to the people of London for close to six hundred years. (The extensive Whittington Charity is still administered by the Mercers Company.) Attending the meeting was the Common Clerk, John Carpenter, a friend of Whittington's and one of the four executors. This was the same John Carpenter who had written the *Liber Albus* of 1419 under Whittington's mayoralty, using the archives to compile an invaluable record of the City's laws and regulations.

The outcome of the meeting at the Bridge House must have been successful, for almost immediately the gate was 'newe begun to be builded in the Yeare 1426'. John Stow records that John Reynwell, the Lord Mayor, laid the first of four foundation stones. For such important work on the Bridge, the blessing of God was still essential: 'IHESUS' was cut on all four stones. Reynwell concerned himself with the Bridge much more than the norm, for he was generous in giving lands and houses to provide funds for the Bridge; and it was due to him that tolls on goods, merchandise, victuals and carriages were withdrawn at the gates at this time.

The Bridge could be damaged on a daily basis. In 1425 and in 1482 the piers and 'grounde werks' were being harmed by fishermen commonly called Petermen, in their boats called Peterboats – the names derived from the apostle Peter. An Act of Common Council as early as around 1400 referred to 'Petermen and others fysshing in the Thames'. There were strict rules about the size of each species allowed to be caught and the methods used, but the adept Petermen, in their double-bowed craft that moved equally well with either end at the front, used nets and '. . . unlawful Engines and Arts in catching Fish in the river Thames'. Also singled out were those who, while collecting whelks and other fish at certain times of year, damaged the piers by keeping their boats too close to them. Additionally, no ship lying at Fresh Wharf, or anywhere else on the east, downstream, side was allowed to cast anchor or fish in the gullies of water flowing through the Bridge nor within a distance of twenty fathoms of any pier of the Bridge. The law was enforced 'under penalty of imprisonment and forfeiture of nets and fish, nets and equipment being publicly burned in the Cheap [at Cheapside]', the main street.

References to Petermen and Peterboats cascaded down the centuries. In about 1668 a William Good, Rope and Twine Maker, could be found at the sign of the Peter Boat and Doublet on London Bridge. A 1930s tradesman's card of Messrs William Good & Son, who were well-known rope-makers at 12 King William Street, reproduced the sign with the date 1688, and on their premises was an old wooden sign to which was attached a plate engraved: 'This business was established in the reign of King Charles II at the Sign of the Peter Boat & Doublet on Old London Bridge'.

Vessels worried those residing on London Bridge in other ways. Some images have an undeniable immediacy. One such was the incident in 1465 when the leaded lights in the windows of a house on the Bridge were smashed by the bowsprit of a foreign ship passing through Drawbridge Lock. The bowsprit bounced off with no further damage, but a sailor had to pay twelvepence for the window to be mended. At the Bridge House wharf, in 1527, a Frenchman was fined for 'brozing [bruising] of a lyytell house upon the Brigge House wharfhe' as his boat rose and fell with the tides.

At dusk on a November evening in 1428 a famous accident occurred under the Bridge. Gregory's Chronicle tells how the Duke of Norfolk boarded his barge at St Mary Overie, above the Bridge, intending to pass through it. A mistake was made in steering, the barge hit one of the piers and at least thirty people drowned. The Duke and two or three others anticipated what was about to happen and jumped on to the pier just before the boat overturned. Ropes were lowered to them and they were hauled up to the bridge street. Even at high tide the arches were dangerous, for the water was then about three feet above the tops of the piers, concealing them from the watermen.

Tough and solid as Old London Bridge appeared to be, it required constant care, and two accounts note that it rocked when a heavy tide was coming in. At the best of times the Bridge was costly to maintain, not only from the damage done by exceptional weather and fire, but from the daily relentless teasing of the water, from the use of the variety of buildings on it and from the incessant traffic. The Bridge was dilapidated during the unstable rule of Henry VI, for the accounts record that the wardens, unusually, were in debt to the Bridge House Fund for £327 9s. 10d., and when it was in poor condition, less money came in from rents and even tolls.

Then, on 14 January 1437 the Great Stone Gate suddenly collapsed, as did the pier on which it stood, affecting both sides of the two arches involved, and houses, although surprisingly no lives were lost. Part of the masonry fell backwards in one piece into the river under the third arch from the bridgefoot. This lock became known as Rock Lock because the obstruction, soon covered in green slime, remained there for the next four hundred years; that is, the rest of the life of the Bridge.

The Wardens faced a difficult decision. Was a temporary structure of wood to be built on one side for light traffic while the stonework on the other side was being rebuilt? Presumably all effort was put into the repair, for the collapse would have had a serious effect on daily life and commerce. But the for once uncomplaining watermen prospered when the Bridge was out of commission.

The next year, 1438, Lord Mayor Stephen Broun asked Richard Beck, clerk of the works to the chapter at Christ Church, Canterbury, to come to London to inspect the damaged Bridge, and to supervise the work needed to keep it standing. Beck was paid four shillings, given 'a convenient house', money for clothes and two pairs of hose 'so long as he may bestir himself, see and walk'. If incapacitated he would receive a good pension for life: another example of how well treated were those who worked for the Bridge. The new structure, according to Stow, was a strong and beautiful piece of work. The cost of rebuilding in what Stow calls 'the voyd place', presumably meaning the gap south of the Great Stone Gate, was assisted by £100 from Richard Gardiner, Lord Mayor in 1478.

On the Drawbridge Gate, the heads of an extraordinary variety of people continued to be displayed, and not just those of the famous, although it did seem to be the favoured place to install the latter. Among the heads and their stories – far too numerous to recount – were people who seemed to seek death. A Benedict Wolman, a 'hostiller' who had been head of the Marshalsea prison, was condemned for conspiring against the King in 1416; he was hanged at Tyburn and his head set upon 'Le Drawebrugge'. In 1431 a William Manderville, also known as Jack Sharpe, a weaver of Abingdon, 'that wolde have made a rysynge in the cytte of London', became famous for saying he would 'to have made Priests' heads as plenty as Sheep's heads, three for a penny'; his head was impaled upon the Bridge. Then there was Sir John Mortimer, who 'brake out of the Tower of London, and was taken upon the towre wharffe, and thar was sore wounded and beaten, and on the morrow brought to Westminster, judged and condemned'. His head too went to the Bridge.

The Bridge had a brief, but symbolic, role following the trial of Eleanor, Duchess of Gloucester, in 1441. The Duchess was married to Humphrey, the brother of King Henry V, and uncle and regent to the young King Henry VI until 1437, a position that was bound to attract jealousy and rivalry. He had an important residence at Greenwich, and in 1433 the ambitious pair were granted a licence 'to empark 200 acres of land, pasture, weed, heath and furze at Estgrenewich', the origin of Greenwich Park, the oldest of London's Royal Parks.

Eleanor's husband was next in line to the throne, and in 1441 she was accused of witchcraft with the intention of harming the King. Perhaps the evidence was weak; perhaps it was too dangerous to impose a more serious punishment. At her trial she was sentenced to do penance by walking through the streets of London on three successive days wearing a white sheet and carrying before her a heavy four-pound candle: a very high-ranking example to set before the excited multitude. On 14 November, the second day, the bridge street was included in her route. She was taken from Westminster by boat to just above the Bridge, where she was met at the Old Swan Stairs by the Lord Mayor, sheriffs and representatives of the Livery Companies, all of whom accompanied her on her walk.

There is an unauthenticated account that she was placed in the pillory believed to have been at the Southwark end of the Bridge. But it was more than enough to be publicly exhibited in such a humiliating way on the bridge street, with the terrifying display of heads in mind and in view. She crossed back over the Bridge and continued up Fish Street Hill, along Gracechurch Street to Christchurch.

The Duchess got off lightly. She had been charged with sorcery along with priest Sir Roger Bolingbroke and two others. At the Guildhall, Bolingbroke was condemned to death, and on the same day as his trial was taken from the Tower to Tyburn, where he was hanged, beheaded and quartered, and his head dispatched to the Bridge.

The Duchess was placed under house arrest. In 1447 Duke Humphrey died mysteriously in prison, but his death caused such agitation among the commons that his body was carried through the streets, in order to demonstrate that there were no marks on it. Many still suspected he had been poisoned. The house and park at Greenwich were immediately seized by Margaret of Anjou, the young queen of Henry VI.

Henry VI had married Margaret, daughter of Réné of Anjou, in April 1445 in yet another attempt to achieve peace between England and France, this time arranged by William de la Pole, Earl of Suffolk. For her coronation a few weeks later the apparel of the officials created a vivid rainbow scene. Riding out to Blackheath to meet the royal pair, the Lord Mayor was robed in scarlet, other civic dignitaries in violet and members of the Livery Companies wore blue gowns with elaborately embroidered sleeves and red hoods. On the return journey, at the Great Stone Gate the first pageant represented Peace and Plenty, where inscribed in Latin on a banner was: 'Enter ye and replenish the earth'. The Queen was welcomed, then proceeded to another pageant on the Bridge itself, where there was a construction of Noah's ark, and verses expressed the wish for peace between England and France.

But the Earl, who had arranged the royal marriage and who had been the virtual prime minister in Henry's disastrous reign, was banished by the King to Flanders in May 1450. On the way he was beheaded in the Straits of Dover by enemies of the King. This murder was intended to be a brutal warning to Henry VI, who, however, ignored it and continued to retain the same people in office. Inexperienced, well-meaning Henry and his hated ministers were themselves largely responsible for the trouble that followed. The name 'Jack Cade' was about to become infamous in a revolt that led to the worst unrest ever seen on London Bridge.

Throughout the country anger simmered and boiled. Fuelled by a near-bankrupt government and misgovernment at all levels, the south-east rebelled in 1450. Kent had always been a hot spot, perhaps due to its unique combination of circumstances, set as it is between and close to both the Continent and London and the influences of both. There were a large number of free peasants, and cloth-working in the Weald of Kent created a generally advanced economy, which also benefited from smuggling. The uprising of Kentish men led by Jack Cade had some similarities to the Peasants' Revolt of 1381, only seventy years earlier, the issues of which had not been resolved.

By 11 June 1450 about 20,000 to 30,000 men were assembled at Blackheath. When Henry returned to London after a visit to Leicester, the rebels retreated to Sevenoaks, and many dispersed. But a small force following the retreat was ambushed and their leader killed, and with this act the uprising gained new strength. They returned to camp at Blackheath from 29 June to 1 July. The Lord Mayor begged the King to stay and deal with the situation, but, consistently weak, Henry abandoned London for Kenilworth Castle in Warwickshire. The City ordered guards to be placed at the City gates and along the wharves both day and night, while on the riverfront projectile-hurling machines were placed.

An attempt was made to find out what the rebels wanted. Sir John Fastolf was a veteran of Agincourt and hero of the 'Battle of the Herrings', when he memorably defeated a French army by creating a circular defensive wall out of herring barrels. At other times, he might have displayed cowardice. Now he took the safe and considered course by sending his servant John Payn on one of his best horses to the Blackheath camp of Jack Cade, the 'Captain of Kent', to try to ascertain their demands.

But the messenger was seized. A vivid impression of life at Cade's headquarters survives in a letter describing the event written years later to John Paston by John Payn. Payn was taken before the Captain of Kent and denounced. He narrowly escaped having his head chopped off when an axe and a block were brought to the Captain, but others intervened, saying '. . . plainly that there should die a hundred me if I died . . .' Instead, he was sent back with their grievances, which included: 'the law serves only to do wrong, '[the King's] false council has lost his law, his merchandise is lost, his common people is destroyed, the sea is lost, France is lost' – and the King cannot even pay for his own meat and drink.

On hearing Payn's description of the strength of Cade's force, Fastolf retreated to the Tower.

Cade and thousands of his men took possession of Southwark on 1 July, making their headquarters at the White Hart on the east side of Borough High Street. The coachyard of this inn, first mentioned in 1404 and the largest in the Borough, was described by Sam Weller in Dickens' *Pickwick Papers*, over 450 years later:

> A double tier of bedroom galleries, with old clumsy balustrades, ran around two sides of the straggling area, and a double row of bells to correspond, sheltered from the weather by a little sloping roof, hung over the door leading to the bar and coffee-room . . . and the occasional heavy tread of a carthorse, or rattling of a chain at the further end of the yard, announced to anybody who cared about the matter that the stable lay in that direction.

There was little stabling in the City itself, so Borough High Street was lined with such inns, also needed by the travellers who arrived after the Bridge gate had been locked at night.

On 2 July Cade cut the ropes of the Drawbridge so it could not be raised, and he may have damaged the lifting machinery. He crossed to St Magnus, where he proclaimed that any of his followers caught plundering would be put to death. Forbidding murder, rape and robbery, he was at first able to control his men. Cade was popular in Southwark and had sympathizers in the City. Somehow he got the keys to the gates of the Bridge, and on 3 July the gates were opened.

Sir James Fiennes, Lord Saye, a leading figure in Kent over the previous decade, was a focus for the mob's hatred as a supporter of the murdered William de la Pole. As the Treasurer of England, he was believed to be responsible for the terrible financial state of the country; in *Henry VI, Part II*, Shakespeare introduces him thus: 'Here's the Lord Saye, which sold the towns in France; he that made us pay one and twenty fifteens, and one shilling to the pound, the last subsidy.'

When Saye refused to plead either guilty or not guilty, Cade had him dragged from where he was imprisoned in the Tower to the Guildhall, where they held a mock trial. Found guilty, he was beheaded in Cheapside, and his head stuck on a spear. Chronicler Robert Fabyan, who was also a clothier and would become a sheriff of London in 1493, described how the body was tied to a horse's tail and dragged across the Bridge to Southwark, where it was put on a gallows and quartered. The head of Sir James Cromer, Saye's father-in-law and the Sheriff of Kent, joined that of Saye to be paraded around the City and Southwark. The increasingly brutal-ized rebels stopped frequently to hold the heads together in a 'kiss', before placing them on the Bridge.

As the robberies, assaults and rapes by Cade's men mounted, what had been an almost friendly attitude to them by the citizens soon turned hostile. According to Shakespeare:

Jack Cade hath gotten London Bridge.
The citizens fly and forsake their houses.

In reality most of the bridge-dwellers tragically did not fly. They furtively watched the drama unfolding before them from within their houses, trying to safeguard shops and homes, where they remained trapped for the duration of a battle in which many were to meet their terrifying fates in the final hours of the rebellion.

On 5 July the rebels retired to Southwark for the night as usual. It was essential for the City to regain control of the Bridge to keep the rebels out of London. A force led by the experienced Captain Matthew Gough, who had served in France under Henry V, took action. Raphael Holinshed's *Chronicles* tell how Gough's men killed the rebel sentries and occupied the Bridge. Cade's men learned at once what had happened. 'The rebelles, which never soundly slep for fear of sudden chances, hearing the bridge to be kept and manned, ran with great haste to open the passage, where between both parties was a ferce and cruell encounter.'

For the only time in the history of Old London Bridge a desperate fight began, and over the hours ahead it raged back and forth over the entire length of the Bridge. Although Gough had been ordered to hold the bridgefoot and advance at daybreak, his men were driven back to the Drawbridge to which Cade then set fire, urging his followers:

> Come, then, let's go fight with them.
> But first go and set London Bridge on fire . . .

As the rebels moved forwards, they fired the houses and shops on either side with the now trapped occupants still inside. *Hall's Chronicle* states that those who tried to escape from being burned in the flames were either killed on the bridge street or drowned in the river.

> Great ruthe it was to behold the miserable state, for some desyrynge [desiring] to eschew the fyre lept on his enemies weapon and so died: fearfull women with chyldren in their armes, amased and appalled, lept for fear into the river: other doubtinge how to save them self betwene fyre, water and swourd, were in their houses suffocat and smoldered.

They fought back and forth all night, sometimes Cade's men, having the upper hand, pushing forward, then Gough's men. Many were killed and thrown into the Thames, weapons and all. As dawn broke the fighting continued. The Londoners had been pushed backwards to 'St Magnus corner', with Shakespeare's Cade exhorting his men: 'Up Fish Street! Down Saint Magnus' corner! Kill and knock down! Throw them into the Thames!' Suddenly and unexpectedly, however, the Londoners repulsed the rebels back over the whole length of the Bridge, and at this point some Kentish men drifted away.

They had fought from ten p.m. to eight a.m. until both sides were so exhausted there was no other option but to arrange an amnesty. Among the many dead were Gough, lamented by chronicler Hall as 'a man of great witte, much experience in feates of chivalri . . .', alderman John Sutton and a 'hardy citizen' named Robert Heysande. The agreement was that Londoners would not go into Southwark, nor rebels into the City, and to 'leave battle' until the next day.

But the amnesty marked the end of the uprising, and Cade and his remaining rebels, weighed down with loot, fled back to Kent.

A proclamation offered a thousand marks to anyone who brought Cade to the King, alive or dead. A day later the rebel leader went down fighting in Sussex; wounded, he died in a cart on his way back to London, recorded in Gregory's Chronicle: '. . . and uppon the morowe he was brought in a carre alle nakyd, [to] the Herte in Sowetheworke.' The landlady of the White Hart was called to identify him. After his naked corpse was mutilated, it was drawn in a hurdle from the King's Bench prison in Southwark, over the Bridge and through London to Newgate. His skull ended up on the Drawbridge Gate, where he had ordered Lord Saye's head to be placed a few days before.

The King soon proclaimed a general pardon, which was honoured in the main, but a large number of executions in Kent still followed, at least thirty at Canterbury, Rochester, Faversham and elsewhere. The Earl of Shrewsbury went to Kent, where he set up a gallows and hanged and beheaded twenty-eight people, including one unfortunate who was mistaken for Cade. Consignments of heads were sent to London, and the number on the Bridge now became so great, it must have been a very gruesome sight indeed, for *Waltham's Annals* notes: 'London said ther shuld no more heads be set upon ther'.

There was immense relief when shops, some makeshift, were soon in business again. Everyday life resumed, fishermen fished, the fisherwomen called out their wares, the swans on the river fiercely protected their cygnets, and the only reported excitement was, refreshingly, the unusual sight of a number of large blowing whales below the Bridge, some trying to pass through it.

By July 1453, at the end of the Hundred Years War, and less than forty years after the great victory of Agincourt, the only English king to have been crowned in France, Lancastrian Henry VI, had lost all of the vast English territories in south-west France. Only Calais remained. Disillusioned soldiers returned home to tell their tales, and the important wine and cloth trades were seriously disrupted.

The new king was popular, handsome Yorkist Edward IV (1461–70, 1471–83). It was another spectacular and colourful occasion when he went from Sheen (Richmond) Palace to the royal apartments in the Tower in June 1461 to prepare for his coronation. In Southwark he was met by the Lord Mayor and aldermen wearing their scarlet robes, and four hundred green-clothed commoners on horseback. The procession rode across the Bridge straight to the Tower, where he spent the night.

Three years later, in 1464, Edward IV married Elizabeth Woodville, and when she was crowned the following year, the Bridge Wardens purchased an abundance of peacocks' feathers to make the angels' wings for the pageant at the Bridge. But the King's popularity was threatened by the favours shown to his wife's relatives, in a reign that was marked both by struggles for power in the Wars of the Roses (1455–85) and by licentiousness. Edward allowed the Earl of Warwick, 'The Kingmaker', to run the country, until Warwick – angered by the royal marriage to Elizabeth Woodville – in a complicated sequence of events briefly deposed Edward IV in favour of Henry VI.

Jack Cade's rebellion was still vividly remembered in 1471,

twenty-one years after it had ended, when there was another uprising, this time led by Thomas 'the Bastard' Fauconbridge. Again, it started in Kent. Fauconbridge was a natural son of William Neville, 1st Lord Fauconbridge, of the powerful Warwick family. The Wars of the Roses provoked and fuelled intrigues, and Fauconbridge supported the Lancastrian Henry VI, who was deranged for several periods during his reign, and who was deposed by the Yorkist Edward IV (who held Henry in the Tower where he was murdered a short time later). At this point, Fauconbridge's intention was to free Henry and restore him to the throne.

He asked for permission to pass through the City with his supporters. Permission was refused: London was held for Edward IV. The City considered Fauconbridge dangerous because he was able to muster a number of ships, which Stow called 'a great navie', as well as 3,000 to 5,000 men. The Common Council 'fortified all along the Thameside' above and below the Bridge from Baynard's Castle (beyond Queenhithe, below St Bride's) to the Tower with armed men and guns.

Mounted scouts were sent out to report on the advance of the rebels. On the Bridge itself the Drawbridge was raised and secured with a thick cable. Three portholes were cut through the raised wooden platform for the guns hidden behind. Sacks of stones and wool were brought on to the Bridge to help deflect both arrows and shot. All related expenses were carefully noted in the Bridge House Records as a special expenditure in May 1471: forty-one yards of canvas sheeting were purchased, soaked in vinegar and hung across the Drawbridge Gate as a protection against the 'wild fire' of these rebels. Twelve new bows and fifty-one sheaves of arrows were bought, as well as candles for the night watches and pails to hold the water to throw on fires. Guns were brought from the Guildhall, and four gunners were requisitioned to man them. Among the variety of payments made by the Wardens for the defence of the Bridge were those to a troop of liverymen who comprised the main body in defence of the Bridge.

On Sunday 12 May the Bridge was attacked. Fauconbridge and a large band of rebels set the Great Stone Gate on fire, which spread to the seven houses on either side up to the Drawbridge. There was not actually a full attack at the Bridge; perhaps it seemed too daunting. Thousands of the rebels crossed the Thames by boat and broke into the City at Aldgate, but they had broken into a trap: after many men had passed through, the portcullis was suddenly lowered, and all the rebels inside were killed. The portcullis was raised again, and a strong force of citizens rushed out to repel those who remained among Fauconbridge's men. Others joined in the pursuit of the insurgents to Mile End, and killed many of them.

Fauconbridge had led the assault at the Bridge, but just as he realized he could not make any headway, he also heard of the failure at Aldgate. When the citizens saw him retreat, the Drawbridge was lowered and they pursued the rebels along Thameside, killing those at the rear and taking prisoners.

Their leader was captured at Southampton some time later, and executed. His head was dispatched to the Bridge built of Kentish ragstone, and *The Paston Letters* wryly record that the next day, 28 September 1471: 'Thomas Fauconbrydge hys hed was yesterdaye sett uppon London Brydge, lokying into Kent warde . . .' towards where his rebellion had begun.

The Drawbridge, perhaps weakened by Fauconbridge's uprising, was suffering from wear and tear. Back in 1463 a faulty winding mechanism had caused a delay to vessels heading upstream to Queenhithe. From then on, when two vessels bound for Queenhithe arrived at the same time, one was required to unload at Billingsgate, but the better vessel or the larger number always went to Queenhithe. In a dispute over the tolls for passing through the Drawbridge, the Common Council ordered that the drawbridge be raised for all ships wanting to pass upstream, and they took a strong line: the Wardens were to charge sixpence, no more, each time the bascule was raised. If the Wardens refused to open the Drawbridge for this exact toll, they would be forced to forfeit three-quarters of their own goods.

In 1481 the Wardens again petitioned the Common Council, complaining of damage done to the tower at the Drawbridge, as well as to the other arches and piers, by the vibrations of the iron-shod carts, which once again were absolutely forbidden. Since the actual raising of the Drawbridge further weakened the structure, now it was to be raised only for great 'necessite and defence' of the City. This development finally spelled the end of what since Saxon times had been the main trading place and port of Queenhithe, which became 'almost forsaken' according to Stow. (At Queenhithe, a small harbour on the City side downstream of the Millennium Bridge can still be seen.)

Also in 1481, perhaps damaged by the attacks, a house known as 'the Common Stage' on London Bridge fell and five men were killed, but the Bridge House workers were not punished, in contrast to what happened in Paris in 1499. There, when houses on the Pont Notre Dame collapsed, killing several people, those who had been responsible for maintaining it were given life imprisonment.

In 1500 Bridge Wardens William Hotte and Edward Grene were notified that Henry VII's barques intended to pass through the Bridge. The Wardens employed carpenters to work day and night to repair 'the full ruynous' structure, desperately preparing it for the King. This was probably the last time the Drawbridge was raised. In spite of all the work done for this occasion, it was not operational in 1506, nor twenty years later. In 1526 the main problem was the weakness of the masonry of the Drawbridge Gateway or tower, and the bascule could not be used until the stonework was strengthened. There were no tolls because the Drawbridge could not be opened, so to keep some money coming in, the decision was made to rent out two chambers in the gateway at 3s. 4d. each.

Skill at arms in a king could be combined with scholarship. Edward IV enthusiastically promoted education, and with the King as patron, William Caxton set up his printing press at Westminster in 1476, his apprentice Wynkyn de Worde taking over in 1491. Customs documents record imports of large numbers of books in manuscript form, over 1,300 in 1480 alone. Stationers and booksellers were always one of the pre-eminent trades represented on Old London Bridge, and now printing, book-binding and bookselling flourished. From 1485 in the reign of Tudor Henry VII there was a Stationer to the King, and in 1501 a Printer to the King. Books might include translations from Virgil and Cicero, Greek mythology, English classics like Chaucer, histories, and pieces giving dissident opinions on the events of the time. And there were 'how to' publications: how to bring up children, how to paint, dance and play sports, all of which sounds familiar to today's book-buyers.

The Lancastrians and Yorks had made their mark on country, City and Bridge. Now came the turn of the astute and vigorous Tudors.

CHAPTER FOUR

'this confusion of wives, so many . . . great personages . . . beheaded'

. . . and among all the straung and beaytifull showes me thinketh there is none so notable, as the Bridge which crosseth the Theames, which is in the manner of a continuall streete, well replenyshed with large and stately houses on both sides, and situate upon twentie Arches whereof each one is made of excellent free stone squared.

John Lyly, *Euphues and his England*, 1580

T HE REIGN OF THE FIRST TUDOR KING, CULTURED, astute Lancastrian Henry VII (1485–1509), marked the end of the Middle Ages. By now the barons were controlled, and the monarchy was more stable, strengthened by the King's marriage to Elizabeth of York, which united the royal houses.

The wealth of the rich cosmopolitan City was built on sea trade. In 1498 a Venetian visitor commented that London benefited from the ebb and flow of the Thames: vessels of a hundred tons could come to the City, while larger ships could get to within five miles of it, yet the water still remained 'fresh' for twenty miles below the Bridge. The river was busy with speedily rowed small boats, ferry boats and mighty merchantmen. By 1514 the watermen's fares were regulated for given distances, and in 1555 a further Act referred to the variety of misfortunes experienced by many of the King's subjects in recent years, caused by 'rude, ignorant and unskilful' watermen.

Old London Bridge joined in the annual Midsummer Day celebrations. The longest day was the happiest of times, a major festival with pageants and morris dancing, and it was when some City officials were elected. Each year on Midsummer's Eve a grand ceremonial muster of thousands of men marched through the streets to music, kept watch all night, and enjoyed a 21 June breakfast that might be served to two thousand. Those crossing over the Bridge saw the gates decorated with flowers and the fresh boughs of leaves, green birch, long fennel, white lilies and St John's wort. The air was sweeter than usual with the scent of the garlands of flowers that also decorated the Bridge House and other houses in Southwark and the City. The amount spent by the Bridge House on flowers for Midsummer Day varied according to their resources. In one year they paid tuppence for pots of fragrant white and yellow jasmine, and some flowers for the occasion were grown in the Bridge House garden among the vegetables and vines. At night the festive but haunting scene was lit by midsummer candles.

London was thriving. An Italian observer in 1497 was amazed by the fifty-two goldsmiths' shops in Cheapside: 'in all the shops in Milan, Rome, Venice and Florence put together, I do not think there would be found so many of the magnificence that are to be seen in London'. But danger lurked on the turbulent streets. A visitor was in Cornhill when he saw his own hood for sale, which had been taken from him some hours earlier in the crowd at Westminster, but before he could get to it, the hood was quickly sold on, and disappeared again. In the turbulent streets a variety of food-sellers plied their trade. The countryman hero of the contemporary satirical ballad 'London Lyckpenny' described them offering ripe strawberries, ribs of beef, mackerel, 'hot shepes feet' and 'many a pye'.

Food played an important part in official life. At the Bridge House in Southwark there was a suitably important-looking chamber – carpeted, no less – to which the City officials retired after completing Bridge business. In 1496 the Bridge House accounts note that a select group of Bridge officials, after 'avewing the remedye of the drawbridge toure' – the Drawbridge had been in a state of decay for some time – enjoyed a repast at a cost of 18s. 11d. provided by Sir William Martyn, Thomas Ward and various commoners. These meals could be memorable: one in 1438 included beef marrowbones, 'chines de pork', cygnets, piglets, geese and plovers. The next year, when there was further concern about 'the daunger and jeopardye of the drawebridge', an inspection was again followed by a dinner for certain aldermen and commoners.

It is most unlikely that the meals at the Bridge House, splendid though they were, could have rivalled the extravagant City feasts, some of which almost defied description and apparently exceeded even those at court. One is described in Philip Massinger's *The City Madam* of 1632, here given in part:

> Man may talk of country christmasses and court gluttony,
> Their thirty-pound buttered eggs, their pies of carps' tongues,
> Their pheasants drenched with ambergris, the carcases
> Of three fat wethers [castrated rams] bruised for gravy, to
> Make sauce for a single peacock; yet their feasts
> Were fasts compared with the city's . . .
>
> Did you not observe it?
> There were three suckling pigs served up in a dish,
> Ta'en from the sow as soon as farrowed,
> A fortnight fed with dates, and muskadine . . .
>
> The dishes were raised one upon another,
> As woodmongers do billets . . .
>
> Three such dinners more would break an alderman
> And make him give up his cloak.

The first instalment of the story of the six wives of Henry VIII began when Catherine of Aragon, the short and 'sweet faced' daughter of Ferdinand and Isabella of Spain, arrived at Plymouth in October 1501 to marry Henry's older brother, the even shorter and immature-looking Arthur, Prince of Wales. Almost sixteen years old, the pleasantly round Princess 'could not have been received with greater rejoicings if she had been the Saviour of the World', according to a member of her entourage. Preparations for the triumphal symbolism of her arrival had begun two years earlier, for her formal welcome was intended to celebrate Henry VII's success in acquiring this Spanish prize – after years of negotiation – which he hoped would establish a powerful alliance between England and Spain against France and make his throne more secure. The detailed arrangements outlined that '. . . the said princess be conveied through Southwerk streight over London Bridge, and so through the Bruge strete [Bridge Street] to Greschurch strete . . .' But when she reached the Bridge on 12 November she was delayed by the pageant there which was the first of six City spectacles, each one entertaining, magnificent and symbolic. Greeting her on the Bridge was a 'St Katherine' holding the saint's Katherine wheel, pointedly paired with a British saint, 'St Ursula', while a number of girls welcomed her with speeches.

Catherine was the last royal princess to be formally and extravagantly greeted on the Bridge. She married Prince Arthur in St Paul's two days later, followed by two weeks of jousting and feasting. But her boy-husband died the next year, and in 1503 the Princess was betrothed to his younger brother Prince Henry, who became Henry VIII when his father Henry VII died.

Flickering flames were seen on the bridge street in 1509 on the day of Henry VII's funeral. The route was lined with torch-carrying members of the Livery Companies: the lowest in rank on the Bridge, the higher the ranking the nearer to St Paul's. On horseback were the Mayor and aldermen, 150 commoners and the Freemen of the City. Also carrying torches were 'strangers' or foreign merchants. The last time flames had been seen on the Bridge was when a serious fire broke out next to the church of St Magnus on 21 November 1504, at the City end. It began at the sign of the pannier (basket-maker), and was extinguished only after six houses had burned down.

Tall, commanding Henry VIII became king. Full of vigour, he was athletic, trim and handsome, showing little indication of the monster he would become. Henry and pretty Catherine were married six weeks after he ascended the throne, and the double crowning was held on Midsummer Day, 1509. They appeared to be happily married for over twenty years, but although five children were born, only Princess Mary survived, and there was no male heir to protect the Tudor dynasty.

The life of every person, great and small, touched on the Bridge. Clever, competent Thomas Wolsey (1475–1530) made himself indispensable to Henry VIII, and by 1515 he was Lord Chancellor and an archbishop. He successfully campaigned for the Pope to make him a cardinal, and in 1515 his greatly anticipated cardinal's hat arrived at Dover. The hat, a valuable ring and the papal bulls to support his authority had been sent in an attendant's pouch. This did not suit Wolsey at all. The carrier was met at Dover and decked out in a rich silken costume. George Cavendish's *Life and Death of Cardinal Wolsey* tells how at Shooter's Hill in Greenwich the attendant accompanying the hat was met by 'a great assembly of prelates and lusty gallant gentlemen [who] conveyed him through London with great triumph'. On the following Sunday, in a splendid ceremony at St Paul's, the tasselled scarlet hat was placed on Thomas Wolsey's head.

In 1518 papal legate Cardinal Lorenzo Campeggio was sent by Pope Leo X on a special mission to England, but Wolsey kept him waiting in Calais for two months until he himself was granted authority equal to Campeggio as an emissary of the Pope. Charles Wriothesley's *Chronicle* describes the procession as Campeggio finally reached the Bridge. Two silver-gilt pillars were carried ahead of him, while Campeggio was 'ridinge in red chamlett [camel's hair], his cardinal's hatt on his head'. From the Bridge all the way to Leadenhall, the route was lined with monks, friars and canons and all the parsons and parish priests of the City. They carried crosses, candlesticks and censers, 'and ever as the legatt passed by them they sensed him'. However, Wolsey kept Campeggio sidelined during his visit.

Every Sunday Wolsey went to visit the King and his court at Greenwich, almost five miles downstream from the Bridge, an event described by Cavendish. Wolsey travelled by barge either from his palatial London home York Place or from upriver Hampton Court as far as the Bridge, but unlike Henry, he always avoided passing through its unpredictable torrents. Instead, he disembarked at The Three Cranes above the Bridge, about where Southwark Bridge now stands. He mounted a mule, a symbol of humility – though this creature was caparisoned in crimson and gold velvet, and the Cardinal's feet rested in bronze gilt stirrups – and rode along Thames Street in splendid procession, surrounded by specially selected handsome attendants, who before him carried two pillars of silver. Tall priests on horseback held two great silver crosses, the first a double cross to indicate his position as legate. The Great Seal in a silk purse was borne by a bare-headed page. When Wolsey arrived at Billingsgate, he rejoined his barge, and continued on to Greenwich.

Although the King travelled through and over London Bridge, he didn't fully trust its strength. Heavy artillery was sent by a different route: a payment was made to a John Johnson 'bycause the Kynge's great gonne [gun] shulde not pass over the bridge, but rather by another way', presumably via Kingston, on the river about twelve miles above London. The King ordered that the twenty-two-piered Kingston Bridge be strengthened, for it had fallen into disrepair in the previous reigns. And Kingston was used when Henry left London on his way to Calais for the summit with Francis I of France in June 1520. Wolsey made the arrangements for both countries, and the extreme richness of every aspect of the encounter – a perhaps unsurpassed combination of politics, athletics, tournaments, music, drama and banquets – led to it being known as the Field of the Cloth of Gold. Those who observed it said it was the eighth wonder of the world.

Wolsey negotiated the second London visit of the Holy Roman Emperor Charles V in 1522. The Emperor, whose vast territories ranged from the Channel to the Adriatic and the Baltic, was the most powerful ruler yet to come to London. Lord Mayor John Melbourne and officers of the City met him at St George's Fields, an area of open ground between Southwark and Lambeth where for centuries dignitaries were received. The speech of welcome was read by Sir Thomas More, who would be executed twelve years later.

Gregory's Chronicle described the scene. On the Bridge at the Drawbridge Gate were placed the figures of giants, on one side Hercules with a club in his hand, and on the other side Samson holding the jawbone of an ass. Together the two figures held a huge inscription listing all the Emperor's titles in golden letters. At the next opening in the Bridge there was an edifice of embattled towers and gates, built to look like black-and-white marble. Above that was a scene showing Jason harnessed with weapons, before him a golden fleece and on the one side a fiery dragon, 'and on the other syde stood two bulles continuously spewing fire'. For this and more the cost to the City was about £1,000, of which the Bridge Fund was responsible for £64.

From 1525 the relationship between Henry VIII and Wolsey began to change, for Wolsey's wealth and palaces far surpassed the King's. Wolsey prudently presented Hampton Court, the finest palace in the kingdom, to the King. At Hampton Court Palace Henry in 1540 installed the fine and elaborate astronomical clock by Nicholas Oursian in the Clock Tower facing the royal apartments. On its essentially original dial, the innermost of three rotating discs still shows the time of high tide at London Bridge.

In 1526 Henry VIII had fallen in love with the obscure Anne Boleyn, a lady-in-waiting to the Queen. Wolsey was in a weakened position when Cardinal Campeggio arrived for his next visit, because it was to hear the complicated matrimonial dispute – 'The King's Great Matter'. They were joint judges in Henry's divorce from Queen Catherine, who argued her case well. Wolsey, both a Cardinal and papal legate who yearned to be pope himself, was unable to procure the divorce the King sought. The greatest gift ever made by an English subject to his monarch did not prevent Wolsey's downfall in 1529. He was dismissed from the Chancellorship, was arrested for treason in York, and died in 1530 on the way to London. The marriage to Catherine of Aragon was annulled, and the break with Rome made.

All of these events had a direct effect on the Bridge and its income. The King was excommunicated by the Pope in 1533, and the Act of Supremacy followed in 1534, making Henry head of the English Church. Work on the Dissolution of the Monasteries began in 1535 to suppress hundreds of monastic institutions. And the immense spoils from the Dissolution went to those connected to the court. To Sir Anthony Browne, Master of the Horse, went the Augustinian Priory of St Mary Overie at the Southwark end of the Bridge, along with much else. The Dissolution freed land for development all over the country, but it severely reduced the income for the Bridge, for example in the loss of quit-rents from some of the great abbeys and priories in 1540–1. The incredible wealth released by the Dissolution was largely dissipated, and in 1550–1 came a fall in the price of silver, which depreciated by twenty-five per cent the value of the silver kept secure with other valuables and documents in the locked Great Chest at the Bridge House.

When Henry changed the Act of Succession, making Elizabeth, daughter of Anne Boleyn, his heir, and bypassing Mary, daughter of Queen Catherine of Aragon, the future bitterness between the half-sisters was guaranteed. Every subject was required to swear an oath of acknowledgement. But there were those in Kent who refused, among them an unbalanced domestic servant named Elizabeth Barton, the 'Maid of Kent', who suffered from religious mania. In 1533 she made increasingly treasonable prophetic utterances against Henry, and – fatally – against his recent marriage to Anne Boleyn. She and her followers were condemned to death, and some of the heads, notably that of 'the Maid', ended up on the Bridge, in view of all those leaving the City on their way to Kent. John Fisher, Bishop of Rochester, and Sir Thomas More, who had been Henry's most highly esteemed first minister, succeeding Wolsey as Lord Chancellor from 1529 to 1532, were innocently caught up in the episode, and their fortunes began to decline.

In 1535 'Harry the Eighth' succeeded in destroying two of the most exceptional men of his reign: John Fisher and Sir Thomas More. They were executed for high treason because they refused to speak the words accepting Henry as supreme head of the Church. Public interest in the executions was intense.

John Fisher, a supporter of Catherine of Aragon, had been held in the Tower since April 1534. Pope Paul III tried to save him by making him a cardinal, but when an already enraged Henry heard this, he declared that if the Pope sent Fisher a hat there would be no head for it. Fisher was executed on 22 June 1535, and the head was kept back from being sent to the Bridge until Anne Boleyn's sparkling black eyes could view it. Richard Hall's *Life of Fisher* describes how the day after the burial, 'the head being somwhat perboyled in hott water, was pricked upon a pole, and sett on high upon London Bridge' to join the heads of some of the monks of the Charterhouse who had maintained the Pope's supremacy. There '. . . the miraculous sight of this head, which after it had stand up the space of xiiii daies upon the bridge could not be perceived to wast nor consume, nether for the weather, which was then verie hott, neither for the parboylinge in hott water, but grew daily fresher and fresher, so that in his life time he never looked so well . . . wherby was notifyed to the whole worlde the innocencie and holines of this blessed father . . .' Thousands came to gaze on this sight, stopping all traffic over the Bridge. After fourteen days the executioner ordered that the head be thrown into the river during the night. Fisher was canonized in the same year.

Sir Thomas More had been living quietly in retirement when Henry forced him to attend raven-haired Anne Boleyn's royal wedding in 1533. Now it was the turn of Sir Thomas. In July the head of More, 'the most blessed and constant Martyr, [Fisher's] companion and fellowe in all his troubles', went to the Bridge. According to J. Hunter's edition of Cresacre More's *Life and Death of Sir Thomas More*, More's head took on somewhat excessive signs of holiness: not decaying after months, a long-missing tooth reputedly restored and grey hair now 'readish or yellow'. Even more extraordinarily, according to antiquarian John Aubrey, More's favourite daughter, Margaret Roper, was passing under the Bridge and looked at his head, saying: 'That head haz layn many a time in my lapp, would to God it would fall into my lap as I pass under' – and it did, or so the story goes. When she died nine years later 'she was buried . . . with her father's head in her arms, as she had desired'. No doubt she purchased the head and placed it in a lead box, for a box containing it was buried with her.

The magnificence of Anne Boleyn's coronation was intended to make up for the earlier secret wedding. The new Queen, wearing cloth of gold and four months pregnant with a future queen, Elizabeth, was met at Greenwich by the Lord Mayor, whose barge was preceded by another in which a dragon continually moved, spewing fire. Anne was conveyed to the Tower where she was greeted by the King, whose almost insane passion for her was reflected in the celebrations. Those accustomed to such royal spectacles reportedly stared in disbelief at the richness and excessiveness of this royal occasion.

The King's palaces were located by the river for obvious ease of travel when the roads were dangerous and frequently almost impassable. However, when the Thames was frozen or semi-frozen, the only option was the rough roads. There is an account of how one cold December day King Henry, Queen Anne Boleyn and Princess Mary rode out over the Bridge, on streets freshly gravelled, past houses hung with luxurious materials, and lined with freezing clergy on each side, on their way to Greenwich by what must have been a frequently used royal road.

There were other love affairs among lesser mortals. Could anyone invent a more romantic tale than that of Edward Osborne and Anne Hewett, told by John Stow? Richard Osborne and his wife Jane were people of some substance in Ashford, Kent. They decided that their son, Edward, should start his career by becoming an apprentice in London, a decision that in due course would elevate the family far above all possible expectations.

Edward was apprenticed with the usual ceremony to William Hewett, a wealthy clothworker who lived with his family on London Bridge. In 1529 Hewett had been given the Freedom of the Clothworkers Company, one of the twelve great Livery Companies. Osborne was to prosper as an apprentice at a time when only about forty per cent completed their seven-year term, for some died and some returned to the country. The Hewett family comprised three sons and one daughter. In 1536 a maid was playing at a window with the young daughter, Anne, who leaned out, lost her balance and fell into the river. The apprentice Osborne, on seeing her fall, instantly and, it has to be said, courageously, leaped from a window and saved her from drowning.

Osborne remained in the household when the family moved soon after this, probably in part for the safety of the child, to Philpot Lane, not far from the Bridge, between Eastcheap and Fenchurch. In 1543 William Hewett became Master of the Company and in 1553 sheriff. In 1559, at a time when his estate was £6,000 a year, he became Lord Mayor and was knighted by Queen Elizabeth. Anne came of marriageable age, and with wealth and position her suitors included the Earl of Shrewsbury. Aware of Osborne's potential, Hewett reputedly said: 'Osborne saved her and Osborne should enjoy her.' Edward proposed and Anne accepted. She was given a most substantial dowry when they married in 1562. Osborne followed in his father-in-law's footsteps, becoming a sheriff in 1575, and Lord Mayor in 1583–4.

As always, work and life went on around London Bridge, and there were lighter moments, apart from the dramas of cruel, despotic kings and selfish, indulgent queens. The Thames was full of fish, including salmon and sturgeon caught with lines. Henry VIII kept a polar bear in the royal zoo at the Tower; the poor creature, wearing a collar and chain, was taken to the river to swim and, it was said, to catch salmon. Whales occasionally came up the river to be pursued to their deaths.

In 1530 the Statute of Bridges had been introduced to protect and repair bridges throughout the kingdom, many of which had been allowed to fall into ruin. If they were damaged, judges were instructed to find out how it had happened and to order that they be fixed at once.

The Thames was deepened and widened in the 1540s. It was Henry who set up shipbuilding yards at Deptford and Woolwich, which became the basis of the Port of London. Wool and cloth were still the main exports, and the river was busy with tall-masted vessels. Several writers observed that it looked like a forest of trees on the water, and the light playing through the masts and sails made the surface of the water look like a glade.

Henry knew the importance of image to power. In 1536, after Anne Boleyn had been executed, and only three days after the chaste Jane Seymour was proclaimed queen at Greenwich, he returned with Jane by royal barge to Westminster, his guards travelling astern in another great barge. As the King passed, the ships all along the Thames shot their guns. The Ambassador of Charles V observed the water procession from an extravagantly bedecked tent on shore. As the King and his third queen approached on the water, the Ambassador sent out boats of trumpeters and music-makers who approached the King making 'a great reverence'. The Ambassador shot off 'fortie great gonns', which were immediately drowned out by more than four hundred pieces of ordnance fired from the Tower, its hard old stones that had witnessed so many cruel scenes softened for the occasion with streamers and banners. 'And so the Kinge passed throwe London Bridge, with his trumpets blowinge before him' as well as drummers and other musicians in barges, 'whiche was a goodlie sight to beholde', according to Wriothesley's *Chronicle*.

The persons whose heads were set on London Bridge and other gates in London included both commoners and lords, doctors and priests, rich and poor: all could easily share the same fate. Loyal, extremely able and unambitious Thomas Cromwell had become Henry's principal adviser, the driving force behind the monarchy, organizer of the Dissolution and the reorganization of government from 1531. (His nephew's great-great-grandson, Oliver Cromwell, would one day make an even greater impact on the country.) All of this counted for nothing. After Jane Seymour died following the birth of the prince who would become Edward VI, the King made a political marriage in 1540 to his fourth wife, the unattractive and unintelligent Anne of Cleves. Henry blamed Cromwell for negotiating this marriage to a woman who was repugnant to him from first sight. He did not present his new wife in the City when the court moved from Greenwich to Westminster a month after the marriage. There was a water pageant with all usual ceremony, but Henry travelled in one barge, while his queen followed in another. When the procession passed the Tower, guns were discharged 'above a thousand chambers of ordnance, which made a noyse like thunder; and that done they passed through London Bridge'. A royal annulment followed six months later.

Thomas Cromwell was sent to the Tower. Regarding the varied accusations made against him, he wrote to the King: 'I have meddled in so many matters under your Highness that I am unable to answer them all', as recounted in B.B. Merriman's *Thomas Cromwell*. From this point on, the King would be his own first minister. Less than six months later, in 1540, the head of Cromwell went to the Bridge. His head may have been visible to the King and his fifth wife, the youngest and most beautiful of them all, Katherine Howard, when he first took her to Greenwich. They travelled by boat through the Bridge, the Lord Mayor's flotilla awaiting them on the downstream side. But within eighteen months, in February 1542, Katherine would be executed at the Tower. Her relative, Francis Derham, had already been hanged at Tyburn in December 1541, and his head placed on the Bridge.

In 1538, the Pope urged Catholic countries to undertake a crusade against this cruel tyrant, Henry VIII. Henry ordered defences to be built along the coasts and in the Thames estuary. In these dangerous times, the City had no choice but to change the dedication of the Chapel from the popular St Thomas of Canterbury to St Thomas the Apostle, but that was not enough. It was not possible for the prominent Chapel to escape Henry VIII's intention to wipe out all references to Thomas Becket. According to the Bridge House Records, the first order in 1538 was that the Chapel must change its dedication. In 1539–40 a painter from Southwark was hired at two shillings for the 'defasynge and mendynge of dyvers pyctures of Thomas Beckett in Our Lady Chapell', and in 1543 an embroiderer was employed to change a representation of the saint into 'the image of Our Lady'. By 1540 only one priest and a clerk remained to continue the offices in the popular Chapel.

A mere name-change, however, did not satisfy the tyrannical

King. In 1549, ten years after Henry had commanded that all images of St Thomas be removed, the order came that the Chapel of St Thomas of Canterbury be defaced, both inside and out. From the Bridge House Records: 'it is agreed that Mr Wylfford and Mr Judde, surveyours of the workes of the brydge, shall tomorrowe begyn to cause the chapell upon the same brydge to be defaced, and to be translated into a dwellyng-house, with as moche spede as they convenyentlye maye'. The beautiful Chapel became a silent shell. But nothing much else happened, and for several years the only work done was by a watchman named Hew Boswell, who was paid two shillings a week.

The major shrines of English saints, worshipped for centuries, had already been destroyed. Short of funds, Henry coveted their immense wealth. From the richest shrine, that of St Thomas à Becket at Canterbury, twenty-six wagonloads of treasure were taken to the Mint, with the order that the saint's bones be removed from the shrine and thrown to the winds.

In 1553 the exquisite Chapel, perhaps the most notable feature ever to grace the Bridge, was turned into a shop and house, and later a warehouse. The Perpendicular Gothic windows and buttresses were gone. In the Chapel's new and sadder life the first leaseholder was a grocer, William Bridger. At this point 'the late chapel upon the Bridge' smelled of cheese and the other provisions that were stored in its undercroft.

For centuries every City church, every building, every street in London had its own smell, dictated by the trades and markets located round about, as noted by Dickens in *The Uncommercial Traveller* of 1861. On wandering past the City of London churches: 'Behind the Monument the service had a flavour of damaged oranges, which, a little further down towards the river, tempered into herrings, and gradually turned into a cosmopolitan blast of fish.' This is still reflected in street names like Fish Street Hill, Bread Street, Poultry and Milk Street. Cannon Street was once Candlewick Street, from which the candle-makers were forced to move because of the unavoidable smell their work created.

Commercial use of the former Chapel carried on until all the

Gent. Mag. Sepr 1753

*The Outside of St Thomas's Chapel, on the great Pier of London Bridge.
fronting towards the Tower.*

The Chapel after its conversion to a house and shop.

buildings were removed from the Bridge. Almost two hundred years later, in 1751–9, stationers Wright and Gill occupied part of what was by then called the Chapel House; from the much defaced but still strong building hung a crane for hauling up goods from boats. Their warehouse was in a cellar ten feet or so below high-water mark, of which *The Morning Advertiser*, 26 April 1798, reported that the excellency of the masonry was such that the stores of paper 'were kept as safe and dry as they would have been in a garret'. The partnership of these two eminent stationers lasted for almost half a century. Each became Lord Mayor, and they died within ten days of one another in 1798. It was said that Gill amassed a fortune of £300,000 and that Wright died with an even larger amount, £2,000 of which he bequeathed to the Stationers Company.

The defaced Chapel building outlasted Henry VIII by almost two hundred years. After his fifth wife Katherine Howard was beheaded, in 1543 he married his sixth wife, genial Catherine Parr. Four years later the end came for Henry VIII. A Venetian, Daniel Barbaro, gave his summary of the reign to the Venetian Senate in 1551: 'In this confusion of wives, so many noblemen and great personages were beheaded, so much church plunder committed and so many acts of disobedience perpetrated that it may be said that in all that ensued and is still going on, is the penalty of that first sin.'

The boy-king Edward VI (1547–53), whose mother, Jane Seymour, had died soon after his birth, ascended the throne at the age of ten. The country was governed by two Protectors, and possibly because there was a child-king there was unrest. In 1549 rioters were anticipated at the Bridge, but the Drawbridge still was not operational, so a false drawbridge was made instead. However, the insurgents never arrived. On a happier note, when the French Ambassador arrived with his entourage in May 1550, he boarded the King's barge in which he 'shott London Bridge'.

In October 1552 the young Edward, who had just returned from a royal progress, heard about the 'Great fishes' that were chased for two days and nights in the Thames before being killed at Woolwich. He wanted to see these 'monster[s] of the whale kind' that very night, so, according to Wriothesley's *Chronicle*, the two 'whirl-pooles' were towed by barges through the Bridge to Westminster to enable the curious fifteen-year-old to have a close look. The precocious youngster died from tuberculosis at Greenwich the next year.

In the very first year of the five-year reign of Mary I, both Bridge and river were prominent in the rebellion of 1554 led by Sir Thomas Wyatt, son of the poet, also Thomas, who had once been attracted to Anne Boleyn.

Discontent began to fester almost as soon as Mary, the Catholic daughter of Henry VIII and Catherine of Aragon, became queen. Her intransigent hated of her Protestant half-sister, Elizabeth, made her refuse to accept her as next of kin. Mary was determined to provide her own heir by marrying the son of Emperor Charles V, Philip of Spain, who was a dozen years her junior. Most people were strongly opposed to a union uniting England with Spain, believing that, under the influence of the Pope, it might lead to war. There was also the fear of religious persecution, which was much more prevalent on the Continent than in England.

When the betrothal was announced in 1554, it sparked the most serious uprising of the time. The aim of the rebels was primarily to prevent the marriage, and perhaps even depose Mary and place Elizabeth on the throne. But news leaked out long before the rebels' preparations were ready, and their plans for March were rushed forward to January. This resulted in defeat for the rebels everywhere except in Kent, a stronghold of Protestantism.

The leader in Kent was the hot-headed Sir Thomas Wyatt, who had fought in the wars in France against Charles V, but was now settled, somewhat impecuniously, in quiet domestic life with his wife and ten children at Allington Castle in Kent. He was not disloyal to the Queen, and a number of important men supported him and his cause.

An Anthony Norton of Trosley in his later confession gave a glimpse of proceedings at Allington Castle just before the uprising. He recalled how Thomas Wyatt had sent for him, and on arriving at the castle, he found Wyatt 'in hys parlor, syttynge by ye fyre'. Wyatt declared that the coming of the King of Spain would be the undoing of the kingdom, for under the guise of friendship Spain would be strengthened while England was subverted, which would ultimately lead to the loss of their country. But Norton warily declined to participate, with the excuse that he lived near the Sheriff of Kent, Sir Robert Southwell, who was to play a major role in suppressing the rebellion.

Wyatt and his men advanced, capturing Rochester Castle along the way, proclaiming that 'we seek no harm to the Queen, but better council and councellors'. He arrived at Blackheath with 7,000 men. A force led by the aged Duke of Norfolk was dispatched to stop him, but these men, on learning that the Kentish men were not against the Queen herself, only her marriage, went over to the other side with cries of 'A Wyatt! A Wyatt!' Wyatt rode on horseback through this addition to his forces, saying: 'So many as will come and tarry with us shall be welcome and as many as will depart, good leave have they.' The men who left crossed back over the Bridge, with bows broken, scabbards emptied and coats turned inside out.

Contrary to expectations, Mary confidently rode to the Guildhall, where she declared to the citizens her determination to remain betrothed. The Queen stated that Wyatt was a rebel, that those in favour of him should join him, and that the way into Kent over the Bridge would be left open to them for a short time.

As the threat neared, the City prepared to defend itself, and the Lord Mayor's officers remained armed even as they served him his dinner. Soon, several thousand of Wyatt's vanguard could be seen from the Tower of London as they marched towards the Bridge with a number of guns in their train. On hearing this news, an outpost of the Queen's troops at St George's Church in Southwark retreated on to the Bridge, an event described in Raphael Holinshed's *Chronicles*: 'The Draw-Bridge was then cut down and thrown into the river; the Bridge gates were shut; ramparts and fortifications were raised around them; ordnance was placed to defend them; and the Mayor and Sheriffs, well armed for the conflict, commanded all persons to shut up their shops and windows and to stand ready harnessed at their doors for any event which might occur.'

As instructed, the bridge-dwellers closed their shops and gathered their weapons. During the night the Bridge was watched by Lord William Howard, the Lord Admiral of England, who had been appointed Captain General for the occasion, and by the Lord Mayor, Sir Thomas White, and three hundred men.

Meeting no opposition in Southwark itself, the rebels sacked the Bishop of Winchester's palace. Wyatt then 'sett 2 peeces of ordnance againste the gate [Great Stone Gate]' at the bridgefoot, and an extensive trench was dug between the Bridge and his men. However, the high state of readiness and the now impassable drawbridge-less Bridge were deeply disconcerting to Wyatt, because he had counted on the support of the City.

Wyatt wanted to take a closer look at the preparations on this famed barbican of the City of London. The Great Stone Gate was apparently far from impregnable, for an opening was made in the wall of a house close to it. At eleven p.m., in the February cold and darkness, Sir Thomas and a few others crawled over the parapet and on to the leads of the gate. To get to the bridge street, they had to go down through the porter's lodge, where they found the porter asleep and his wife and others sitting before a coal fire. They were shocked when they saw him, but he said, 'as you love your lives sit still, you shall have no hurt', and they remained quiet. The rebels crept out on to the roadway, and went as far as the drawbridge gap. From there they saw the Admiral, the Lord Mayor and Sir Andrew Judd discussing the defence of the Bridge. 'It troubled Wiat and all his companie very sore to see that London did so stiffelie stand and hold out against them: for in the assistance which they looked to have had in that of the citie, all their hope of prosperous speed consisted.' Wyatt had a long look, then returned to Southwark, saying, 'This place, Sirs, is too hot for us.'

He could have taken his forces on to the Bridge as far as the gap, and launched a surprise attack. But Wyatt was basically honourable; he did not want to pillage London in an uprising that had perhaps started somewhat light-heartedly. The rebels paused to assess all options, but the very next night an unplanned encounter precipitated events.

Above the Bridge, a Thomas Menschen, employed by Sir John Brydges, the Lieutenant of the Tower of London, was being rowed downstream towards the Bridge. The oarsman was hailed by a waterman who worked from Tower Stairs, and who wanted to cross the river. Menschen told the oarsman to pick up this man. Crossing the river was forbidden in the emergency, and so attracted the attention of a party of armed rebels. When Menschen refused to land the man as ordered, weapons were fired, probably at close range: the Tower Stairs waterman was killed, the oarsman wounded, but 'with much paine' rowed through the Bridge and to the Tower wharf. The Lieutenant of the Tower decided on vengeance. Stow recorded that the same night and the next morning from the Tower the Lieutenant pointed seven 'great pieces of ordnance', heavy cannons and demi-cannons, at the foot of the Bridge and Southwark, as well as at the steeples of St Olave and St Mary Overie, backed up by the weapons at the White Tower, the Divelling Tower and over the Watergate.

On seeing this, Stow reported, the alarmed inhabitants of Southwark went to Wyatt: 'Sir, we are all likely to be undone, and destroyed for your sake, our houses shall by and bye bee throwne downe upon our heads, to the utter spoyle of this burrough, with the shot of the Tower, already bent and charged against us; for the love of God take pity on us.' Wyatt replied: 'I pray you my friends bee content for a while, and I will soon ease you of this mischief, for God forbid that you, or the least of you, should be killed or hurt on my behalfe.'

Wyatt then decided to make a diversion to Kingston Bridge, the only other bridge over the Thames near London. The next day the rebels marched the twelve miles to Kingston in ten hours. But the bridge there had been partially destroyed by the locals, who repulsed them. They left their guns behind, but somehow crossed the river to avoid a return to Southwark and London Bridge. Wyatt arrived back in London at the locked Ludgate with his exhausted men to hear Lord William Howard say: 'Avaunt thee, traitor, thou shalt not come in here.'

The leader of the narrowly defeated rising surrendered at Temple Bar, which marks the boundary of the City on the west side, and

The cage and stocks on the Bridge.

was taken to the Tower to be met by Sir John Brydges, whose threat of bombardment had made him leave Southwark only a short time before. Wyatt and a hundred rebels were later executed, but Wyatt's head was not placed on the Bridge; rather on the gibbet at Hay Hill, near the present Berkeley Square, from where it was stolen. Other parts of his body were distributed to places where it was thought the sight of them would be most effective, one spot being at Pepper Alley immediately west of the bridgefoot in Southwark.

The turmoil and perceived threat created an excellent opportunity for the Queen to get rid of her rival, the unfortunate Lady Jane Grey, as well as the Lady's husband, father and uncle. The sixteen-year-old Protestant Lady Jane, the chosen heir of young Edward VI, had reigned for nine days before being deposed by Mary. Her beheading was presided over by Sir William Hewett, who had been made sheriff the year before. A painting attributed to Antonio Morro in the Museum of London depicts Hewett in the robes of that office. This rich merchant, whose daughter had been rescued from the river by Edward Osborne as a child, had greeted Queen Mary in the City on her accession, and was loyal to her.

Princess Elizabeth was also in grave danger, for Queen Mary suspected her half-sister's involvement in the uprising. Elizabeth was informed by the Marquess of Winchester and the Earl of Surrey that she must go to the Tower. Although the barge and 'the tide which waited for no one' were ready, Elizabeth delayed, requesting that she might wait for the next tide 'trusting that the next would be better and more comfortable'; then that she might write to Mary, who was furious at the delay, but a letter was finally allowed. The next tide fell around midnight, and there was nervousness that popular Elizabeth might be rescued by Protestant supporters. Jean Froissart tells how on Palm Sunday, a day of grey and steady drizzle, Elizabeth eventually entered the barge. With her those on the Bridge saw the two lords, two of Queen Mary's ladies-in-waiting, three of her own, her gentleman-usher and two of her grooms. With the Tower of London in sight, the bridge weir conspired to delay Elizabeth's incarceration, for the water proved to be particularly troublesome. The bargemen had difficulty in shooting the Bridge, the barge hitting the ground in the shallow water under it, and immediately before them they saw the great drop at the rapids. The unhappy party remained dangerously stuck under the Bridge for a time before proceeding.

The party having finally shot the Bridge, those on the Bridge rushed to the other side to see Elizabeth arrive at the Watergate entrance to the Tower. All the while the Princess obdurately insisted that she was not a traitor. Implicated or not, no evidence against her emerged, and in May 1554 she was released. At mid-afternoon, those on the Bridge once again saw her pass through, being taken to a royal residence at Woodstock.

Mary married Philip in July 1554 at Winchester, against the wishes of Privy Councillors, Parliament and many of her subjects. In August the royal couple arrived from Richmond in separate barges, landing above the Bridge at St Mary Overie Stairs, and from there went to nearby Winchester House, home of Bishop

Gardiner, the Lord Chancellor. They hunted in the Bishop's park, and stayed at Suffolk Place, the manor house of the Duke of Suffolk, principal landlord and steward of Southwark.

A day or two later came the state entry over the Bridge. According to chronicler Holinshed, 'a vain great spectacle' was set up at the Drawbridge – which must have been repaired very quickly indeed after Wyatt's uprising – with 'two images representing Corineus, and the other Gogmagog' holding Latin verses between them, the excessiveness of which the author could not bear to describe.

Mary and Philip ruled jointly, confirming the worst fears of Wyatt and so many others. Philip became King of Spain in 1556. He soon involved his wife and England in a war with France, an action with the most disastrous symbolic and economic result possible: England lost Calais. Calais was England's final foothold in France, and had a special place in the national consciousness. It represented the glorious campaigns of the Black Prince and Henry V. Even more important was its commercial value as an official and vital market for England's most important export, wool. Mary's brief, austere reign ended in November 1558 when she died childless and unmourned, and with her death Philip's rights in England ended.

The Bridge prepared to greet its sixteenth English monarch: Queen Elizabeth I.

CHAPTER FIVE

'. . . one of the wonders of the world'

. . . to consider the forme and beauty of this famous Bridge . . . it is adorned with sumptuous buildings, and statelie and beautifull houses on either side, inhabited by wealthy citizens and furnished with all matter of trades, comparable in itselfe to a little Citie, whose buildings are so artificially contrived, and so firmly combined, as it seemth more than an ordinary streete, for it is one continuous vaulte or roofe . . .

John Norden, *c.* 1600

A T MID-MORNING ONE DECEMBER DAY IN 1558, the twenty-five-year-old Elizabeth, daughter of Henry VIII's second wife, Anne Boleyn, went through the Bridge as Queen. Only four and a half years earlier the clever princess blessed by luck had passed through the structure to the Tower for her brief stay. Now her progress by royal barge to Somerset House from Greenwich was witnessed by the commons she was to rule for almost fifty years, ever expertly promoting the cult of Gloriana.

By now the initial immense shock of Henry's Dissolution of the Monasteries in 1537 and the Reformation had largely been absorbed. The great changes became a great stimulus, and minds opened to the genius of the Renaissance. There was an explosion of printing, energizing developments in every sphere. Elizabeth's kingdom was poised for greatness, but the country she had inherited was weak, divided, near bankrupt and politically hemmed in between rivals France and Spain. The ongoing conflict with the latter, then the most powerful country in the world, was to include an encounter with the Spanish Armada. But Elizabeth, as well as being an instinctive politician, was more than able to hold her own. The Protestant Queen ruled with guile and moderation: her approach to the all-important subject of religion was at least initially neither to persecute Catholics nor to allow them to worship in public.

The dynamism of the era was reflected on every level. In its 622-year history, Old London Bridge attained its peak of prestige and magnificence during Elizabeth's reign. It would be adorned with extravagant Nonesuch House, which replaced the Drawbridge Gate. Of all the highly decorated inhabited bridges in Europe, no other was ornamented on this scale, although its most outstanding features – the Chapel and Nonesuch House – were not on it at the same time. By now the Bridge had been illustrated by several artists, it was a central feature on the maps of London that were appearing, and it was described by a traveller in Elizabethan England, Baron Waldstein, in his diary as 'easily one of the finest bridges in the whole of Europe both for size and beauty'.

There was a rapid expansion in culture and building, and the latter included the embankment of the river at Bankside, complete with water stairs and landings. Trade expanded and life became a little easier; waterwheels were built by the arches of the Bridge to pump water to homes in the City, and romance attached itself to the old structure.

The 'peerless sovereign Queen' used the river as a setting for royal spectacle to enhance her charisma and popularity. Although she did not fear for her safety in crowds, she did not like going over the Bridge. Only once in her forty-five-year reign did she enter the high, narrow, dark, tunnel-like structure. The 'one continuous vaulte or roof' of the bridge street must have felt threatening, for she never repeated the experience.

An example of her avoidance occurred in 1566 when she secretly came from Greenwich to Southwark to meet her great favourite,

Robert Dudley, Earl of Leicester. James Gairdner, in *Three Fifteenth Century Chronicles*, recounts how they almost missed each other, probably due to the wary Queen revealing neither her intentions nor her route. Leicester entered the City with his great train 'all in theyr riche cotes and to ye nombar of 700'. He reached Temple Bar, then proceeded through Ludgate and St Paul's Churchyard to London Stone, where he awaited his queen at Lord Oxford's house in St Swithin's Churchyard, a little to the north-east of the Bridge.

Meanwhile, in telling contrast, Elizabeth, with only two ladies, entered a 'whiry' with a single pair of oars just above the Bridge at St Mary Overie Stairs, and without ceremony was rowed across to the stairs at The Three Cranes in the Vintry, an area of wine warehouses. At the top of the steps they 'entryd a cowche cyveryd with blewe and so rode . . . to mett with ye sayd Earle of Lescestar'. But impatient Leicester had already left Lord Oxford's house because she was not there when he arrived. Leicester proceeded along Candlewick Street (Cannon Street), Eastcheap, New Fish Street and over the Bridge to Southwark. Just beyond St George's Church he halted to wait for his queen. Meanwhile, Elizabeth crossed back to Southwark by wherry the way she had come, then drove on in her coach. On overtaking Leicester she left her coach, and embraced and kissed the Earl three times. Then they rode on together to Greenwich, where she had been born, as had her father. There, at the often-used Palace of Placentia, she enjoyed the space and the luxury. Greenwich was where ambassadors were received to then be rowed upstream in an eight-oared barge, suitably outfitted with a cabin and a red satin awning.

London was already famed as a tourist attraction. The main sights in the City and in Southwark were well known and listed, and the wondrous Bridge, perhaps the most famous of them, linked the two disparate centres. The Bridge was described in *The London Journal of Allesandro Magno* in 1562 as 'a remarkable sight even among the beauties of London'.

The sights were recounted by D. Lupton in *London and the Countrey Carbonadoed* of 1632. Southwark could boast of the Paris

Gardens (from 'Paradise'), an animal show on the South Bank; play-houses; fencing schools; and dancing schools. On the City side there was the Tower of London (to which Shakespeare made more references than to any other London building) and St Paul's; north-west of the Bridge was Cheapside with its abundance of jewellers; Sir Thomas Gresham's Royal Exchange; Turnbull Street, a prostitutes' quarter – 'their chiefest desire is to bee well mann'd'; Bedlam (the Hospital of St Mary of Bethlehem for the care of the insane); Artillery (the military training ground 'three fields from Moorgate and next to the six windmills'); and the fisherwomen.

The fisherwomen were highly visible and highly audible, the very kind of characterful subject to whom Hogarth would later be attracted, confirmed in his wonderful portrait of *The Shrimp Seller*, alert, smiling, looking for customers, her basket on her head. 'These Crying, Wandering, and Travailing creatures carry their shops on their heads, and their story-house is ordinarily Billingsgate on the Bridgefoot . . . they set up every morning their Trade afresh . . . They are merriest when all their ware is gone: in the morning they delight to have their shop full, at Even they desire to have it empty', a description found in Annette Hope's *Londoners' Larder*. A shop of 'some two yards compass' might hold all kinds of fish, herbs, roots, strawberries, apples or plums, even nuts, oranges and lemons. 'If they drinke out their whole Stock, it's but pawning a Petticoat in Long-lane, or themselves in Turnbull-street for to set up againe . . .' Surprisingly, they did not necessarily specialize: 'She that was this day for Fish, may be tomorrow for Fruit; next day for Herbs, another for Roots: so that you must hear them cry before you know what they are furnished withall.'

As was to be expected, the fisherwomen were seen in the greatest numbers near the markets that sold fish. The main ones, Billingsgate, Fish Street Hill and New Fish Street, were all close to the Bridge, as was the Hall of the Fishmongers Company, one of the leading Livery Companies. Fishing was important. Strength in maritime fishing was equated with maritime power: England's supremacy in the immensely valuable Newfoundland fisheries was achieved only after the defeat of the Armada. And for economic reasons, all fishing was encouraged. To promote more fish being consumed in this now non-Catholic country, the number of fish-days – on which fish, not meat, was to be eaten – was increased to comprise more than half the days in the year.

At the time when the Bridge peaked in beauty, it again became a focus for romance, with a wedding held on 20 July 1562, when a Miss Nicholls was given in marriage by her father to a Mr Coke in the church of St Olave which adjoined the Bridge House in Southwark. The wedding sermon was preached by an eminent theologian, Mr Becon. The Form of Solemnization of Matrimony used would have been very similar to today's. After the couple had consented together in holy wedlock, a wedding celebration which lasted for at least two days was held at the Bridge House. The Lord Mayor attended and all the aldermen 'with many Ladies, and many other worshipful Men and Women'. Then all the company went back to the Bridge House to dinner, 'Where was as Good Cheer as ever was known, with all manner of Musick and Dancing all the Remainder of the Day: And at night a goodly Supper; and then followed a Masque till Midnight'.

On the following day 'the Wedding was kept at the Bridge House with great Cheer', according to John Stow. A supper was again provided and the masquers came in: 'One was in Cloth of Gold. The next Masque consisted of Friars, the third of Nuns. And after, they danced by Times: And lastly, the Friars and the Nuns danced together.' Unfortunately, we don't know much about the individuals who warranted such celebrations. Neither Mr Nicholls nor Mr Coke was a Bridge Warden, but the bride's father may have been the Tide Carpenter or the important Clerk of the Works who supervised the daily work, or in some other permanent position closely connected to the Bridge. We are left only with the cheering description of the festivities.

The most romantic of all the stories connected with the Bridge now reached its apogee. That same Edward Osborne – the apprentice who rescued from the Thames his employer's little daughter, whom he later married – became Lord Mayor of London, and was knighted by Queen Elizabeth on 2 February 1584 at Westminster.

His proud wife, who was to die only two years later, looked on as he reached the highest civic position in the land. He also became the first governor of the Turkey Company, trading with Spain, the Levant and Turkey.

Osborne's grandson, also called Edward Osborne, was created a baronet in 1629, and his great-grandson, Sir Thomas, the second baronet, in 1694 became the first Duke of Leeds, a dukedom being the highest rank possible for a commoner. It jars the flow of this happy tale to learn that the Earl of Shaftesbury described the characteristics of the new Duke as: a liar, proud, ambitious, revengeful, false, prodigal and as covetous as was humanly possible. John Evelyn, the Duke's long-time close acquaintance, said, somewhat carefully, that he was 'a man of excellent natural parts' but never generous or grateful.

The populous City needed ever-increasing amounts of water. In 1574 Dutchman Peter Morris first made a proposal to install and operate a waterwheel set upstream before the arch nearest the City end, which would pump river water to the upper City. Morris had a most powerful supporter in Sir Christopher Hatton, a favourite of Elizabeth's, and to whom she forced the Bishop of Ely to lease today's Hatton Garden, then acres of roses, the rent to be paid in bushels of this floral emblem of England. On 26 May 1580, Hatton, who a few years later would be Lord Chancellor, wrote to the Lord Mayor and aldermen regarding an agreement between 'his servant' Peter Morris and the Corporation of London for conveying water from the Thames as far as Leadenhall (the site of a mansion donated to the Corporation, where Leadenhall Market stands today) and requesting more time to complete the work. Only the 'poor water-bearers' were opposed.

In 1580 – to encourage the City to give him the promised funding – Morris had conducted a demonstration for the Lord Mayor and aldermen, in which he used a pump to shoot a jet of water, reputedly over the steeple of St Magnus. Morris undertook to supply water with every tide, and the City granted the lease for the use of the river water, the place where the waterwheel stood, as well as the most northerly arch of the Bridge. The City also gave financial aid to Morris during the initial difficulties with the hydraulic machinery.

How did the first waterwheel of 1582 function? Although anchored to the Bridge, it was not positioned right under an arch, but was set slightly upstream before the north arch. The waterwheel drove a shaft which in turn through a connecting rod semi-rotated a disc, and this by means of chains drove the piston rods of two pumps. It required careful maintenance, worked only when the tide was flowing, and usefully could be raised or lowered with the tide by one man operating a windlass.

In 1582 a lease for a second waterwheel was granted on the same terms as the first. Ten years later the water flowed to a water cistern at the four-way intersection at the east end of Cornhill where it meets Gracechurch, Leadenhall and Bishopsgate. A fifth of the water was lost as it was directed uphill through large lead pipes from the north end of the Bridge

into diverse men's houses in Thames Street, new fish streete and Grasse street [Gracechurch Street], up to the north west corner of Leaden hall, the highest ground of all the Citie, where the waste of the main pipe rising into this standarde (provided at the charges of the Citie) with four spoutes did at every tyde runne (according to covenant) foure ways, plentifully serving to the commoditie of the inhabitants neare adjoyning in their houses, and also cleansed the Chanels of the streete towarde Bishopgate, Aldgate, the bridge, and the Stocks Market . . .

The waterwheels were yet another, and a serious, blockage at the bridge weir, where the water now dangerously bunched up even more at both the ebb and the flow. The open space under the arches had totalled 245 feet at half-tide, and there was the additional obstruction in Lock Rock near the Southwark end where a piece of the Bridge had fallen in. By 1588 the mighty river had been reduced to about one-sixth of its natural width.

In the next reign these waterwheels would be supplemented when Sir Hugh Myddelton completed construction of the New River in 1609–13, using the gravity of the land itself to bring pure water about forty miles down from rural Hertfordshire to a reservoir at Clerkenwell, then on to 30,000 houses in the City.

The waterwheels – eventually five of them – on the north end of the Bridge were matched by corn mills at the south end. When mills there first began is not known, but there is a record in 1523 of a 'mill now lying in one of the gullies which breaketh the right course of the stream', doing 'great hurt' to the woodwork of the Bridge, although nothing else is known about it. From the very beginning all the mills and waterworks changed the flow of the water and harmed the Bridge.

In 1591 the Common Council ordered that mills to grind the corn be built at the Southwark end on the west side (opposite the warehouses for corn on the east side), making use of the two piers between the Great Stone Gateway and the Southwark bank. These corn granaries and mills are visible in the early watercolour *London Bridge on Fire,** although oddly no fire can be seen in it. As with the waterwheels, a watermill was not placed right under an arch but upstream in front of it, where twelve feet away from the Bridge a shed was built over it all on three piers, all joined by a very extensive roof which covered a large space on the west side of the Bridge. The wheels at the Southwark end were used both to grind corn and eventually to pump water to houses in Southwark.

As far back as around 1520 a system had also existed for storing corn and grain near the Bridge to help feed the poor in times of need. Near the Bridge House there were ten large corn warehouses, each with an oven to bake the bread of the poorer citizens. In 1545, when large quantities of corn arrived, the City companies were required to purchase a quota, and to stock the warehouses with 10,000 'quarters' of grain. Payment was made the day agreement was reached, but the corn remained in the Bridge House granaries

---

*Anon., of an early but unknown date: Pepysian Collection, Magdalene College, Cambridge.

where it was 'turned and screened' to keep it fresh. If the corn went mouldy, the bakers were still compelled to buy it from this source, even though, if a baker was convicted of selling bad bread, fairly serious penalties included the pillory. The ongoing strong protestations of the bakers were ignored. A City Council ordinance of 1520 described the bakers as being 'of pure malyce and envye' and who 'daily sow scismes and grugges against the purveyors and buyers of whete conveyed to the garnardes at the Briggehouse for the good provision of the said City . . .' But the bakers never stopped their vehement protests and unwisely accused the Wardens of making a profit on the wheat and the ovens they built so the poor could bake their bread. In fact the Bridge House lost money on their charitable endeavour.

Although few people ventured far from where they had been born, what was happening on the Continent could easily affect their lives. It could mean success or failure in business and trade, war or peace, life or death. Antwerp was the biggest trading centre for England's main export, wool, and Antwerp was controlled by Spain.

Glamorous, amoral Captain Francis Drake held a privateer's licence from the Queen, her indirect – but effective and richly rewarding – way of attacking the Spanish treasure ships. He became the first Englishman to circumnavigate the world, and on his return after three years in 1580 the *Golden Hind* became an immediate tourist attraction. The Queen too wanted to see it and to hear Drake's stories. She travelled to Deptford Creek on the River Effra; this now hidden river flows into the Thames above Vauxhall Bridge (and may have been part of Cnut's route to avoid London's bridge in 1014). Her share of the takings from Drake's voyage equalled a whole year's revenue. Although the Spanish protested, the 'phoenix of the world' knighted Drake before a huge crowd, then dined with him in his cabin. It was her wish that the ship remain in Deptford Creek 'as a memorial to national honour and imperial enterprise', and there it stayed until it fell apart, as bits were taken for souvenirs.

Protestant Elizabeth always favoured subtle means to avoid conflict. But in 1587 she ended the intrigue surrounding her

Catholic cousin and rival Mary Stuart, Queen of Scots. The sentence of execution was read out at London Bridge before the sombre Lord Mayor and aldermen on horseback. The news quickly spread throughout Europe, and gave Philip of Spain the excuse he needed to attack. This led to one of the most famous events of Elizabeth's reign, one that is now part of English folklore: the defeat of the Spanish Armada.

Preparations were made all over the south of England in 1588 against a possible landing by the powerful enemy, and lookouts were posted to sight enemy sails. On the Bridge all the gates were closed at night, the Great Stone Gate was checked, and the portcullises were repaired. There was a clear plan of action laid out for such occasions, for each City ward was required to provide a specific number of men and arms. For the ward of Bridge Within on this occasion it was 383 men, including 115 men with shot or firearms, 92 with garments to support pikes, 31 with bows and 61 with pikes. Many of the Thames watermen, who had received their royal charter from Henry VIII, volunteered to fight and made excellent sailors.

In early August 1588 the Spanish Armada of 20,000 men and 130 ocean-going but cumbersome ships was harassed and defeated by the skirmishes and fire-ships of the fleet of fewer and smaller English ships. Drake, a vice admiral, was in the midst of the action, but it was the vile weather that chose the victor. The commemorative Armada Jewel was inscribed: 'God blew and they were scattered'.

There was a grand procession to St Paul's. The Queen attended the service of thanksgiving there, as did Sir Edward Osborne, former Lord Mayor and senior civic figure. The lower battlements of the cathedral were decorated with ten flags and a streamer captured from the Spanish warships. The latter, with 'an image of our Ladie, with her sonne in her armes', was held over the pulpit during the sermon. The next day these trophies of war were transferred to the most prestigious site in the City: the Great Stone Gate on London Bridge, visible to all those going to the first day of Southwark Fair.

Traditionally, the citizens of the Borough had the right to hold an annual three-day fair on every 7, 8 and 9 September, set out in a charter of 1462. Hogarth's much later superb etching, *Southwark Fair*, forces one's eye across the numerous strands of exuberance, coarseness, frivolity and cruelty. Controversy over the valuable rights to a fair in Southwark had led to the creation of the new ward of Bridge Without. Reginald R. Sharpe, in *London and the Kingdom*, recounts how, when the City had claimed the right to hold a market on two days of the week each September, Sir John Gate, the King's bailiff, protested. To resolve the matter once and for all, on 23 April 1550, £647 2s. 1d. was paid by the City to the King, who in return gave them a charter conveying 'divers messuages' (houses and their lands) in Southwark, and for a further 500 marks surrendered all the royal liberties (lands owned by the King) and franchises held in the borough of Southwark. Thus, the ward of Bridge Without (the City) came into being on 31 July 1550.

There was no large open place for the fair in Southwark, so it took place in streets, inn yards and courtyards and extended almost on to the Bridge. On a chosen day during each fair, the Lord Mayor and sheriffs rode to St Magnus after dinner, where they were received by the aldermen with all due ceremony. The Mayor's sword-bearer carried his sword (several eighteenth-century mayors' sword-rests remain in the church to this day). After prayers they rode through the fair and on to St George's in Southwark or to the stones marking the areas that were under the jurisdiction of the City, and then returned to the Bridge House for a banquet. But Southwark Fair became too riotous, and was suppressed in 1763.

Foreign travellers carried information in both directions, and left valuable records of their impressions. News came in 1591 that the Ponte di Rialto, where there had been a bridge since at least 1250, had been completed. This Venetian bridge, on a single level, used its space to the maximum, for shops lined both the inside and outside walkways. It has one supremely elegant arch, and at the highest point an open place for viewing the Grand Canal in both directions. To an effusive observer, the twenty-arched bridge at London defiantly became 'Twenty Rialtos'.

Visitors were amused, intrigued, even apparently frightened by the street criers of London, who 'carried and cried' their goods, and added much colour and character to the City. Strangers going about their business or sightseeing in London were often mocked and insulted by the commons. Jacob Rathgeb, private secretary to Duke Friedrich von Württemberg, noted in 1592 that '. . . they care little for foreigners, but scoff and laugh at them; and moreover one dare not oppose them, else the street-boys and apprentices collect together in immense crowds and strike to the right and left unmercifully without regard to person; and because they are the strongest, one is obliged to put up with the insult as well as the injury'.

The roads could be impossible, so a cloak and stout shoes were needed for splashing through narrow streets awash from the dripping roofs and worse. A refugee-visitor, Giordano Bruno – friar, philosopher, perhaps a spy – in *The Ash Wednesday Supper* told of the short journey to a dinner in Whitehall. For speed, he and his friends went to a private pier and called for 'oars'. It took so long for a boat to come they could have walked 'and performed some errands on the way'. At last a boat with two boatmen slowly appeared 'as if they were going to their own hanging'. After much discussion they were helped on board by a man 'who looked like the ancient ferryman from the kingdom of Tartarus', while the other, his son, 'seemed to be about 65'. They proceeded 'through much time but little space' until the men turned suddenly towards the bank and would go no further: they were at their own house. Now on foot, Bruno and his friends were in a street which began as a mudhole and from which there was no detour. He fell so deeply into a hole he could not pull his legs out. By helping one another, 'ever sinking into the liquid mire', they reached the main street to find that they were 'about twenty-two steps' from where they had started out.

It was a time of public execution everywhere in Europe. In England the worst of crimes was treason, but in London on the frequent 'law days' at least twenty to thirty men and women were hanged, as German traveller Thomas Platter reported in 1599. Gibbets or gallows were everywhere. Fetter Lane, for example, had a gallows at each end. Of the various places for displaying the heads and quarters, especially of traitors, the Bridge was the premier choice. And there was no rush to remove the skulls. In Antony van den Wyngaerde's drawing of around 1550, there are five heads on the Drawbridge Gate. They were left on the poles for what could be a considerable time – until space ran out. For a time heads were exhibited at Temple Bar where, Horace Walpole later reported, youths with nothing better to do rented out small telescopes at a halfpenny a time for a closer look. Whether this form of enterprise was duplicated in Southwark is not known.

Around 1560 the skulls on the Bridge were put to use. Skilled German and Dutch workers had been brought to London to work at the Mint within the Tower. A large quantity of withdrawn debased coins were to be melted down and refined, mixed with arsenic. Most of the workers became ill, probably from arsenic fumes. In an age when the remedy for a tumour was stroking it with a dead man's hand, the cure in this case was to drink from a dead man's skull. The aldermen and others in charge of the Mint tried to help by obtaining a warrant from the Court of Common Council authorizing the removal of the heads from London Bridge. Cups were made from the skulls, from which the afflicted men drank. Supposedly there was some relief, although most of the workers still died.

Usually, there were many heads to be seen on the Bridge. In 1592 Jacob Rathgeb saw about thirty-four heads 'of persons of distinction who had in former times been condemned and beheaded for creating riots and from other causes'. *The Diary of the Duke of Stettin's Journey through England* of 1602 recorded: 'Near the end of the bridge, on the suburb sidde, were stuck up the heads of 30 gentlemen of high standing who had been beheaded on account of treason and secret practises against the Queen.' In Claes Jansz Visscher's *Long Prospect of London*, published in 1616, the Great Stone Gate is topped by almost twenty heads. And there seemed to be no disgrace in having had an ancestor's head appear on the Bridge; on the contrary, Thomas Platter in 1599 noted that '. . . descendants are apt to boast of this'. In 1566 the heads on the Bridge appeared, to scholar Joseph Justus Scaliger, like 'masts of ships and at the top of them quarters of men's corpses'.

Platter also observed that the City was run by a merchant class, all of whom were members of one of the Livery Companies and Freemen of the City; and that only they could trade or open a shop within the City, including on the Bridge: 'Most of the inhabitants are employed in commerce. They buy, sell and trade in all corners of the globe, for which purpose the water serves them well, since ships from France, the Netherlands and Germany and other countries land in this city, bringing goods with them and loading others in exchange.'

When Rathgeb arrived in 1592, he wrote that London was '. . . a large, excellent and mighty city of business, and the most important in the whole kingdom, most of the inhabitants are employed in buying and selling merchandise, and trading in almost every corner of the world . . .' He also commented on the dress of the Londoners:

> The inhabitants are magnificently apparelled, and are extremely proud and overbearing; and because the greater part, and especially the tradespeople, seldom go into other countries . . . The women . . . are dressed out in exceedingly fine clothes, and give all their attention to their ruffs and stuffs, to such a degree indeed, that . . . many a one does not hesitate to wear velvet in the streets, which is common with them, whilst at home perhaps they have not a piece of rye bread . . .

No one approached – dared approach – the Queen in magnificence. This was the woman who in the first days of her reign had demanded that all crimson-coloured silk be held by the customs officers at the Port of London, for her to take her pick 'for the furniture of her coronation' (the Bridge House contributed £4 to her coronation procession, which seems a modest amount). Every detail of her triumphant portraits is symbolic, the monarch herself ever youthful even in later years, in red wig 'of a colour never made by nature' and an all-seeing mask of white-lead face paint. In a period of costly, impractical clothing, which might be embroidered, padded, slashed, frilled and winged, the rich often gave or left their wardrobes to their servants. The latter were forbidden by law to wear them, so sold them on to the players of one of the usually feuding theatre companies.

Shakespeare referred to the Bridge in his plays, as did his clever friend and rival, dramatist Ben Jonson. A Londoner born and bred, Jonson aimed to depict human foibles, as in this passage from one of his farces, *Epicoene* or *The Silent Woman* of 1609, which also outlines the principal and noisiest sights of London:

> She had a peruke that's like a pound of hemp, made up in shoe threads . . . All her teeth were made in the Blackfriars, both her eyebrows in the Strand, and her hair in Silver-street. Every part of the town owns a piece of her . . . She takes herself asunder still when she goes to bed, into some twenty boxes; and about next day noon is put together again, like a great German clock.
>
> So it would rid me of her! – and, that I did supererogatory penance in a belfry, at Westminster Hall, in the Cockpit, at the fall of a stag, the Tower-wharf – what place is there else? – London-bridge, Paris Garden, Billingsgate, when their noises are at their height and loudest.

Literally on top of the noise of the river traffic, the bridge street was one of the most ear-splitting places in London, and the variations of the din were ever-changing: frightened, confused cattle worried by dogs or being beaten as they searched for a way through the throng, perhaps falling over the side; the hammering in dozens of workshops; the cheeky apprentices calling out 'What lack ye?' followed by a list of their wares, from 'flea-tormentors' to 'delicate cowcumbers to pickle'; jokes and insults; a man blowing a trumpet while selling toy hobby-horses carried on his shoulder; and the ballad-sellers:

> Antique Ballads, sung to crowds of old,
> Now cheaply bought at twice their weight in gold.

Then there were the rival gangs of fighting schoolboys; the moans of the frequently injured or dying; horses' hoofs tapping; seagulls screaming. And it started early. The rattle of cart wheels over the Bridge began at five a.m., and was soon joined by the imploring cries of the characterful street-sellers: 'Twelvepence a peck, oysters', 'Buy a fine singing bird', 'Hot spiced gingerbread'.

By this period there was a committee to regulate the stalls and shops, and to settle the frequent disputes. With the sun rising over the river downstream in the east, the shop flaps were opened at around six a.m; these shelves were permitted to extend only four inches beyond the shop fronts. From E. Guilpin's *Skialetheia* of 1598: 'There squeaks a cart-wheel; here a tumbril rumbles; Here scolds an old brawl; there a porter grumbles; Here two tough car-men combat for the way.'

Traffic on the Bridge worsened. Then there was the thudding of the waterwheels with the tides and the churning of the rapids.

Ned Ward, host of the King's Head Tavern near Gray's Inn, and author of *The London Spy*, first published 1698–1703, recorded his impressions of 'the surprizing Novelty': 'We now turn'd down to the *Thames-side*, where the frightful roar of the *Bridge* Water-falls so astonish'd my Eyes, and terrified my Ears, that, like *Roger* in his *Mill*, or the inhabitants of the Cateracts of the *Nile*, I could hear no voice softer than a *Speaking Trumpet*, or the audible Organ of a *Scolding Fish Woman* . . .'

As dusk fell the daytime noise subsided. Each house was supposed to be lit with a lantern in front, but darkness and silence prevailed. The defenceless, and wise, stayed in and safe, and went to bed after a day that had started at five or six a.m. The watchman, with dog, staff and bell called out:

Twelve of the clock, look well to your locks,
Your fire and your light, and God give you good night.

In the darkness dogs howled. Guilpin continued: 'Two swaggering knaves here brabble for a whore; There brawls an ale-knight for his fat-grown score.' Unidentifiable outbursts, screams and grunts were even more fearsome. The atmosphere was usually treacherous, as described by Shakespeare in *Richard II*:

> When the searching eye of heaven is hid
> Behind the globe, and lights the lower world,
> Then thieves and robbers range abroad unseen,
> In murders, and in outrage bloody here.

The third of the seven stages of London Bridge dates from around 1600. The Bridge by now had been depicted from several viewpoints, and what a view they give. Van den Wyngaerde's, the earliest one, is from the south-east, giving the Bridge in perspective (1594). The anonymous late-Tudor illustration *London Bridge on Fire* shows the Bridge from the west or upriver side in great detail: the buildings facing the Square by the Chapel are ornate, the waterwheels thud at both ends, and there are eighteen weather-vanes along its length. It can be paired with John Norden's view from the east or

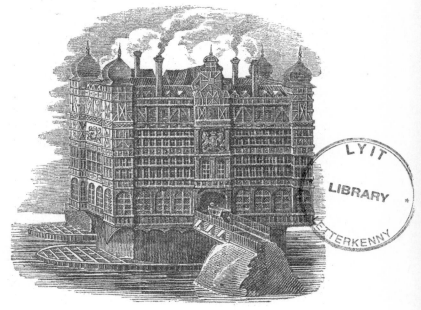

Nonesuch House from the south-west or Southwark side.

Nonesuch House from the west or upstream side.

downriver side, published in 1624, and also detailed. In this the Drawbridge Gate is gone and the heads (fourteen in the anonymous drawing) have been transferred to the Great Stone Gate. Replacing the Drawbridge Gate is ornate Nonesuch House with all its filials; the Chapel is now a dwelling; there are windows in the gables of the buildings; from several windows buckets are being lowered to the river; and from enclosed hanging balconies with their leaded windows, if anyone is looking they can see that a boat has overturned in the rapids and three people are struggling in the water.

Adding to the 'artistic' appearance of the Bridge, most of the houses were out of plumb, and the line of buildings was uneven, for those on the piers were deeper than those on the arches, allowing for either more or larger rooms. Just as the buildings appealingly jutted out to different depths, the number of floors varied and there might be as many as five above a shop. Both drawings show an extraordinary jumble of styles, elevations, hanging extensions, windows and roof lines, yet there is an overall harmony.

John Norden was surveyor to Henry, Prince of Wales, the eldest son of James I. This topographical engraver made two line engravings of City and Bridge, both about 1600, as the reign of Elizabeth I was coming to a close. His detailed engravings are from the east, and from the south-west. He gives a description with the dedication on the drawing: 'I present unto you this simple modell of one of the wonders of the world.'

It is Norden's engravings and the description in his lengthy dedication that have been the basis for models made of the Bridge. There were sumptuous buildings, and stately houses on either side inhabited by wealthy citizens, and all kinds of trades were located there: 'It was comparable in itselfe to a little Citie.'

Claes Jansz Visscher's famous 1616 detailed engraving, *Long Prospect of London,* was an accurate long view of the Bridge from the south-west. The Great Stone Gate, with the heads, is prominent in the foreground in his overview of Bridge, river and City.

Then there were the maps and bird's-eye views. Added to surveyor Ralph Agas's *Plan of London,* about 1560–70, was Hoefnagel's *Plan of London* (from Georg Braun and Frans Hohenburg's *Civitates Orbis Terrarum,* 1572), which is a view from the south where gardens and fields can be seen surprisingly close to the centre of the City.

What Rathgeb saw was a '. . . beautiful long bridge, with quite splendid, handsome, and well-built houses, which are occupied by merchants of consequence'. Platter described 'many tall handsome merchant dwellings, and expensive shops, where all manner of wares are for sale, resembling a long street'.

It was a time when Old London Bridge was undergoing dramatic change. The architectural extravagance and overelaboration of the Renaissance was appropriately reflected in a new building: Nonesuch House – 'none such like it'. The structure that had no equal in England replaced the brutal, be-headed Drawbridge Gate on the pier between the eighth and ninth arches from the Southwark end.

The first stone of the fantastic 'new Frame upon London Bridge' was laid on 28 August 1577 by Sir John Langely, the Lord Mayor, in a ceremony observed by the sheriffs and the Wardens. Only the foundations were of stone; as with all other buildings on the Bridge, the use of timber reduced the weight on the overall structure. The framing had been constructed in Holland – a kind of pre-fab. When the extraordinary jigsaw was completed more than two years later, the elaborate design – and the fact that it was held together solely with wooden pegs – reinforced its fame. The building protruded considerably beyond the line of the Bridge, making it look substantial on all sides, including its very much narrower east and west sides. In itself, it was a sight to see in London Town.

Above the roadway arch on the south front of Nonesuch House, a shallow portico with pilasters on the three main floors terminated in a curious gable supported with main scrolls and much ornamental woodwork. At each of the four corners a projecting turret rose the full height of the four floors, each one surmounted by a Russian-style onion-shaped cupola which was topped by a gilded weather-vane.

The lavish exterior decoration of Nonesuch House can be seen in Visscher's view. It was extensively carved, both on its broad principal front facing Southwark – where two sundials told travellers the time almost a century and a half before St Magnus' clock at the City end. The walls of the building seemed to be comprised of closely placed windows, the number of windows delightfully decreasing in size the higher up they were. Overhanging the water on each side of the building were broad bay windows suggesting well-lighted interiors. Coats of arms with supporters had pride of place on the south, east and west fronts. Panels adorned with sculptured wood, gilded pilasters and balustraded galleries were beneath the windows of the main (south) front.

The building was also painted, the colours unknown except for an entry in a sixteenth-century account book at Coventry: 'Paid to Durram, the paynter, to bye Coulors to paynt . . . as the newe house on London Bridge.' All the rails were painted to look like stone, the small pillars were painted in white lead and the large pillars in 'perfect greene'.

Residence in Nonesuch House was coveted by rich merchants, mainly mercers and haberdashers. The interiors can be imagined: panelled walls hung with glowing paintings and tapestries, silver and pewter glistening, carved and plumply cushioned oak furniture. John Stow, who saw the building, described it as 'a beautifull and chargeable peece of worke'.

At about the same time, there was another new and ornate feature on the Bridge: 'the house with many windows', so called because no other name for it has come down to us. From the Southwark end it was the first building after the Great Stone Gate, forming yet another gateway at the other end of the first river arch.

'The house with many windows' – the imperfections of the hand-made glass catching the light and reflections from the ever-changing water – was smaller and less elaborate than Nonesuch House. It had four semicircular turrets, but was notable for the seemingly continuous line of transomed windows on the three upper floors which included the turrets, the tops of which were protected by heavily overhung eaves under battlemented parapets.

Dark and cavern-like was the entry to the bridge street, with its high gabled houses that ran all the way along on both sides to the Drawbridge arch and the 'gateway' of Nonesuch House. The fronts of shops and houses must have had richly carved spandrels over the doors, and been decorated with sculptured panels and moulded beams.

Interestingly, although the Bridge was clearly controlled by the Lord Mayor and aldermen, the Court also influenced decisions. In one example, in 1579, the most powerful person after the Queen was involved in the granting of leases for new buildings on the Bridge: William Cecil, Lord Burghley, was Lord Treasurer and as the Queen's most important adviser helped her govern the kingdom in a remarkable partnership that lasted for forty years. Some houses were rebuilt because they had become so ruinous that the tenants had been afraid to occupy them. It was Burghley who took up the former tenants' cause; he wrote to the Lord Mayor and aldermen on behalf of the tenants to ask that they be allowed to again occupy the premises at increased, but affordable, rents, even though others might pay more. For their part, the original tenants consented to relinquish the unexpired term of the old leases, and so the new leases were granted.

Records such as leases had been kept in the earliest days in a chamber of the Guildhall, and later in the Chapel on the Bridge. In the 1790s a Muniment (or document) Room for the archives would be built in the middle of the garden at the Bridge House. The Bridge House and yard would be painted in watercolour in 1837 – a calm and pleasing scene, so unlike what it must have been like when the old Bridge required its essential daily services – presumably just before the Bridge Wardens' offices and archives were moved to the Guildhall.

There is a glimpse into the detail of some of the houses on the Bridge from a lease of 1613 in the Bridge House Muniment Room. For the tenement on the central part on the western side, the accommodation (on 18 May 1613) comprised twelve rooms, two little dark chambers and a cellar. There were three floors and an attic, common to the larger houses, arranged as:

1. Ground/street floor: shop and counting house, with a 'hanging cellar', which either projected at the back on the same level, or was built out between the piers below the roadway.
2. First floor: a hall and a chamber, and a 'little dark chamber'. The kitchen may have been on this floor, but seemingly was on the one above with 'a little void room' and a chamber behind it.
3. Second floor: over the kitchen three small rooms.
4. Gables in roof: three other small rooms, possibly in the roof (Norden's engraving shows gables).

Wonder of the world or not, so terrifying was the sight of the swirling torrent below that some country people refused to cross over the Bridge: they were rowed across instead. Their queen seemingly shared this apprehension. When, in 1579, Elizabeth signalled that she would come to London by land and pass over the Bridge, the City was quick to ensure an ostentatious display and great rejoicing. But the night before this significant occasion the Queen sent a sequence of couriers: the first to order that there was not to be a great crowd; half an hour later, the second to command that no citizen was to receive the Queen armed; and shortly thereafter, the third to state that she would come by water instead. There was great disappointment, and a lot of money must have been wasted on preparations by the Bridge Wardens and City officials.

But the Queen enjoyed the river as much or more than anyone. A.L. Rowse quotes the *Diary of Henry Machyn*: '. . . the Queen's grace supped at Baynard Castle . . . and after supper the Queen's grace rowed up and down the Thames, and a hundred boats about her grace, with trumpets and guns and flutes and guns, and squibs hurling on high to and fro, till 10 at night ere her grace departed and all the water-side stood with a thousand people looking at her grace'.

The design of the magnificent royal barge included gangways and two cabins with carving, paintings and glass windows. The elaborate vessel resided in its own boathouse on dry land close to one of the Southwark theatres, along with its steerage boat. The latter, lashed to the royal conveyance to add stability, was for the sweating oarsmen.

Elizabeth also relished expeditions to the bear-pits in Southwark in an age when viewing such cruelty gave pleasure, and only a few Puritans protested at the grossness of it. Animal-baiting pre-dated the theatres, and had the patronage of both the Queen and her successor, James I. It would be banned during the Commonwealth (1649–60), after which Charles II would revive it.

The Bear Garden was a large wooden building, three storeys high with galleries round the top. Around 120 to 200 large English dogs were kept in separate wooden kennels, along with a dozen bears and some bulls. The show Thomas Platter saw in 1599 was of a sequence of bears, each on a long rope staked in the middle. The bears were an investment, and so were not killed; in fact, some became stars. As one bear tired another was brought in. A clever old bear effortlessly swept the dogs aside with its paws, while a blind bear knew how to untie the rope and then scampered back to its kennel.

In 1584, a German traveller, Lupold von Wedel, described how dogs fought individually with a bear, the largest kept till last, how a horse was brought in to be chased by the dogs, and then a bull who 'defended himself bravely'. A number of men and women entered from another area, and danced, fought and conversed with one another, while one man threw white bread into the audience, who scrambled for it. A rose hung overhead in the middle of the structure which, when set alight by a rocket, released hundreds of apples and pears down on to the audience. As they chased after them, fireworks and rockets were set off among the crowd, marking the end of the performance.

Gambling was rife in the dicing houses, and it seemed that everyone was besotted by the tobacco that had been introduced by Sir Walter Raleigh from the New World. The narcotic weed would have been on sale on the Bridge, among a huge range of goods. In the eighteenth century a tobacconist, John Winkley, was 'near ye Bridge' in Southwark, but there must have been many more. His tradesman's card depicted a 'coarse rude engraving of a negro smoking and holding a roll of tobacco' with a crown above his head, two ships in full sail behind, and in the foreground four smaller negroes planting and packing tobacco.

In about 1587, among the numerous people who arrived from the country each year was Shakespeare, and, as with many new arrivals, he initially stayed in Southwark. He would have looked at the Bridge with an intense and personal interest, for the head of one of his mother's Catholic relatives, Edward Arden, High Sheriff of the country of Warwickshire in 1575, had been placed on it only four years earlier. In 1592 Shakespeare's name first appeared in a pamphlet by Robert Greene where he was listed as an actor/player. He had played alongside Richard Burbage as a member of the Lord Chamberlain's Men, performing before Elizabeth I at Christmas 1594. The Queen commissioned some of his plays, and his work became the ultimate expression of the cultural riches of her reign.

One place his plays were performed at was the galleried George inn, which survives in Borough High Street, not far from where the Bridge once stood. The first theatres brought together the secular plays that were performed in inn yards, and the animal-baiting which took place in amphitheatre-like pits. The appetite for the drama and excitement of the theatre was enormous. After a major rebuilding of the Rose in Southwark in 1592, in the first nineteen weeks there were 105 performances of twenty-three plays. The Swan was another early theatre, as was the most famous and successful one of all, the Globe. All are clearly depicted in Visscher's engraving. In Elizabeth's reign it was estimated that 20,000 people a week went to the theatre.

Richard Burbage's playhouse of 1576, the Theatre, was in Shoreditch (as was the Curtain), in almost a straight line north of the Bridge and outside the City wall. After a dispute over the rent, the building was dismantled in the winter of 1598–9. In this very cold winter there was no need to use the Bridge. Over the Christmas period the timber was carted across the frozen Thames to its new Bankside site on a plot near the Rose, where it was reconstructed as the Globe. The Globe was a summer theatre, the biggest and the best equipped in Southwark, with a huge stage and 'cellarage' below and a balcony above, allowing for quick scene changes. The Burbage brothers had not been able to afford to rebuild the Globe themselves, so they had offered their five leading players shares to raise funds. With this Shakespeare became a part owner of the playhouse.

The theatre's name was taken from its sign and the flag which flew to announce that a play was in progress and which could be seen across the river by would-be theatre-goers. It showed Hercules with the world on his shoulders, and on it was the motto *Totus Mundus Agit Histrionem* ('All the World's a Stage').

By 1596 there was a total ban on theatres in the City, which made Southwark even more popular, and the watermen busier than ever. Shakespeare would have been rowed across the river many times, often, it is believed, by the 'Water Poet' and wherryman John Taylor (1580–1653), who worked on the river near the Bridge. The river attracted great characters, and he was one of the most memorable. Accounts of him appeared in Southey's *Observations on Uneducated Poets*, and elsewhere. The Water Poet was a larger-than-life figure, whose own life was extraordinary. Among other things, he was pressed into the navy to serve at the siege of Cadiz, and was also an innkeeper. In 1618 he made a journey on foot from London to Edinburgh which he wrote about, having taken advance orders for his planned book, and in the same year he built a boat of 'brown paper' – hemp – in which he sailed from London downstream and around to Queenborough in the Medway estuary, and then wrote *In Praise of Hempseed*. The Thames was his inspiration:

> But noble Thames, whilst I can hold a pen,
> I will disclose thy glory unto men;
> Thou in the morning when my coin is scant
> Before the evening doth supply my want.

Taylor was extremely agitated when in his later years private coaches suddenly appeared: 'This infernal swarm of coaches have overrun the land and we can get no living on the water.' He led a hopeless campaign against the coaches, then popularly kept an inn from where he sold his poems along with the ale.

The many inns in Southwark entertained the theatre-goers until performances started mid-afternoon. This was preceded by a lively scene on the river. Platter observed that 'a number of tiny streets lead to the Thames from both ends of the town; the boatmen wait there in great crowds, each one eager to be the first to catch one [a theatre-goer]'. In two- or four-oared light rowing boats, 'charmingly upholstered' with embroidered cushions, and perhaps with awnings to deflect sun or rain, they were conveyed to the pleasures of the south bank to join the rest of the motley, lively audience when the flag was flying above the playhouse. Stephen Gosson, in *The School of Abuse* (1579), described such a crowd:

> . . . you shall see such heaving, and shoving, such itching and shouldering to sit by women, such care for their garments,

that they shall not be trod on: such eyes to their laps, that no chips light in them: such pillows to their backs, that they take no hurt: such masking in their ears, I know not what: such giving them pippins to pass the time: such playing at foot-saunt without cards; such tickling, such toying, such smiling, such winking, and such manning them home, when the sports are ended, that it is a right comedy to mark their behaviour, to watch their conceits . . .

According to John Chamberlain, writing in 1624, everyone attended: the 'old and young, rich and poor, master and servants, papists and puritans'. It was cheapest to be one of the groundlings – those who stood in the open uncovered space in front of the stage – described by playwright Thomas Dekker: 'Their houses smoakt every after none with Stinkards who were so glued together in crowdes with the Steames of strong breath, that when they came foorth, their faces lookt as if they had beene per boylde.' At the Globe, Shakespeare's 'wooden O', they ate cherries and plums, drank, heckled the actors, broke into fights, threw whatever was to hand at the actors, hissed and clapped at the action. As Shakespeare himself put it in *Henry VIII*: 'These are youths that thunder at a playhouse and fight for bitten apples.'

Any activity that attracted crowds was a potential threat to public order, and Southwark positively heaved with such activities. One Lord Mayor after another tried to ban plays: they distracted apprentices and workmen from their jobs, were thought to be a breeding ground for the plague, and were a danger to morality. But drama came under the protection of the Royal Court. Elizabeth, who herself sang and danced every day, loved being entertained. Her Privy Council protected the theatres, perhaps partly so they could supply well-practised and professional players to perform before the Queen, while not being trained at her expense.

Another powerful group that wanted to see plays banned was the Puritans. Thomas White, in a 1578 sermon, at a time when plays were banned during an outbreak of the plague, as they often were, stated: '. . . the cause of sin are plays: therefore the cause of plagues are plays'. When the playhouses in the City and suburbs were frequently closed during the summer months because of recurrent plague, it was a severe blow to the earnings of both actors and watermen. After the Rose was closed during an outbreak, the watermen, lacking such a lucrative trade, took action by petitioning Lord Admiral Howard for help and relief, asking that Philip Henslowe be allowed to keep his playhouse open.

Aside from these attractions, what was Southwark like in 1622? Crossing the Bridge into Southwark, on the High Street on the right was a row of butchers' shops with a few other shops such as shoemakers and tailors. After the Hospital Gate corner there was a saddler, a grocer, a barber-surgeon, an ironmonger, another grocer, a vintner, two more grocers, a linen-draper and a turner, then a house occupied by two men who were wealthy enough not to practise a trade. Men were usually head of the household, and those in the High Street were well off enough to contribute to the poor rate. Down one of the narrow, tortuous alleys, such as Little Horseshoe Alley, were at least sixty households headed by artisans such as tailors, shoemakers and about a dozen poor widows.

The appealingly jumbled, lively scene was described by the poet William d'Avenant (whose father was the publican in an Oxford tavern frequented by Shakespeare): 'Here a palace, there a wood-yard; here a garden, there a brewhouse; here dwelt a lord, there a dyer.' Among it all were brothels; their trade sign was a hand or a hand holding a cup.

Southwark had been the site of immensely profitable brothels for hundreds of years. They were owned by the Bishop of Winchester – religion and brothels went side by side in Southwark. Henry I (1100–35) had created the Liberty of the See of Winchester in the Borough of Southwark, confirmed by Henry II in 1161, for the governance of the twenty-two licensed brothels along Bankside (seconded by Thomas Becket). The Bishop's residence, Winchester House, sat almost next to the church of St Mary Overie. The prostitutes were nicknamed 'Winchester Geese', and from 1531, Stephen Gardiner, Bishop of Winchester, appointed a Henry Frances 'Bayliffe of the Clinke and Capteyn of the Stewes and all the whores'.

Even in Southwark punishment was never far away; its symbols and implements, usually in full or over-use, were everywhere. From 1577 heads were displayed on the Great Stone Gate, and pillories stood in the middle of the street at the Southwark end of the Bridge, just before the gateway. Cages, stocks and a whipping post sat beside the nearby Clink prison. During Mary's dangerous reign, when three hundred people had been burned for heresy at Smithfield alone, the Queen ordered that cages and stocks be erected in every parish; there was a pillory or stocks on the Bridge on the west side just inside the Great Stone Gate with a cage beside it. At one point an oak cage sat at the entrance to the Bridge, and it was used on the death of Pope Julius III, when prayers and dirges were ordered to be sung at St Magnus. A passing woman enquired what was happening; on being told that she must pray for the Pope, she refused, saying that the Pope was 'cleane' and had no need of her prayers. In Mary's unhappy time, this was interpreted as edging towards heresy and the woman was carried across the Bridge to the cage at the Southwark end and told to 'coole herself there'. Five prisons were located in Southwark: the Clink, the King's Bench, the Marshalsea, the White Lion and the Counter.

Death from the gibbet, disease, or even old age was ever present irrespective of rank or wealth. On 24 March 1603 Elizabeth died at Richmond Palace. The death of a monarch might presage trouble, so householders kept a watch and guard at every street and City gate. Her coffin was taken by river to the substantial royal, and public, landing, Whitehall Stairs, adjoining the Palace of Whitehall. At her funeral the people crowded the streets, windows and roofs, weeping and groaning at the sight of her lifelike effigy.

During Elizabeth's reign London Bridge, in its third stage, enjoyed the most vibrant chapter in its story. Life was becoming more comfortable for the population of London, which, by the end of the reign, was about 200,000. The country was clearly Protestant, resolving the religious turmoil of previous reigns. Trade thrived, with new markets in India and America, and the wonders of the New World were being revealed. The Virgin Queen's adventurers had laid the basis for the world power and industrial leader the country would become.

When the first of the Stuarts, James I, came to the throne of England and to London, he had already been King of Scotland (James VI) for thirty-six years, a country to which he never returned. One conspiracy, among a number, and only two years after his accession, aimed to destroy King and Parliament because of a lack of tolerance towards Catholics: Guy Fawkes and the Gunpowder Plot entered folklore. One of the conspirators, Father Henry Garnet, an English Jesuit, was hanged in St Paul's Churchyard, his head placed on the Bridge, where crowds gathered to view his face which – the proof of his innocence – retained its colour for twenty days.

But such drama aside, the minutiae of life continued on the Bridge and elsewhere. By now the Bridge was run by a standing committee of management and the role of the Bridge Wardens had declined in importance. Soon the Common Council took over the granting of leases from the Wardens, and by the late seventeenth century a committee inspected the accounts. There were fewer workmen at the Bridge House by this time because tenants were responsible for the repairs themselves.

There is an impression of life on the Bridge in 1615 in B.F. Phillpott's translation of the *Life of Jón Olafsson*, a visiting Icelander: 'London Bridge is built in such a fashion that a strong foundation at the very bottom is of hewn rocks nearly all across the width of the river, the thickness of width of the bridge I cannot tell, as a great part of the town is built on it; on it stand three of the largest chief churches, and, if I am not mistaken, several smaller.' His imagination or memory may have played tricks on him, but his impressions are still of interest: 'In the floor of every eating house on the bridge there is a square trap door, over the hole through which the water for household purposes is daily drawn up, and when there is fish in the river they are caught with lines and drawn up through the trap-door, and so brought living to the kitchen . . .'

There were rings in the walls of the piers, and 'boatmen catch them with boathooks by those who pass through in cutters, praams, ships and boats bearing every kind of merchandise too and fro'. But the piers were irresistible to the boatmen. They tied up there, causing damage, and efforts continued to be made to stop it. An Act of Common Council of 5 October 1620 set out the penalties for those who allowed their boats to harm any part of the structure, or who tied up to the piers, or who linked vessels in such a way as to hinder passage, or who removed any part of the filling of the piers.

Southwark's role in colonizing the New World was the creation of tough, adaptable people. Some of the 'Pilgrim Fathers' came from Southwark, and some had been imprisoned in the Clink there. When the *Mayflower* sailed from Drake's port of Plymouth to Massachusetts in 1620, there were 101 pilgrims and fifty crew on board. Among them was John Billington from Southwark. Members of his family were apparently the only ones who didn't become seriously ill or die during the first winter. In the opinion of one descendant, they survived because they had been hardened by the Southwark germs.

John Harvard did not survive long in the New World, yet he famously lives on. Born in Southwark in 1607, he had been christened at St Saviour's (now Southwark Cathedral, where there is a Harvard Chapel). His father was a 'fleshmonger'– a butcher – and reputedly met John's mother, Katherine, on a visit to Stratford-upon-Avon accompanied by Shakespeare, who may have introduced them. John's father left him a considerable sum, and his mother bequeathed the Queen's Head Inn in Borough High Street to him. He sold the tavern, and in 1637 sailed to America with his young wife and four hundred books. He died the next year but left one half of his estate and all of his library towards the erection of a college – what became Harvard University.

The period that excelled in larger-than-life figures left a great legacy. The pilgrims took with them Shakespeare's English – speech and literature vibrantly absorbing common language and life, which had come to fruition in the plays presented round about river and Bridge – and successfully planted it in the New World.

CHAPTER SIX

'the late terrible fire on London Bridge'

Let the whole Earth now all her wonders *count*
This Bridg of Wonders is the Paramount.
James Howell, *Londinopolis*, 1657

IN THE SUMMER OF 1625 THE NEW KING, CHARLES I, brought his French bride, Henrietta Maria, home. At Gravesend, they boarded the royal barge, accompanied by a welcoming flotilla. When they reached the Tower at five p.m. thunder and lightning was echoed by the salvoes of fifty ships

James I in a Thames procession.

of war. It was raining as they passed through the Bridge, but the windows of the royal barge remained open and the sixteen-year-old Queen stuck out her arm and waved. It was noted that the royal partners were clothed in unlucky green.

Under the Bridge the danger was ever present, as noted by a visitor, M. de Montconys, in 1663. 'To avoid the rude English coaches and the ruder paved streets of London. "They never go below the bridge . . . it is considered dangerous for these small boats to go under the bridge when the tide is running up, for the water has there an extreme rapidity, even greater than when it is returning, and the two currents are mixed." Even with a fall of only two feet the Bridge was avoided . . .'

Over the Bridge, the volume of traffic increased. By 1631 where there had been mainly carts there were now hackney carriages as well, providing serious competition to the furious watermen. Soon, however, there would be more urgent things to worry about.

From 1630, just before the first of the two great fires of the 1600s, the Dutch painter and draughtsman Claude de Jongh (*c.* 1600–63) depicted the Bridge four times. All were from the west, upriver, side. The oil paintings were *Three Cranes at Low Water* and *The View of Old London Bridge* (1630); there were also two drawings, dated 1627. He painted boldly and simply, using contrast, and his London paintings were among his best work, but are all very similar because, although he lived in England several times, his reference may have been an inaccurate line drawing by an Antwerp artist. However, the scenes are atmospheric and evocative, and a sadness clings to the Bridge.

After a period of comparative quiet came the first of the two great fires of the seventeenth century, both of which would seriously imperil the Bridge. Unlike the devastating fire in 1212 which started in Southwark, the fire that began on the night of 11 February 1633 broke out at the other end of the Bridge near St Magnus, ominously close to where the Great Fire of London would start thirty-three years later. The 1633 fire was even more serious for the Bridge than would be the more famous one of 1666.

On a cold night the maidservant of John Briggs, a needle-maker, right at the City end of the Bridge, looked out of the window; the moon was casting the shadow of the church of St Magnus on to the Thames. The streams of turbulence passing through the constriction of the twenty piers of the Bridge were furiously fighting the ice forming on the river, and even this late she saw children, one with a candle, most unshod, playing tentatively at the edges of the freezing water. She checked that everything was in order before going to bed, so her mistress would have nothing to complain of in the morning. She placed a tub full of hot ashes under the stairs, as she had done on so many nights before, to be sure of a fire the next morning when her bones would creak with cold. After a day that had started at six that morning, she fell asleep.

A witness to the fire was Nehemiah Wallington, a turner of Little Eastcheap. His sleep had been penetrated by the cries for water, and he soon saw the fire vaulting over the tops of houses 'neere tenn of the clocke att night'. Briggs's house was burned down, and the next one with all its contents. Briggs, his wife and child escaped with only 'their shurt and smoke; and the fire burnt downe all the houses on both sides of the way, from S. Magnes Church to the first open place [the Square by the Chapel]'. The water conduits nearby were opened, and the water pipes in the streets were cut open, from which they used brooms to sweep the water down towards the fire. In Southwark the brewers brought water in vessels on their drays. Luckily, there was little wind. Unluckily, it was impossible to get water from the river because the tide was out and most of what was there was frozen.

In the flight to escape the fire many were injured, and many died. This fire destroyed houses on both sides of the Bridge, burning fiercely all night and part of the next day, and it continued smouldering until 19 February. On the Bridge all hands worked night and day 'to carry away timber, and brickes, and tiles, and rubbish cast down into the liters, So that on Wensday the Bridge was cleared that passengers might goe over.'

Wallington gives a valuable detailed list of 'The Names, and Trades, and number of the Houses burnt upon the Bridge . . .':

[West side, Southwark end to City end]

1. Mr William Vyner — Haberdasher of Smal Wares
2. Mr John Broome — Hosier
3. Mr Arthur Lee — Haberdasher of smal Wares
4. M^ris Iohane Broome — Hosier
5. Mr Ralph Panne — Shewmaker
6. Mr Abraham Marten — Haberdasher of Hattes
7. Mr Jeremiah Champney — Hosier
8. Mr John Terrill — Silke man
9. Mr Ellis Midmore — Milliner
10. Mr Francis Finch — Hosier
11. Mr Andrewe Bouth — Haberdasher of Small Wares
12. Mr Samuel Petty — Glover
13. Mr Valentin Beale — Mercer
14. M^ris Chambers, Senior — ---------
15. Mr Jeremiah Chamley — Silke man
16. The Blew Bore [Blue Boar] — Empti
17. Mr John Glover — Stiller of Strong Waters
18. Mr John Wilding, Junior — Girdler
19. Mr Daniel Conney — Silke man
20. Mr Stephen Beale — Lyning Draper

[East side, Southwark end to City end]

[Adjoining the square]

21. M^ris Jane Langham — Mercer
22. Mr James Dunkin — Wolling Draper
23. Mr Matthew Harding — Salter

[The Chapel]

24. Mr Abraham Chambers — Haberdasher of Smal Wares
25. Mr Lyne Daniel ⎫ — Haberdasher of Hattes,
26. ⎭ a double house
27. M^ris ----- Brookes — Glover
28. Mr ----- Coverley — Hosier
29. Mr John Dransfielde — Grocer
30. Mr Newman — Emptie
31. Mr Edward Warnett ⎫ — Partoners. Haberdashers of
32. Mr Samuel Wood ⎭ Small Wares

33. Mr Iohn Greene	Haberdasher of Hattes
34. Mr Heugh Powel	Haberdasher of Hattes
35. Mr Samuel Armitage	Haberdasher of Small Wares
36. Mr John Sherley	Haberdasher of Small Wares
37. Mr John Lawrymore	Grocer
38. Mr Timothy Drake	Woolling Draper
39. Mr John Brigges	Needle-maker [where the fire began]
40. Mr Richard Shelbuery	Scrivener
41. Mr Edward Greene	Hosier
42. Mr Hazard	the Curate [presumably of St Magnus]
43. Mr Hewlett	the Clarke at St Magnus Cloyster

At this period the buildings were occupied mainly by merchants who dealt in aspects of the clothing trade. There was only one needle-maker and, unusually, no book-seller.

One-third of the houses on the bridge were destroyed, as was a large portion of the City. In the affected 354-foot-long section, the fire created a useful opportunity to extend the bridge street from fifteen feet in width to eighteen feet. For the safety of pedestrians, wooden fencing ten and a half feet high was erected on each side, with a five-foot-deep recess for foot passengers to escape from the traffic and the onward rush of 'beastes made wild and furious through the indiscreete and violent usage of their drivers'.

Vulnerably placed St Magnus was not damaged in the 'late terrible fire on London Bridge' in 1640. Whether this referred to the 1633 fire or a later one is not known. In St Magnus the large Table of Benefaction (Gifts), with lettering in gold type, remains high on the west wall of the church and records the close escape from what must have been a considerable fire. There is the provision for a sermon to be preached on every twelfth day of February to commemorate the preservation of the church. A Susanna Chambers, a parishioner of St Magnus and possibly the 'Mris Chambers' who had resided on the Bridge, left twenty shillings a year for the parson to preach an annual sermon of thanksgiving that the church had been spared.

The political and intellectual ferment of the 1640s made it a busy time for book-sellers, and the commercial appeal of the Bridge continued to be particularly attractive to these tradesmen and to stationers throughout much of the life of the Bridge. The first recorded book-seller on the Bridge itself (1556–71) was a William Pickering whose address was 'under St Magnus Church' at the City end, and a similar business had been run by a Hugh Astley, also described as living under the church, from 1588 to 1608. Between 1600 and 1621 book-seller John Tapp's name was associated with the Bridge. Another, Henry Gosson, was there in about 1610 and 1628 'on London Bridge near to the Gate' in Southwark, by now the only remaining gate on the Bridge. As noted, no book-sellers are on the list of houses burned in 1633, but Gosson was still in business 'near the Gate' in 1635, and book-seller Charles Tyus was there in 1659 and 1664.

By the reign of Charles I a disproportionately large number of book-sellers on the Bridge printed and sold their popular chap-books (small books of stories and ballads), ready reckoners, accounts of political debate, crime stories and religious tracts. A mere twenty-four book-sellers in the City in 1640 had increased to a stupendous 2,134 by 1642. And they had competition among the numerous entertaining street-criers, including those selling horn books, ink-horns, or ink – 'Fine Writeing Ink!' – which was carried in a little barrel on the ink-seller's back, with a funnel at his belt, and quill pens clasped in one hand.

Underneath the Bridge, the dangerous bridge weir was comparatively safe to pass through at high and low tides when there was 'still' or 'standing water'. At all other times it was approached with great caution or avoided. The hazards were well known, and at the very least one could expect to be 'soundly washed' going through the Bridge.

According to folklore an English queen had never died by drowning. Such luck did not extend to one of Queen Henrietta Maria's ladies-in-waiting, Mrs Anna Kirke, whose husband's family had long been royal courtiers. She had taken her place as a Lady of the Bedchamber, while her husband, George, was a Gentleman of the Bedchamber and Keeper of the Palace of Whitehall. The Calendar of State Papers records that the Queen herself was not on board on 6 July 1641 when her royal barge was passing through the Bridge, hit a log and 'over-tossed'. Everyone was thrown into the water; all were rescued except Mrs Kirke.

Lord Cork recorded the disaster: 'This daie Mrs Kirke was drowned coming through London bridge; the earle of denbigh, and his daughter, my deer, deer daughter in Lawe, the ladie Kynalmeaky thorough gods great providence and mercie beinge alsoe caste away in the Thames were miraceulously preserved; ffor which great delivery god made me and her ever moste thanckfull. Sir Frederick cornwallys his Lady, was saved.'

Of the many thousands of people who drowned at the Bridge, an image of only one – Anna Kirke – is known. She was twice painted by Anthony Van Dyck, who had become court painter in 1632; unsurprisingly, he depicted her with corkscrew ringlets like Henrietta Maria, and clothed in pale silken satin as so often was her queen, who took the news 'very heavily' and now wept for her.

The daily newssheets of 1641 were concerned exclusively with King and Parliament, but the drowning was recorded in correspondence and in a poem. Mrs Kirke's niece, Miss Killigrew, was a painter and a poet from a family also linked to the court. A collection of her poetry published in 1686 included a poem entitled 'On my aunt Mrs A. K[irke] Drown'd under London Bridge in the Queen's Bardge, Anno 1641'. It concludes:

> So noble was her aire, so great her meen,
> She seem'd afriend, not servant to the queen.
> To sin, if known, she never did give way,
> Vice could not storm her, could it not betray.
> When angry Heav'n extinguish[t] her fair light,
> It seem'd to say, *Nought's precious in my sight;*
> *And I in waves this paragon have drown'd,*
> *The nation next, and king I will confound.*

Miss Killigrew's words seemed to predict the fate of Charles I.

For eleven years, from 1629 to 1640, Charles had ruled without Parliament. To the essential, insurmountable problem – the King's belief in the Divine Right of Kings – were added the equally intransigent conflict between Protestant and Roman Catholic Europe, and the King's utter inability to balance the books.

In January 1642, at the very time that a new block of houses was finally being planned for the Bridge, replacing those lost in the 1633 fire, City and country reached crisis point. In a complicated sequence of events during which Charles intended to summon and dissolve Parliament as he wished, he failed in his attempt to arrest five members of Parliament in the council chamber. Alarmed by the vehemence of the crowds, he left London, abandoning his kingdom's greatest asset with all its symbolism and immense resources, including the armoury, to the Parliamentarians. The result was a civil war that continued for the next seven years, only ending with the execution of Charles I in 1649.

Events favoured one side then the other, but by 1647 the King had surrendered himself and was handed over to Parliament. As a prisoner he was moved from place to place, and in 1647, at a time when he was kept at Hampton Court Palace, attention was again concentrated on the Bridge in its role as a fortification and a boundary of the City. There was great tension and fear as Cromwell's New Model Army ominously moved towards St Albans, Uxbridge and Reading; the City fathers, who had no wish to be controlled by any army, requested of the Commander-in-Chief, Lord Fairfax, that the army remain thirty miles away to prevent prices from being driven up. This may have bought a little time, but not much.

At the beginning of August few slept soundly on the Bridge or in the City, for news came that the army was approaching London and was already as close as Hounslow Heath. Colonel Edmund Ludlow made the observation that the Common Council of the City, under increasing pressure, decided it was 'ready to admit the army as friends not being able to oppose them as enemies'.

The commissioners sent by the Common Council to Fairfax on 2 August returned the same night to report his demands, recorded by Bulstrode Whitelock in *Memorials of English Affairs during the Reign of Charles I*: 'To have the forts on the west side of London delivered up to him, that security being given, he would bring the numbers of both Houses who were forced from Parliament to Westminster to sit in a free House and of this, Answer was to be returned to the General by twelve a Clock at night.'

The Council consented, but set conditions: soldiers and ordnance were to be withdrawn, and the redoubts on Southwark were to be quitted. They emphasized that they relied on Fairfax for protection from his soldiers. Fairfax, with the army now at Hammersmith, gave these assurances.

The Borough of Southwark as usual jealously asserted its defiance of its overweening rival, the City, by responding independently to Fairfax on the same day as did the City. Some believed that Southwark wooed the Parliamentary forces because the shopkeepers wanted the soldiers' money.

However, the day before, the officers of Southwark's trained bands (the trained bands gave London considerable military strength), had declared themselves unwilling to fight under the command of the City. Their message to Fairfax stated that they 'disliked the proceedings of London against the army, and desired assistance from the General who sent Colonel Rainsborough's Brigade [the force approaching] towards them'.

At two a.m. the next day, this brigade marched into Southwark, 'the soldiers carrying themselves very civilly', only to find the Bridge gates shut, the portcullis down and soldiers within, in spite of the assurances by the City that the gates would be open. They immediately 'planted two pieces of Ordnance against the Gate and set a guard without, and in a short time after the great Fort was yielded to them'. During that night, when the bridge-dwellers must have kept their weapons nearby and waited fearfully, the Common Council debated and accepted Fairfax's demands. It was a smooth operation, and there was no loss of life. On 4 August the gates of the Bridge were formally opened, and the army marched over the Bridge and into the City, the last time that the gates of London Bridge would welcome an armed force.

The Lord Mayor, Sir John Gayer, and the aldermen went out to meet the troops in Hyde Park. The 'great Iron Chaines . . . to keepe Horsemen out were all taken away by command and made a prey to the Souldiers and others'. The following day, exhibiting the discipline on which they prided themselves, the Parliamentarian troops marched through the City and back out over the Bridge – so close to the first-floor hall windows that the bridge-dwellers smelled them and heard their comments. Did they break step to march over the Bridge, so as not to rock it?

During an alarm in April 1648 and another in June, the gates of London Bridge were closed, for there was news that a rising of Kentish Royalists was approaching under the command of the Earl of Norwich, even though there were many in the City who still supported the King.

During the Civil War the Bridge House was compelled to borrow money, a reversal of the situation in earlier times when with their carefully accumulated funds they were in a strong enough position to lend money for public projects, such as £290 to Christ's Church Hospital in 1604.

Royalists were vacating London in increasing numbers to seek safety on the Continent. A popular Civil War song commemorated the image of London's Bridge:

> Farewell, Bridge-foot, and Bear thereby,
> And those bald pates that stand so high.
> We wish it, from our very soules,
> That other heads were on those poles.

The devastating fire of 1633 and the Civil War were foretastes of what was to come for Bridge and City. It is to Wenceslaus Hollar's *Panorama of London* (1647) that we turn for the fourth of the seven stages, 1651 to 1666, of the appearance of London Bridge: around the time of the Restoration. This stage covers the period after the fire of 1633 and before the Great Fire of London in 1666.

Everyone had heard of London Bridge. Hollar, an exiled Bohemian artist, knew the popular saying 'London Bridge is made for wise men to go over and fools to go under'; indeed, the Charles Bridge in his native Prague was often measured against London Bridge, as was every bridge. Forced to flee his native city, on his travels as an etcher and engraver Hollar may even have seen the sculptured plaque of London Bridge, dated 1617, and oddly gracing the front of a house in Dordrecht. He first arrived in England in 1637 as an 'artist in residence' in the entourage of the Earl of Arundel and Surrey. He had experienced the rule of Charles I, the Civil War and the Commonwealth, and was now well placed to witness the return of Charles II and the two greatest disasters ever to befall the City.

The angle of the *Panorama* tells us that the artist made his carefully observed and accurate reference sketches from the top of the tower of St Saviour's in Southwark. Climbing the steeply winding stone, then wooden, steps to the tower roof of St Saviour's, he would have been able to smell the tanneries of Southwark, and hear the cries of the watermen, hawkers and apprentices, and the protests of animals being driven towards the slaughterhouses. Facing the river, to his right, he looked down on the curious sight of a town on a bridge. Beyond, on the opposite shore, was the threatening Tower of London and on his extreme right in the far distance Shooter's Hill at Greenwich; to his left on the other side of the river he saw St Paul's Cathedral and, looking across the bulging curve in the river, the Banqueting House at the Palace of Whitehall, both dominating flattish London. According to visiting Count Lorenzo Magalotti, who recorded the travels of Cosmo, the third Grand Duke of Tuscany, in 1669, in the green fields around the City and its suburbs 'vast hordes of cattle' waited to be driven in.

Just below his viewpoint at the Southwark end of the nine-hundred-foot-long structure stood the Great Stone Gate with its display of heads. Next, after an open arch, his *Panorama* depicts for the first time the notable gateway 'house with many windows' on the second pier. Few other changes are apparent looking along the Bridge as far as the former Chapel.

Beyond the Chapel, the Bridge appeared very different. The Square was now part of the long open space where a number of

After the 1633 fire, Hollar's view shows the palisaded gap at the north end.

houses had been destroyed in the fire of 1633. In normal times, repair would have been swift under the eyes of the Wardens. Agitation and confusion among those who governed meant that construction had been delayed. Instead, along this open place Hollar's drawing shows the attempt to prevent travellers from being blown into the Thames: the wooden palisading that had been erected on each side, this insecure fencing itself frequently ending up in the river. For strength, the Wardens had ordered that the palings be tied together by overhead beams. To light the way on what was a dangerous place in the dark, lanterns were hung from the beams, swaying in the river breezes and casting strange shadows in an at times already ghostly scene.

So important was London's bridge that, even in these days of unprecedented difficulty, an effort had been made at reconstruction: one house on the east side had been built in 1639. Six years later work finally began on a large block, sited over the waterwheels at the City end. A contemporary account records that the timber framing was started in Bridge House yard: 'The one half of these houses begaine to be new built . . . on Munday the 12 day of May 1645; And were finally finished in a stately manner on Saturday the 7 day of June 1651.'

The new houses built between 1645 and 1651 were quite unlike what had preceded them. They were designed as one complete block of three storeys, and the rooms in the garrets had dormer windows. The roofs were 'stately platforms leaded and railed with Ballasters'. Large as it was, the whole block at the north end filled only one-third of the available space, leaving a large gap between it and the Chapel. The timber block was described as being carried out 'in a very substantial and beautiful manner'.

At ground level, Hollar's view of the City and its suburbs was of slums and mansions, churches, markets and hawkers, and street life that was dirty, drab and colourful, sometimes funny, often dangerous, and usually noisy. There might be the piercing squeals of a pig being gelded in the street, or the snorting of passing rival stallions. On tenterhooks pushed into the earth, dyed and finished cloth hung to dry in the open air, for London was the main cloth market; cloth in 1640 comprised a massive eighty-seven per cent of the nation's exports.

Newly arrived from the country, Kent-born Thomas Passinger, an apprentice to book-seller Charles Tyus on the Bridge, was astonished by the strange and exotic sights. All humanity passed before his eyes: there were street-sellers, rogues and beggars of every description; one minute a lord in a velvet-lined coach drawn by six fine horses might pass, the next a blind water-carrier with a wooden keg on his shoulders and led by a little dog carrying a lantern, or a lady in a sedan chair escorted by liveried servants and African slave boys, or more likely the raucous fisherwomen, their shops on their heads and themselves one of the noted sights.

To those accustomed to fine country air, another shock would have been the polluted atmosphere hanging over the City, a fact deplored by diarist John Evelyn. He lamented in *Fumifugium, or the Inconvenience if the Aer and Smoake of London Dissipated* of 1661 that 'this glorious and antient city should wrap her stately head in clouds of smoke and sulphur'. Most of the pollution was caused by the sea coal used in domestic and working fires, and a large number of these were located by the river near the Bridge, which stood at the centre of the hubbub.

Charles I's assertion of his God-given right to govern unchallenged and his defiance of Parliament finally came to an end in January 1649, when he was tried and executed by the English Parliament. The rule of Cromwell and the Commonwealth (1649–60) began, and the commons learned how to respond to a new master. Such was the financial exhaustion during these years that no copper was coined by the government. Ever adaptable, traders throughout the country, and especially in London (including those on the Bridge), devised their own illegal currency: traders' tokens. Among the establishments that used these tokens were publican Cornelius Cooke's Bear at the bridgefoot, and book-seller Charles Tyus's The Three Bibles on the Bridge, a usual sign for a book-seller. On this token the obverse shows: 'AT . THE . 3 BIBLES . ON (C.S.T.)' – for 'Charles and Sarah Tyus'; on the reverse: 'LONDON . BRIDGE (three Bibles)'. This is the only token known for book-sellers on London Bridge; indeed only eleven tokens have been recorded for book-sellers in all of London.

Other traders' tokens have left some of the few clues as to the traders on or near the Bridge at this time. There is a token for Thomas Beson, of The King's Head Tavern in New Fish Street (head of Henry VIII), leased to him in 1647 for twenty-five years at a rental of £80. Gilbert Brandon and his wife Elizabeth had a token issued in 1657 for Ye Swan & Bridge at 57 New Fish Street (charmingly depicting a swan walking on a bridge lined with houses); here Samuel Pepys had dined, but was not impressed with such 'a poor house and ill dressed', but the fish and poultry were good. There is one for 'At the Whit. Lyon' (a lion rampant) 'Neir London Bridge'; and a 1666 token for Nicholas Harrison, 'At Blak' (a bull) 'On London Bridge'.

When the Lord Protector, Oliver Cromwell, died in 1658, there was no one to take his place. The nation now grasped a seldom-given second chance. Both nobility and commons had had enough after seven years of civil war, followed by ten years of the harsh regime of the Commonwealth. Charles II, who had bided his time on the Continent, proclaimed his intentions. The decision was made to invite him back, and vengeance on the Commonwealth leaders, alive and dead, was swift. Such duties underway, it was finally time for London to relax, enjoy itself and prepare for the royal return.

Just as in 1647, when the gates of Old London Bridge had been symbolically opened to the Parliamentarians, so in 1660 the Bridge was to witness 'the return of banished majesty'. Decades had passed since the Bridge had been decorated for a national occasion, and Bridge Wardens Francis Kirby and Robert Hussey had few if any appropriate decorative materials stored in Bridge House yard. Nor could statues, silks and feathers be rented, since theatres had been closed during the Commonwealth, singing and dancing banned. For the Herald to proclaim Charles's return, a rich coat of arms had to be borrowed from Henry VII's Chapel at Westminster Abbey and returned the next day.

Because every tradesman on the Bridge was required to be a member of a Livery Company, it was easy to borrow rich tapestries with which to drape the buildings on this bridge of humble Kentish ragstone. The Wardens upped the order for candles so the tidemen could continue to work by candlelight to complete repairs. An order was made for the Drawbridge to be speedily mended. The stonemasons repaired the stone work, the paviors the surface of the bridge street; the wood-carvers created the giant decorations, then the painters and stainers took over.

Unlike his father Charles I, who disappeared from public view just when an affirmation of royal authority was desperately needed, Charles II understood the value of public ceremony within a robust setting of theatrical extravagance. He returned to the capital on his thirtieth birthday, 29 May, with all the elements carefully arranged – heraldry, symbols of authority and power, trumpeters, an entourage, military strength – to place himself before his people.

Hopes were high that the Restoration, the re-establishment of the monarchy and a legal government would bring stability to life and business. The streets were strewn with flowers and hung with tapestries, and 'fountains flowed with wine'. First the procession of the Lord Mayor, Thomas Alleyne, a rich silk merchant and twice Lord Mayor, made its way across the Bridge from the City to Southwark to greet the King at St George's Fields. Here the Lord Mayor, who had publicly proclaimed Charles king three weeks earlier, was knighted. It was meticulously noted in the Bridge House Records that the plate, linen and glasses for this reception alone had cost the Bridge Wardens £7 0s. 4d.

People jostled for the few available vantage points on the bridge street, while those who lived on the Bridge had an unsurpassed view from windows, rooftops and the new balustraded roof plat-forms. The spectacle began, and we can only marvel at the detail of it. Major-General Brown led a troop of three hundred gentlemen in cloth of silver, flourishing their swords. Next came three hundred men in velvet coats attended by 'footmen and lacquies' in purple. The repression of extravagance – and joy – in the previous seven-teen years was now eclipsed by music, sound and colour. Indeed, every rich and exotic colour imaginable, all embellished with gold and silver, flashing in the sunshine appeared on the Bridge – then followed troops, some in buff coats with cloth-of-silver sleeves and rich green scarves, others in blue liveries inlaid with silver, then trumpeters and footmen clothed in sea-green garments decorated with gold and silver.

The King's procession was led by seven hundred horsemen. Two trumpets bearing His Majesty's arms were followed by seventy-two sheriff's men, red cloaks laced with silver and carrying their half pikes, followed on horseback by the gentlemen of the City Livery Companies dressed in black velvet, their chains of gold glittering.

'The chiefest Ray of Lustre' rode towards the Bridge, between his two brothers, the Dukes of York (later James II) and Gloucester, through the daunting Great Stone Gate and on to the narrow confines of the bridge street. The King, jaunty red plume in his hat, looked up and around with interest and satisfaction at 'the Bridg of Wonders'. As he clattered on to the granite cobblestone paving of the Bridge and into view at the Rock Lock, then at the Drawbridge, the immense crowds on every available surface responded. From his youth Charles II remembered well the greatest engineering feat in his kingdom, and so far it looked much the same as when he had last seen it. In the small scale of the Bridge, shopkeepers like Tyus and his family at the first-floor windows would have been at eye-level with the riding monarch, an obviously large man 'more than two yards in length' (so described on a 'wanted poster' during the Civil War) with a dark complexion, whose fleshy, swarthy face would have been flushed with pleasure and excitement, his long, dark periwig curling in the heat.

Maypoles have been symbols of rebirth since at least Celtic times, but they had been banned during the Commonwealth, including a 'most prodigious maypole' that had always stood in the Strand opposite Somerset House. On the day of the King's return maypoles sprouted everywhere.

On 14 April 1661, the Strand maypole was replaced by permission of the King, and paid for by the local parishioners. The 134-foot-high cedar pole, '. . . a most choice and remarkable Piece, 'twas made below Bridg, and brought in two parts to Scotland Yard', the Royal Office of Works. From there it was conveyed to the Strand, 'a Streamer flourishing before it, Drums beating all the way, and other sorts of Musick'. It was erected by twelve sailors, the only ones capable of handling a mast of this size, with 'their Cables, Pullies, and other tacklins, with six great Anchors'. An early publication, *The Cities Loyalty Display'd* also records that 'Little children did much rejoice, and ancient people did clap their hands saying, golden days begin to appear'.

Now Christmas was declared legal again, as were the theatres, and the annual Lord Mayor's Parade, a procession and pageant on the river traditionally held on 9 November, the day a new Lord Mayor was installed, became part of civic life and ritual once more.

Poor little Charles I had gone, the Commonwealth had come and gone, and now a king with perhaps too much robust red wine in his veins had arrived. When Charles II passed by the Bear at the bridgefoot in Southwark on that day of the Restoration, did publican Cornelius Cooke – a colonel in Cromwell's army who had been on the commission to dispose of royal property – note the cynicism in the face, and the full, indulgent lips, an indication of what would be? Soon, not only the ladies and the dandies of the court – and Cooke would have known many of them well – but even the Royal Horse Guard would wear long wigs and muffs, as well as face-paint and perfume. Led by the King, gambling and bear-baiting thrived. And then there were the King's *amours*; by 1662 an ambassador reported that Londoners were already saying that their monarch 'only hunts and lusts'.

At this time of great change, the figure of Samuel Pepys appears. Raised a Puritan, Pepys nonetheless embraced the Royalist cause with gusto, and was among the party that had gone to bring the King home from Holland. He now strove to become the important Clerk of the Acts at the Navy Board, a principal office of the Navy. There, once he began 'to mind his business', his exceptional industry and rare honesty increasingly placed him in a position of power. His *Diary* (1660–9), written in code, partly to prevent his French wife Elizabeth from learning about his sexual adventures, is an insight into both great events in the kingdom and small personal triumphs – often endearingly mingled together. The couple had moved to a Navy Office house with office attached in Seething Lane, close to Tower Wharf, below and not far from the Bridge itself. The frequent references to the old structure in his Diary as he daily went about his official and private life confirm its central role to the people of the City and of Southwark.

In May 1662 Charles married the convent-educated Catherine of Braganza, who spoke no English. The antagonism between the royal pair was soon common knowledge, and not unexpected, for the King's mistresses were handily tucked away in the rambling Palace of Whitehall with its hundreds of apartments. All was reported by gossiping courtiers and their ladies at the Bear at the bridgefoot in Southwark. This tavern, built in 1319, had been favoured by royal courtiers since Elizabethan times. Dramatist William Wycherley noted that 'persons of better condition' had resorted to the Bear for pleasure and privacy for a very long time. The preferred drink was canary, a sweet wine like Madeira, which as a compliment a man sometimes filtered through the bottom of a lady's smock, one observer noting it was a filthy as well as an indecent custom.

Pepys, an expert on food, drink and the places that provided them, frequently visited this tavern. 'I away back again to the Beare at the Bridge foot, being full of wind and out of order, and there called for a biscuit and a piece of cheese and a gill of sacke . . .' When a law was passed in 1663 to force taverns along the river to keep their back doors locked in order to hinder access to the river and so cut down on unlawful activities, the Bear was exempted 'for the convenience of passengers to Greenwich'.

The latter half of the seventeenth century was a busy time for the Keeper of the Heads. As the regicides and traitors were executed, their heads appeared on top of the Great Stone Gate. Following Venner's Rising in 1661, the heads of fourteen rebels went up, including that of Thomas Venner, the leader of the obscure sect known as the Fifth Monarchy men about whom little is known. What in reality was a minor rising took the government by surprise, and they initially believed the threat to be much more serious: guards were set at the dockyards and arsenals. These religious fanatics had been captured after two days of frantic fighting in the streets, and Pepys had accidentally been a witness to Venner's fate: '. . . in our way meeting Venner and Pritchard upon a sledge, who with two more Fifth Monarchy men were hanged to-day and the first two drawn and quartered . . .'

Such was the state of the roads and the congestion of the City and its suburbs, the Thames was the obvious main avenue of transport, and especially so for Samuel Pepys on his frequent trips to the Navy Office at Deptford. He often went by water for very short journeys, even from Westminster to Whitehall – recalling the use of the vaporetti in Venice today. Among the perks of his position were an official yacht and waterman; when the *Diary* began, this was a man called Payne. There was an easy-going relationship between them which endured even after Payne asked for Pepys' help in getting a new position as waterman to the Lord Chamberlain. Pepys also had a regular 'pair of oars', a sculler on whose boat his arms were painted.

Many people refused point blank to go 'through the Bridge', such was the frequent loss of life, and the death of Mrs Anna Kirke would not have been forgotten. When Pepys and his portrait-painter acquaintance Salisbury went to Whitehall on the river, nothing could persuade the wary artist to go through the Bridge. 'Come Mr Salisbury to see me, and showed me a face or two of his painting, and indeed I perceive that he will be a great master. I took him to White Hall with me by water, but could not by any means be moved to go through the bridge, and we were fain to go round by the Old Swan.'

For as long as anyone could remember, the steps by the Old Swan tavern on the City side had been a well-sited feature above the Bridge. In order westwards from the Bridge and above it were the Old Swan, Coleharbour, the Three Cranes, Queenhithe, Broken Wharf, Paul's Wharf, Puddlewharf and the Wardrobe (where royal state robes were stored).

To avoid the bridge weir when travelling downstream, the prudent landed at the pier at the Three Cranes (Pepys complained that the best room in this tavern was 'like a narrow dogg-hole' when he was forced to entertain poor relations there) or at the Old Swan, and walked to the steps beyond the Bridge. Or they transferred to a safer boat, then landed at Billingsgate on the other side of the Bridge and boarded the original craft. When going upstream they landed below the Bridge and reversed the procedure.

The canny watermen's charges varied, and to settle disputes their rates were fixed by the Guildhall on 23 April 1655:

> From London Bridge to the bridgefoot westward, as above, and all other places not exceeding the Poultry, Cheapside, Newgate market, for xiii c weight, not exceeding xviii c weight – xviii *d*.
>
> And from all other wharfs and places between London bridge and Temple Barre to the same, and places of like distance, for every load of coalls – xii *d*.

From years of experience the watermen instinctively knew the times of the tides, which varied considerably each day. They were especially wary at spring high tide, when at the Bridge the river could be as much as sixteen feet higher than at its lowest, allowing only about eight feet between the surface of the water and the underside of the structure. The intrepid diarist Pepys knew when to approach the bridge weir with caution, especially at night after a day of work or merry-making, either up or down the river. He was frightened when returning home by water in the dark, and against the tide – the watermen had to grope with poles the whole way – but he finally got through the Bridge. He also knew the time to opt for a safer course; to avoid his boat being trapped against the Bridge in the unpredictable currents, he 'was fain to shooting the Bridge, walk over the piles through the bridge, while Sir William Batten and Sir J. Minnes [in another boat] were aground against the bridge, and could not in a great while get through'.

Both Bridge and Bear were often noted in Pepys's excursions and give a zestful idea of how they were entwined with life in the City. He, his wife and friends went by barge from the Tower to Greenwich, then 'so home to the Bridge, bringing night home with us and it raining hard, but we got them on foot to the Beare and there put them in a boat; and I back to my wife in the barge and so to the Tower wharf and home'.

He includes a rare reference to games at the busy location of the Bridge, with waterman Payne in the middle of the excitement:

'Being through the bridge I found the Thames full of boats and galleys, and upon enquiry found that there was a wager to be run this morning. So spying of Payne in a gally, I went unto him, and there staid, thinking to have gone to Chelsy with them. But upon the start, the wager boats fell foul of one another, till at last one of them goes over, pretending foul play, and so the other row away alone, and all our sport was lost.'

The Bridge was constantly assailed by traffic, by the river and by storms. The effect of one severe storm in January 1666 at ebb tide was recorded by Pepys:

> . . . the wind again being very furious, and so we durst not go by water, walked to London quite round the Bridge, no boat being able to Stirre; . . . It was dangerous to walk the streets . . . But above all, the pales on London Bridge on both sides were blown away, so that we were fain to stoop very low, for fear of blowing off of the bridge. We could see no boats in the Thames affloat but what were broke loose and carried through the bridge . . . And the greatest sight of all, among other parcels of ships here and there in clusters together, one was quite overset, and lay with her masts all along in the water and keel above water . . .

So great was the traffic over the Bridge that the structure, especially the wooden Drawbridge, although no longer raised, required constant repair. If ignored, decline was rapid. By 1666, no one could remember when it had last been rebuilt. Pepys had gone to Woolwich for the launch of the *Royal Catharine*, and came back on the river. 'Dark when we come to London, and a stop of coaches in Southwark. Into the Bear, at the Bridge-foot, to Sir William Batten. Presently the stop is removed, and there going out to find my coach, I could not find it: so I was fain to go through the dark and dirt over the bridge, and I fell in a hole broke on the bridge [probably on the Drawbridge], but, the constable standing there to keep people from it, I catched up, otherwise I had broke my leg: for which mercy the Lord be praised!' The Bridge House Records note that three years later the Master Carpenter reported that the Bridge was again in a state of decay; the estimated cost of repairs was £200.

The bridge street teemed with people and with animals, many on the hoof to feed the City. Over the twenty arches came livestock, drays and goods from the fields of Kent, royal and ducal carriages, people on foot, including women from the country hoping to sell their produce, and single horsemen. So burdened was it with traffic converging from both directions, it could take an hour or more to cross. For people and for animals it was often quicker and safer to cross by boat, and there were ferries of every description all along the river. One livestock ferry, also for horse and carts, operated from Lambeth to today's Horseferry Road in Westminster.

Above the bridge weir, the narrow passageways between the stone piers with their protective starlings ground and trapped boats, corpses, rubbish of every kind and raw sewage. Everyone knew of the ultimate use to which the book-sellers' flimsy ballads and chapbooks were so often put. The watermen frequently complained that the very bulk of it endangered navigation at the Bridge, and it was unhealthy.

The whole of the teeming City was unhealthy. Filth everywhere was combined with intense overcrowding. There was almost no sanitation, and the privies that existed often projected out over ditches, streams and even, or especially, Royal Thames itself, into which also flowed waste from the slaughterhouses. Rubbish was thrown into the streets, where it may or may not have been collected, to join dead animals there, and rats roamed freely in the thatch and in the wattle-and-daub walls of almost every dwelling.

The question of removing houses from the Bridge first arose after the fire of 1633. A report by Trinity House analysed the situation, noting that even the depth of the Pool of London was decreasing because so much waste from the houses on the Bridge went into it. From the 1200s the Wardens had been told that they were responsible for keeping and repairing a public latrine with two entrances on the Bridge; some individual residences as well had their own arrangements projecting out over the river. There was a privy over the Fleet in the 1200s near where the river entered the

Thames which caused disease and death. The general unwholesomeness was the worst it had ever been.

Seldom a year passed without a few cases of the plague, and a serious outbreak was not unusual. The watermen and those who lived on or near the Bridge, even the fishmongers in Fish Street Hill, believed that they would be protected from virulent pestilence in the future as they had been in the past. Dr E. Barnard, somewhat oddly and the only source for this information, recounted in his *History of Cold Bathing* of 1709: 'And I have been lately told, by several eminent Men, living on *London-Bridge*, that they have observed, that for the quantity of Houses, that the Bridge scapes better than other parts of the City, in any Contagious time whatsoever: as also Fishmongers on the Hill [Fish Street Hill] are generally healthful . . .' Life on the Bridge may well have been healthier because, unlike the narrow dark streets of the City, there was sun and light and it was almost impossible to prevent fresh air from blowing through every room. There were no cesspits, blocked drains or graveyards to contaminate air and water. And, possibly, because of all this, it was slightly less appealing to the black rats.

News came in 1663–4 that the plague was strong in England's trading partner, Holland. In the frosty winter of 1664–5 predictions of an outbreak increased, and ominous signs, real or imagined, were reported: a comet with a tail of sickly hue – 'a warning shot from heaven' – the sun setting in streams of blood and, according to Daniel Defoe in *A Journal of the Plague Year* of 1722, 'a marvellous double tide at London Bridge', perhaps referring to an abnormal tide back in 1641 when, an hour and a half after one tide, another one violently and noisily came in and alarmingly was six feet higher than the first one.

Five cases of the plague were recorded in 1664, and controls on shipping and quarantine for ships coming from plague-ridden ports hindered river life. In June 1665, Pepys was going down Holborn in a hackney coach when it came to a sudden stop and the coachman staggered down, crying that he was 'stroke very sick, and almost blind . . .' Sadly, Pepys alighted and took another coach. By late summer he was deeply shocked to hear that his former waterman,

Payne, had buried a child and that Payne himself '. . . fell sick as soon as he had landed me on Friday morning last, when I had been all night upon the water (and I believe he did get his infection that day at Brainford) is now dead of the plague . . . did put me in to great apprehension of melancholy and with good reason . . .' But Pepys's information was wrong on one point, for waterman Payne was a survivor in every respect.

Reverend Thomas Vincent, a Nonconformist fanatic, reported that 'the great orbs begin to move first'. But the greatest orb was not among them. Whatever the faults of Charles II, throughout his life he seemed exceedingly careless of his own safety. At the very end of July 1665, King and court finally left London in a progress that ended in Oxford, where Parliament was convened in October.

The rich could leave, the poor could not. The wealthy merchants, along with the majority of doctors and churchmen – claiming to seek their patients and parishioners in the country – were not slow in leaving. The flood of people had begun as early as May; in the panic 'each man became a porter to himself', some rolling a barrel of wine before them. A contemporary illustration depicts 'Multitudes flying from London in boats and barges' and 'Flying by land'. For a time there had been great traffic of people and of wagons full of goods heading north and west out through Holborn, and south out over the Bridge, as London emptied itself into the terrified countryside.

Some stayed. Samuel Pepys was one, the only one to remain at the Navy Office in Seething Lane, fearful but still quietly businesslike. In August he wrote to Sir William Coventry: 'You, sir, took your turn at the sword, I must therefore not grudge to take mine at the pestilence.' By mid-August he was ordered to move his work to Greenwich. John Evelyn continued to write and work, now missing the cacophony of noise that, along with the polluted air, had so recently been intolerable to him. Bravely, Reverend Vincent stayed, praying over the abandoned sick and dying, and followed by desperate crowds everywhere; in his own household of eight, three died within seven days.

The courageous Lord Mayor, Sir John Lawrence, and the

aldermen remained. It was not by accident that London had become the greatest port, financial centre and hub of commerce in the kingdom: the City would be governed. The outbreak of the plague in 1485 was recalled, when two Lord Mayors in succession died, the second only four days after the first. Every precaution was taken, and the party of the Venetian Ambassador complained that the Lord Mayor of London supervised affairs and conducted audiences while standing in a glass case which he had had constructed specifically for this purpose, as recorded in the *Calendar of State Papers Domestic.*

Enforced death by execution had stopped in June, overwhelmed by indiscriminate death everywhere. Thousands were dying in the City; the use of coffins was soon abandoned, and shrouds were used instead. At the beginning of July it was four thousand people a week. By August the night was too short to bury the dead, and daytime burials commenced. By the first days of September the toll peaked at ten thousand per week. For Hollar, it was 'no patrons, no artist'. His wife and mainstay had died the previous year, and he now lost to the pestilence his only son, 'an ingeniose youth' who 'drew delicately' according to antiquary John Aubrey. Talented James Hollar, the focus of all his father's hopes, died in Hollar's studio where the artist's etching plates for Holbein's *Dance of Death* reputedly lay nearby. But the plague brought some comfort: Hollar was to marry a second time, a woman who had apparently taken refuge in his house.

Now contagion-ridden corpses were pulled by the tides, but few boats. By August it was unlawful to carry goods on the Thames. By September grass grew in some deserted by-ways in Whitehall. Abandoned flower gardens were left untouched, for it was believed that the sweetness of flowers could attract infection. Church sextons, who buried the dead, smoked furiously, for tobacco was believed to give protection; their clay pipes have been found in great numbers in excavated plague pits. Children were encouraged to smoke, and the boys at Eton were whipped for not smoking.

In September, the worst month of 'the blacke Pestilence', a desperate effort was made to cleanse the air. The Lord Mayor

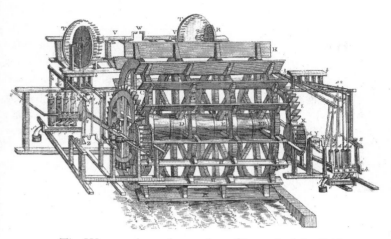

The Waterworks at the north or City end of the Bridge.

ordered that fires be lit in all the streets, one in front of every sixth house, to burn for three successive days. The Bridge may have been a focal point – now defending the City against attack by disease – for a great bonfire was constructed near St Magnus the Martyr. On 7 September Pepys '. . . saw Fires burning in the street, as it is through the whole City by the Lord Mayors order'. On the river he saw 'All the way fires on each side of the Thames . . .' The number of deaths slipped, then rose higher than ever.

At the height of the plague the sense of unreality was intensified by brilliant sunshine and impossibly blue skies. Virtually all work had ceased, and the air was clear for once of the noise, the polluting smoke and the smells of the fires of the soap-boilers, the dyers and the brewers located round about the Bridge. Those few who paused to look at the Bridge saw it sitting low above the water with an eerie and unusual clarity, Bridge and City seemingly put to sleep by a malevolent spell. The deep silence was broken only by church bells tolling and the bells of the plague carts which collected up the dead. Those who ventured out strained to identify an unusually clear sound: the waterwheels churning with the tides under the Bridge.

Finally, the sickness ran its course and started to abate with the onset of colder weather in November. It is now known that the bite of the flea living on the hairs of the black rat was the carrier of the bacterium *Yersinia pestis*. All cats and dogs in the City had been killed – more than four thousand – but there was little thought of rats. As recently as 1631 Charles I's Huguenot physician, Sir Theodore de Mayerne, had been asked to recommend actions to lessen the impact of the next outbreak. Among other sensible suggestions – none implemented – he told the King that he believed rodents rather than cats and dogs to be plague-carriers. Had well-meaning Charles acted on this, history might remember him differently.

Deaths were more numerous in the nearby suburbs than in the City. At least 100,000 people in London had perished. The true figure will never be known. According to Dr E. Barnard, who said he heard it from an apothecary who lived on the Bridge, only two people residing on the Bridge had died. Now there was a deficiency of workers everywhere, coupled with 'no business doing' in London. According to John Taylor, the Water Poet:

> All trades are dead, or almost out of breath,
> But such as live by sickness and by death.

When winter came, the Bridge Wardens tallied up the survivors among the men based at Bridge House yard – from the clerk and the tidemen to the cook. Some survivors bore scars of the disease: some limped and some had tumours. The Keeper of Dogs in the yard had no dogs to keep. Added to the competition for able-bodied men was the ongoing war against the Dutch and the French. The press gangs were more heartless than ever, grabbing unwilling recruits off the streets to serve in the navy. At such a time, the law specifically forbidding impressment of workers on London Bridge was a great encouragement to be part of the team caring for the Bridge.

Slowly the economy began to revive and social life returned, although the number of deaths from the plague continued to be much higher than in normal times. As traffic over the Bridge and into the City increased, each trader on the Bridge let down the wooden flap at the front of his small, dark shop to make a shelf for selling goods. Charles Tyus had died in 1664, and his widow, Sarah, became sole proprietor; she married the former apprentice, Thomas Passinger, possibly because only a Freeman of the City could have a shop. Passinger advertised his wares in bright red letters on 'posts', sheets nailed to the front of his shop, along with the pages of new books, hot from the press. Such nails often caught the clothing of passers-by with the expected curses, as people 'jostled for the wall' and safety from the animals and traffic. After Passinger's death, the business descended through relatives who were still working on the Bridge as late as 1722.

On 5 January 1666 Pepys wrote: 'It is a delightful thing to see the town full of people again . . . and shops begin to open.' In February 1666, King and court returned to London. By the summer of 1666 the Venetian Ambassador was able to record a charming picture of City and Bridge:

The City of London renders itself worthy to be styled the metropolis of the kingdom, and the abode of royalty. It is three miles long and very densely populated. Two thirds of its extent consists in suburbs where the nobility and the people also reside and where all the royal palaces, parks and gardens are situated. In the third part are the principal merchants from whom they select the chief magistrates of the City, called the Lord Mayor and officials . . . They are connected by a very noble stone bridge of twenty very lofty arches, on each side of which are convenient houses and shops, so that it has rather the air of a long suburb than a handsome structure such as a bridge.

The congestion on the most famous street in London, spreading well beyond the approaches at the bridgefoot, must have often been as much a hindrance as a bonus to business. Yet the shopkeepers on the Bridge and round about were anxious about their livelihoods if more ferries or another bridge were allowed. The Lord Mayor had petitioned the King back in 1663 to set up two ferries 'on account of the straitness [narrowness] and trouble of passing on London Bridge'. The Royal Surveyor had added his piece – this 'being the only expedient to ease the Bridge . . . from the multitude of carts, drays and drifts of cattle, since his Majesty would not admit of another bridge'. The King had said he would consider it. Nothing happened regarding this, nor about the detailed plan the King was given in 1664 for a bridge between Westminster and Lambeth.

Fires were frequent. The commons now sensed the danger and became restless with the increasing predictions by religious leaders of the destruction of London by fire. To some, London represented the very essence of sin and thus would be punished by God. Nonconformist religious leaders were united at least on this point. Eight years earlier, in 1658, Walter Gostelo had published *The Coming of God in Mercy, in Vengeance, Beginning with Fire, to Convert or Consume all this so Sinful City London*. Added to such writings was a notable nervousness caused by the war against the Dutch and the French, and a real fear of attack.

John Evelyn had despaired in his 1661 report to the King 'that the buildings [in the City] should be composed of such a congestion of mis-shapen and extravagant houses: that the streets should be so narrow and incommodious in the very centre and busiest places of intercourse'.

Charles II had written to the Lord Mayor in April 1665 warning of the danger of fire in the narrow, overcrowded streets with their overhanging timber houses. It was an even worse situation on the Bridge, where there were also hautpas joining the buildings overhead. And there were combustible materials everywhere around the bridgefeet and in the City.

In an unusually dry summer, 1 September 1666 had been a typically busy Saturday. The soon-to-be-infamous Pudding Lane, as with most of the City, had remained relatively unchanged for longer than anyone could remember. John Stow reported that it was

'. . . commonly called Pudding Lane, because the butchers of Eastcheap having their scalding houses for hogs there, and their puddings, with other filth of beasts, are voided down that way to their dung boats on the Thames . . .'

Only a few yards west of and parallel to Pudding Lane was Fish Street Hill, which led on to the Bridge. The house of Thomas Farynor, the King's baker, was on the west side of the lane, about ten doors up from Thames Street, itself only eleven feet wide and a service road for the wharves and warehouses along the river.

As the inhabitants on the Bridge settled down to sleep on the night of 1 September, they heard the trade signs creaking in the wind – unusually blowing strongly from the east. A final thought before sleep could well have been: When will it rain?

Those living on the Bridge were first awakened by the bells of St Clements, Eastcheap, and cries of 'Help!' They looked out to see St Margaret's on Fish Street Hill already ablaze. A crowd quickly gathered on the Bridge to watch the fire cross Thames Street and immediately catch on to St Magnus the Martyr hard by the foot of the Bridge. The bridge-dwellers watching the fire saw the parish clerk in his nightshirt rush in and out trying to save the parish registers. The flames caught at once, and the belfry was quickly ablaze, alerting all of London.

The conflagration raced across the gatehouse and on to the Bridge itself. Soon alight was the much admired multi-storeyed new block of buildings where the first floor overhung both street and river continuously. To avoid additional weight being put on the already overburdened structure, the Bridge had been excluded from the law of 1621 requiring the forefront and outer walls of all new buildings to be of brick or stone. Even in the City this edict had been largely ignored. Timber was used instead.

Reverend Vincent, who was present on the night of 1 September, applied his passion for religion to his description of the fire in *God's Terrible Voice in the City* of 1667:

It was in the depth and the dead of the night, when most doors and fences were lockt up in the City, that the Fire doth break forth and appear abroad; and like a mighty Giant refreshed with Wine, doth awake and arm itself, quickly gathers strength, when it hath made havok of some houses; rusheth down the hill towards the Bridge, crosseth Thames-street, invadeth Magnus-church, at the Bridgefoot; and though that church were so great, yet it was not a sufficient Barricado [barricade] against this Conqueror; but having scaled this Fort, it shooteth flames with so much the greater the advantage into all places round about; and a great building of houses upon the Bridge is quickly thrown to the ground . . .

In a mocking twist of fate, the falling beams from the over-hanging buildings had landed on the waterwheels and transformed them into charred ruins before anyone even thought of using them. Glowing timbers filled the bridge street and thus blocked the Bridge, removing a vital escape route from the burning City and preventing those in Southwark from helping.

The Lord Mayor, Sir Thomas Bludwell, had been awakened for the first time at three a.m. Variously described as vain, silly and indecisive, he had gone to observe the houses burning in Pudding Lane and witnessed St Magnus catch fire. Before going back to bed, he memorably commented: 'Pish! A woman might piss it out!' He was soon awakened again, but this time he did not return to bed. The City fathers, so adept even when ten thousand a week were dying of the plague, now seemed helpless, as Reverend Vincent noted: 'The Lord Mayor comes with his Officers; a confusion there is: councell is taken away; and London, so famous for wisodom and dexterity, can now find neither brains nor hands to prevent its ruine.'

At the start of the fire, one-third of the buildings on the Bridge were soon gone. Showers of 'fire-drops' blew on the strong easterly wind towards those quietly watching, their faces lit up. Strangely, the space left by the fire of 1633 – where houses had not yet been rebuilt – together with the thirty-foot-long open place at the Square by the Chapel created an essential fire-break and preserved the remaining two-thirds of the Bridge. The wind carried sparks across the river to the Southwark end of the Bridge, where a stable in

Shoe Lane caught fire. When two houses were alight, a third was pulled down to form a fire-break, so the fire in Southwark was quickly extinguished.

This fire was different from earlier ones. There was the dry summer and the easterly wind, and the conflagration had started near the north bank of the river by the Bridge where there were numerous fuel-rich structures and materials. There were no hoses at this date to fight a fire, and when the few fire appliances such as the small manual 'worm-drive fire squirt' were found, no one could get down the narrow by-ways, nor through the crowds, with the appliances, and some fell into the river.

On the west side of Fish Street Hill, Fishmongers Hall, beside the Bridge, caught fire. Thomas Tanner, Clerk of the Fishmongers Company, recorded that the fire rushed suddenly over a number of houses to the lantern of Fishmongers Hall. Clerks rushed to save the precious records, deeds and charters to put them in waiting lighters and boats, largely in vain, for the roof fell in quickly. The Hall was surrounded by a slum of timber buildings, intersected by narrow footways. On the wharves were timber warehouses, sometimes thatched, and sheds, cellars and storehouses containing every type of combustible goods, including tallow, oil and spirits, shipped goods and, crucially, barrels of pitch. Flames exploded through this densely packed area.

There were later reports that a strange atmosphere of apathy, hysteria and terror had prevailed, and the commons had been almost as quick to blame fellow citizens as they did foreigners. In a not unique incident a widow in Moorgate, fleeing the fire into Moorfield with her apron filled with baby chickens, was accused by a panicked mob of carrying fire-balls. She was attacked, and her breasts cut off. Wenceslaus Hollar, a foreigner with an East European accent, was forced to hide for fear of being lynched.

In the rush to escape the fire, Payne was no doubt among the watermen, who normally carried people, and the lightermen, who usually carried goods, as they forgot all such demarcations and rushed to offer assistance. Calculatingly, they set the price before taking anyone, no matter how stricken. The day before, the fare to go 'over the water directly' had been threepence for one man with sculls, fourpence for two men with oars. The rate now tripled. When they heard about it, the enemy, the Dutch, were delighted by the fire and produced a succession of sensational maps and prints depicting its progress, including an unlikely one of weeping watermen, who in reality were making fortunes.

The river itself was a spectacle, with clouds of smoke billowing along it in the easterly wind, the water reflecting the flames. Boats of every description were filled with an extraordinary array of people and goods – from the new-born to the near-dead, from beds to virginals – and on the water floated possessions that had fallen in as a result of collisions. Trying to keep well under the structure and away from the sparks on the wind, people huddled on the stinking, muddy river banks and sheltered on the piers of the Bridge, while boats full of people stayed near and under the protection of the Bridge, a scene painted a century later by Philippe Jacques de Loutherbourg, J.M.W. Turner's mentor.

In the flames, smoke and heat, could there have been a more chilling sight than the Great Stone Gate? The rotting heads, skulls and quarters emerged through the swirling smoke, one minute casting shadows, the next reflecting flames. John Dryden, in his *Annus Mirabilis* of 1667, described it thus:

> The ghost of traitors from the Bridge descend,
> With bold fanatic spectres to rejoice,
> About the fire into a dance they bend
> And sing this Sabbath's notes with feeble voice.

On Tuesday 4 September the fire neared St Paul's and its large courtyard which was the centre of the book trade in the City. By Thursday, the 579-year-old cathedral, once the largest in Europe, was threatened. Pepys knew this area well since the days when it had been close by his school, and he had continued to frequent it. He watched as the cathedral caught fire in three places and was damaged beyond repair. Thousands of books burned, including three hundred copies of Sir William Dugdale's *History of St Paul's*, which Hollar had lovingly illustrated with forty engravings.

Finally, the wind abated. But as late as Friday 7 September there was still a danger to the Bridge, as Evelyn recorded in his *Diary*. He went on foot from Whitehall as far as London Bridge 'through the late Fleet-Street . . . with extraordinary difficulty, clambering overe heaps of yet smoking rubbish'. The King had gone to the Tower by water, and ordered that the houses so densely built around the moat be demolished, for they had 'taken fire and attacked the White Tower, where the magazines of powder lay, [and] would undoubtedly not only have beaten down and destroyed all the bridge, but sunk and torn the vessels in the river, and rendered the demolition beyond all expression for several miles about the country . . .'

The fire subsided, although hot embers were found months afterwards in cellars and in dangerous no-go areas taken over by criminals. Twelve book-sellers remained on Old London Bridge, among whom were Thomas Passinger and his wife Sarah. Waterman Payne was still on the river, perhaps richer, no doubt sadder, but happy to have survived both the plague and the Great Fire. In 1667 Payne helped Pepys procure household staff, including his own daughter, Nell, who became the 'cook maid', then maid before she left, probably because Elizabeth Pepys correctly sensed 'a dalliance'; when they later met by chance, Pepys sometimes still had 'a bout' with Nell. In 1668 Payne saw Pepys at the puppet show of *Dick Whittington* in Southwark, and was quick to take in hand his former benefactor's well-being, as Pepys records: 'I away with Payne the waterman; he seeing me at the play did get me a link to light me, and so light me to the Beare, where Bland, my waterman waited' with Pepys's valuables, for he feared that his pockets would be cut at the fair. 'So by link-light through the Bridge, it being mighty dark, but still water; and so home . . .'

Samuel Pepys kept his *Diary* until 1669, the year of his wife's death at a time when he was embroiled in controversy and vigorously defending his actions at the Navy Office. He continued to relish all the pleasures life offered and to thrive in his notable career. Elizabeth and Samuel Pepys (died 1703) were buried in St Olave's, Hart Street, 'our own church', only yards from where they had lived and from the Navy Office. This was also the church to which a grateful Princess Elizabeth had come to give thanks for her release from the Tower more than 150 years earlier. St Olave's is one of only eight churches that survived the Great Fire and that still exist today. It is satisfying to know that the church's patron saint, 'St Olaf', was Olaf Haraldsson, martyred king and patron saint of Norway (1014–30), who in 1014 led the battle of the timber London Bridge, the probable source of the nursery rhyme 'London Bridge is Falling Down'.

On the restoration of Charles II, Wenceslaus Hollar had petitioned the King for work, and specifically for financial support to enable him to finish a very large, very detailed map of London, which he himself described as being a stupendous '10 Foot in bredth, and 5 Foot upward' in extent. The King, who as a child had been taught to draw by Hollar, heartlessly side-stepped the artist's appeal by passing it on to the Lord Mayor. Tantalizingly, the progress and fate of what Hollar intended to be his masterpiece is unknown.

His beloved St Paul's had been beyond saving, but he had etched it numerous times and was pleased that he had 'thus preserved its memory'. Now his prints of London were in demand for their topographical accuracy, rarity and evocation of the past. His plan of London was later used by Evelyn 'as the most accurate hitherto extant' in promoting his own scheme for rebuilding the City. But Hollar's fortunes never recovered from the deaths of his patron, the Earl of Arundel and Surrey, his first wife and his only son, the plague of 1665 and the Great Fire of London in 1666.

The life of this gifted and modest man was destined to be a struggle to the end. George Vertue – artist, engraver and his first biographer – noted that Hollar's 'painful and laborious life [was] always attended with difficulties'. With age his sight began to fail and the quality of his work suffered. Increasingly besieged by creditors, he hid his portfolios, then stopped signing his work to try to retain the pittance he was paid. Hollar died in London in 1703 just after the bailiffs arrived.

A superb etcher, engraver and topographer, Hollar had produced a plate a week for half a century. He left 2,733 engravings, including one of the most valuable topographical records of the seventeenth century, *A Panorama of London*, showing river, Bridge and City after the 1633 fire and before the 1666 fire. Fittingly, the illustration is framed by allegorical figures of London and the Thames, and at 108 by 90 inches in dimension, six plates were required to print it. There was also his most popular print, giving two views, *London Before and After the Great Fire* of 1666 (27 $\frac{1}{4}$ by 18 inches), which he completed for publication only three months after the fire itself.

In Southwark Cathedral, once the St Saviour's from the tower of which he had made his reference drawings, a memorial plaque to Hollar begins:

> The works of nature and of men
> by thee preserved, takes life again.
> And ev'n thy Prague serenely shines.
> Secure from ravage in thy lines . . .

A remarkable survival, the Bridge still stood, although seriously damaged, having been subjected to intense heat twice in just over thirty years. The 1651 block of houses over two arches at the City end had been destroyed, as had the waterwheels. When the embers cooled, Wardens Robert Hussey and Anthony Scarlett paid workmen four shillings to unblock the bridge street by torchlight, and the irrepressible shopkeepers set up sheds from which to haggle over their wares. In its 622-year-long history Old London Bridge, a formidable fortification second only to the Tower of London, was never taken in battle. But once again the most fearsome enemy – fire – had almost accomplished its destruction with ease.

Much worse was the devastation of the City and the kingdom's greatest port, the engines driving the country's business and trade. One-sixth of the population of London, at least 100,000 people, 'late of London, now of the Fields' in Reverend Vincent's inimitable words, were homeless, for 13,400 houses had disappeared, along with forty-four Company Halls, the Royal Exchange, the Custom House, St Paul's Cathedral, the Guildhall, the Bridewell and other City prisons, three City gates and the bridges over the Fleet River that ran along the west wall of the City.

Among the six chapels and eighty-seven parish churches destroyed were the parish and church of St Mary Colechurch on the corner of Poultry and Old Jewry, where the founder-builder of Old London Bridge, Peter de Colechurch, had been chaplain almost five hundred years earlier. In 1205 his bones had been interred in the undercroft of what – until 1548–9 – had been the Chapel on the Bridge. The architect-priest's burial place was by now forgotten, and throughout strife, plague and fire he reposed peacefully at one with his Bridge.

After the fire, the River Thames still ebbed and flowed, bringing goods and people to the City once more. The commons' old friend – the wounded Bridge – stolidly endured, binding together the City and Southwark, London and south-east England, home and abroad. For the deeply astonished Londoners, river and Bridge were the only remaining certainties.

The trade card of Christopher Stedman. ➤

CHAPTER SEVEN

'keep to the left'

The Knight in the triumph of his heart made several reflections on the greatness of the British *Nation . . . that the* Thames *was the noblest river in* Europe; *that* London Bridge *was a greater piece of work than any of the Seven Wonders of the World; with many other honest prejudices which naturally cleave to the heart of a true* Englishman.
Joseph Addison, 1672–1719, *The Spectator*

HAPPILY, AMID THE GREYNESS AND GLOOM FOLLOWING THE FIRE, the small yellow flowers of London Rocket (*Sisymbrium irio*) bloomed in the stonework on the Bridge and on wasteground round about. Hot,

mustardy and biting, they flowered freely from July to September in the nooks and crannies of the Bridge, thriving in the cracks between the old stones that absorbed the sun during the day and reflected the heat back after sunset. This cheerful role played by London Rocket in 1667, noted by Richard Thomson in *Chronicles of London Bridge*, was echoed almost three hundred years later, when the star-shaped pink flowers of London Pride (*Saxifraga* x *urbium*) colonized World War II rubble in the City.

Shopkeepers were quick to set up sheds in the ruins on the Bridge – their very livelihood depended on it – and as the rubble from the fire was cleared, much of it was used to extend the quays or simply dumped into the Thames. In the City the merchants were rehoused so business could resume. As early as the Thursday after the fire, markets were reopened and agreements made as to how to share those unscathed sites that remained. Leadenhall, for example, normally a market for fish, meal, hides and leather, became the meat market, but on Thursdays the clothiers took over. In the crisis Aldersgate Street and around the pump in Bishopsgate Street were designated areas for vegetable stalls.

At first there were ambitious schemes to build a new city. Christopher Wren and John Evelyn presented their plans to the King; one aim among many was to improve communications across London Bridge. But such plans were set aside. To save time, the City was rebuilt to its medieval layout. A priority, oddly, was the building of the Monument to the Great Fire of London, as outlined in the first Act of Parliament following the fire (1667): the construction of a 'column or pillar of brass or stone', which was designed by Wren and Robert Hooke. The Monument was built on the site of ancient St Margaret, New Fish Street, the first church to be burned down; this parish was now united with St Magnus. The Great Fire provided a broad canvas on which Wren's genius could flourish, and he rebuilt more than fifty of the City's churches.

Not unexpectedly, taverns and alehouses quickly re-established themselves, one being Ye Swan & Bridge. The urgency was to rehouse people quickly, without the delays that would have been caused by fighting vested interests or negotiating property rights, as would have been the case if streets had been replanned. It was essential to get the economy moving again.

The waterwheels had been destroyed, and the 1667 Act empowered the descendants of Peter Morris to rebuild in timber the essential 'water house' with waterwheels in two arches.

At a time when excellent sites were available for very little, at least one bridge-dweller had a role in the rebuilding of London, although we don't know the outcome. In November 1667, an ambitious scrivener or copyist named James Peters who lived 'at the Sign of The Sugar loaf near the drawbridge on London Bridge' announced in the *London Gazette* that all who wished to buy or sell ground in the City should go to his dwelling.

On the Bridge itself, after two intense fires the masonry of the arches and piers needed costly repairs before work could start on the houses, and this included 'six cellars' that had been damaged. The cost in the end for structural repairs was £1,500.

Meanwhile, the old St Paul's was being demolished by Wren, who each night crossed the Thames to what some believe was his house on the river near the Globe Theatre, from where he could keep the daily reducing bulk of the cathedral ruins in his sight and in his mind. The rubble of Kentish ragstone was purchased by the City to pave the streets. Pulling down walls eighty feet high and five feet thick was exceedingly risky, and there were casualties. The workmen refused to go near the dangerous two-hundred-foot cathedral tower, so Wren blew it up with gunpowder in a series of explosions. The noise and dust of these could be heard and seen from the Bridge and added to the confused wreckage of the scene in the City.

The great houses upriver from the Bridge, with their gardens down to the Thames, were not rebuilt, and this land became the site for courts and alleys. Within the City after the fire there were four thousand more houses in the same space than there had been before. Much character and many remarkable buildings had gone, but a cleaner, safer London emerged, rebuilt in stone.

On the Bridge, the authorities granted leases of sixty-one years, with rents based on the frontage at a rate of ten shillings per foot, as noted in W. Maitland's *History and Survey of London*. Rather than have one organizational body, it was more effective for each tenant to be responsible for building his own premises, but following strict rules regarding the materials and style.

In the fifth stage of Old London Bridge, around 1710, after all the rebuilding was complete, the appearance of the Bridge from the east and west is seen in an engraving by Sutton Nicholls. Almost all the medieval houses had been rebuilt in the Restoration style with the exception of those at the Southwark end; some of the latter may have dated back to 1471 but would themselves burn down in 1725. The Bridge looked distinctly different.

City ladies shopping on the bridge street saw the entire space on both sides to the first opening north of the Chapel filled with a double row of regularly built timber houses four storeys high. These new houses were built in a style popular in the Restoration period of Charles II, with dormer windows and hipped and over-hung roofs (still to be seen in the red-brick houses in King's Bench Walk in the Temple, an evocative scene where the gas street lanterns are lit every evening). The upper portions of the houses had projecting bays for latrines; there was no worry about sanitation with the supposedly cleansing Thames flowing beneath, although in reality the tides simply pulled the excrement back and forth. The houses almost in the middle, between Nonesuch House and the former Chapel, had leads on their flat roofs and balustrades, where roof-gardens gave London's best views high above the turmoil and in total contrast to the dark shops beneath.

As the new structures were being built, the width of the bridge street was increased to twenty feet. To achieve this symmetry – unusual for the Bridge, where the width was never completely regular all the way across until all the houses were removed in 1760 – the front of the structures just rested on the arches. The bulk of the Bridge was held up by the piers, which were joined by wooden girdering, each girder being strong enough to support five or six struts. This girdering unfortunately hid the top of the arches, except at the three openings between the blocks of houses, and so reduced the charm of the Bridge.

The trade card of Walter Watkins, a trader on the Bridge.

The fortunes of the Bridge had been totally reversed. Now it was no longer a favoured place to live, with its noise, congestion and strange smells. To those of refined tastes, some of the most objectionable trades were concentrated around the Southwark end, and involved the use of animal products. Bermondsey, just east of Southwark, was the main place for the manufacture of leather. The skinners and tanners, round about the slaughterhouses, treated the skins with dog faeces and urine. There was the clinging smell of the fat used by the soap-boilers, and the bones used by the glue-makers. The dyers and their associated odours had been established in Southwark from about 1680. Wealthy women wisely carried pomanders or scent bottles.

The proximity of the tanneries in Southwark and Bermondsey meant there were leather-sellers on the Bridge. In 1750 Walter Watkins was a breeches-maker, leather-seller and glover at the sign of the Breeches and Glove. About the same time John Grant, brush-maker, was at the Four Brushes at one corner of the Square; among other things, he made and sold 'all sorts of Ship & House Brushes', and his trade was two-way: he would give 'The most ready Money for good Bees Wax, Hogs Hair & Horse Hair'.

The once-wondrous Nonesuch House had by now become near ruinous, but still stood, still held together by its wooden pegs. The accommodation on the Bridge, so highly prized in Elizabethan days when the rich preferred to live on a main thoroughfare with the poor hidden away in back-street slums, was by the early Georgian years reduced to lodgings above shops. New suburbs, such as Hampstead and Islington, with clean air, were preferred.

But there was still only one Bridge, and it was still famous. The contents page of a 1708 guidebook and directory of London, Edward Hatton's *New View of London*, listed streets, markets, churches, the halls of City Companies, palaces, houses of nobility, colleges, libraries, museums, free-schools, hospitals, prisons, work-houses, followed by: 'Of Fountains, Bridges, Conduits, Ferries, Docks, Keys, Wharves, Plying-places for Boats and their distances from London Bridge'.

Tradesmen's cards were issued mainly after 1760. The cards or handbills were a form of advertising, and great care was taken in their extravagant design, each incorporating fascinating details and illustrations of the trade and wares being advertised by the tradesman, and the important image on the sign that hung in front of the shop. The surviving cards tell us something about who was on the Bridge and what they did. With the daily influx of visitors, and sailors nearby, the Bridge was the most obvious location for map-sellers. John Laban, Map and Print Seller at the sign of the Lamb and the Three Stars, advertised: 'Pictures Carefully Cleaned, Lined and Mended; Carved and Gilt Frames for Pictures; Pear-tree and all other Sorts of Frames for Prints.'

And what could be better than a globe as a trade sign for a map-seller? In 1749, print- and map-seller William Herbert was at the sign of the Golden Globe under the Piazza on the east side, the third house from the south end of the new block. His tradesman's card proclaimed: 'Great Variety of English Maps and Prints Chiefly Collected from the Works of the most Celebrated artists . . . N.B. Prints neatly Framed & Glazed for Exportation, Rooms and Staircases fitted up in the Modern Indian Taste.' The latter reflected fashionable trends prompted by the East India trade; the East India Company, chartered in 1600 during Elizabeth's reign, was one of the foundation stones of the Empire, with its monopoly on trade to the East Indies, then to India.

A globe might also be the sign of scientific instrument makers. Christopher Stedman, a mathematical instrument maker, was 'At the Globe on London Bridge' about 1750. He sold instruments for sea or land, including navigation, and his wonderfully detailed engraved card depicted a globe, cupids and his mathematical and navigational instruments resting all around the rococo frame. His widow Elizabeth carried on after he died, almost the only circumstance in which a woman ran a business, and widows usually quickly remarried.

In the same tradition of fine instruments on the Bridge, about 1690 there had been a surgical instrument maker, Samuel Grover, at the Sceptre and Heart, who 'maketh all sorts of Chirurgeons Instruments the best sort of Razors penkniues Scissers & Launcetts there are sold the best Hoans and Fine Fish Skin Cases'. On his card, in the centre, is the device of the Sceptre and Heart enclosed by two palm branches, around which is displayed a terrifying arrangement of lancets, trepans, saws, scissors and knives.

A tradesman's address was important, and proximity to the Bear tavern was almost as good a one to have as was Old London Bridge itself. Robert Vincent was a scale-maker 'At the Hand & Scales on

London Bridge, the Second Door from the Bear Tavern Southwark-side'. The famous Bear, dating back to at least 1319, would be pulled down in December 1761, but the Hand & Scales, only two doors away, must have escaped demolition, because its 1793 address was No. 1, High Street, Borough, and in 1802: 'Vincent & Chancellor was at No. 1, Bridge Foot, Borough'.

The taverns were joined by their unwelcome rivals the coffee houses — taverns or inns selling coffee, perhaps tea and chocolate as well — which popped up after coffee was introduced into the country in the early 1600s. By 1632 there were about three thousand in London. Like the taverns, many could be found near the Bridge. It was said that 'coffee and the Commonwealth came in together' in 1660. Soon, they were deemed nurseries of sedition, and places where dissenting pamphlets were distributed. And wives strongly disapproved of the influence of the new stimulant. In 1674 'The Women's Petition against Coffee' appeared in which they complained at length that there was '. . . a very sensible Decay of that true Old English Vigour . . . Never did Man wear greater Breeches, or carry less in them of any Mettle whatsoever . . .' all due to the 'Excessive use of that Newfangled, Abominable, Heathenish Liquor called COFFEE . . .'

The coffee houses had a relaxed, club-like atmosphere where politics, finance and gambling flourished. One of the most famous, Garraway's Coffee House, was near the Royal Exchange, north of the Bridge. Like the others it was a place where wine was auctioned off 'by the candle': the person bidding when the candle went out got the goods. And at Garraway's the first public sale of Hudson's Bay Company furs from Canada was held, in 1671. Coffee houses were also a venue for the first insurance companies, and Sun Fire Insurance initially set up business in two rented rooms at Garraway's in 1711.

By the early 1700s there were coffee houses at both ends of the Bridge. A famous one, Shades, was 'a low dark room built out from Fishmongers Hall. It was divided into compartments overlooking the river', and was the last tavern in London where wine was drawn into silver tankards. There may well have been coffee houses on the

Bridge, but the only one recorded was in the early 1800s, that of 'Strachan & Softlaw, Tavern. Bridge House Hotel, Tavern & Coffee House, London Bridge Southwark'. Goods in the Blue Boar on the Bridge reflected the new fashions: coffee and chocolate mills and nutmeg grinders were now among the huge range of stock.

The vintners were vehemently opposed to the unexpected new arrival – but the Bear still thrived, and seemed to have been there for ever, as proclaimed in a poem of 1691, 'The Last Search after Claret in Southwark':

> We came to the Bear, which we soon understood,
> Was the first house in Southwark built after the Flood.

Punch was another popular drink. On one day in April 1722 there was a unique sight on the bridge street: the shopkeepers held a party in the middle of it. The Drawbridge had been following its usual pattern of 'decay and rebuild' for centuries, and when it was decided, yet again, to replace it, the bridge street, most unusually, was closed for a time. Only the bridge-dwellers and those coming to make purchases were allowed on to it. Shopkeepers relished this rare opportunity to place tables in the middle of the roadway, where they had a party for a whole afternoon. In future they boasted that they had once sat leisurely drinking punch in the centre of the busiest street in London. This may have occurred at the Southwark end, for there was a London Bridge Punch House adjoining the gate there in 1755.

The Bridge often touched on the stories of individuals, great and small. Sometimes there is a glimpse of personal suffering unrelated to plague, strife or natural disaster. In February 1667 Pepys was told by his waterman that the wife of the publican of the Bear had committed suicide by throwing herself into the river. Troubled Pepys, a Puritan at heart but ever susceptible to feminine appeal, recalled that she was 'a beautiful a woman as most I have seen', who had sadly tried to take her own life before.

Beauty, Bridge and Bear had a place in another small drama, and one indicative of life at the court of Charles II in the Restoration period. Frances Teresa Stuart, the daughter of a Catholic Scottish royalist, had been sent to court in 1662, where her elfin looks soon attracted the attention of the King. Either clever and virtuous, or disarmingly feather-headed, Frances refused either to surrender herself to the King – at least initially – or to interest herself in political affairs. From 1666 she had been much in favour; in 1667 'la Belle Stuart' became the model for the image of Britannia on numerous medals and coins. In addition to her royal lover, 'Old Rowley' (his nickname coming from his favourite racehorse), she stirred deep passions in others, including the King's cousin, the Duke of Richmond and Lennox. Even Pepys was torn between his admiration of her beauty and the way she was able to maintain her ambiguous position at court.

The King disliked his cousin, perhaps sensing a true rival. Although Charles didn't want to part with Frances, she had become tired of fending him off. The Duke and Frances Stuart were a love match, but their marriage had to be clandestine. She fled her apartment overlooking the Thames at the Palace of Whitehall to join the Duke at the Bear, where a coach was supposed to be waiting. But it was not there. As they huddled at the bridgefoot in the darkness of a stormy night, a patron of the Bear almost discovered them, but one of their companions provided a distraction by stumbling into him, and after apologies he went on his way. Within twenty-four hours they were married, without royal permission, at the Duke's Cobham Hall in Kent. Charles banned them both from court, and was even more furious when the new Duchess sent back the jewels and presents he had given her. However, they were soon accepted again at court. The new Duchess survived smallpox, although she was badly disfigured, and she outlived the King by almost twenty years, the Duke by thirty, a parrot remaining her companion for forty years.

All were deeply alarmed by a Dutch attack on the undefended Medway estuary in 1667, when English warships were burned. There was nothing to stop an attack on London and the Bridge. The Duke of Richmond and Lennox commanded a troop of the horse, and ships were sunk in Barking Creek as a defence in the preparations ordered by Charles II. So frightened was Pepys that at two hours' notice – with his wife and his gold – he left London. The Dutch, however, withdrew.

In the dark, the streets were menacing enough even without the threat of attack, and efforts were made to light the way. Count Lorenzo Magalotti, in the account of his travels in England, noted that the 'streets are lighted till a certain hour in the morning by large lanterns'. When the lanterns go out, 'you may find boys at every step, who run before you with lighted torches'. On the Bridge and elsewhere it was the duty of every householder in winter to hang out a candle or lantern from dusk until nine p.m. This ruling was largely ignored, and the streets remained dark and ill-lit. On the bridge street globe lamps burning whale oil were set at regular intervals, to be replaced in the nineteenth century by gas lamps.

The barbarous role of the Bridge finally ended in 1678, when the last head was exposed on it. The head was that of the unfortunate William Stayley, Catholic banker and goldsmith, who became one of a number of innocent victims in the very strange and complicated story of Titus Oates. When Oates fabricated a plot and swore on the Bible to the authorities that it was all true, the common people exploded with fear and anger, and Oates became a hero. The tragic results included what can be called the judicial murder of innocent Stayley and at least thirty-four others. Due to a petition by Stayley's friends, and his penitent attitude, his quarters were buried without being exhibited. But his funeral on 29 November at St Paul's, Covent Garden, attracted so much attention that Charles II heard of it, and ordered the body to be dug up, the quarters exposed and the head set upon the Bridge. In this suitably gruesome way ended a tradition that had started with the brutal execution of Scottish patriot William Wallace almost four hundred years earlier.

In happy contrast, the severe winter of 1683–4 set the scene for one of the most famous of the frost fairs. The occurrence of frost fairs and the structure of the Bridge were closely linked, for in extreme cold the damming effect of the piers in a much shallower and wider river than today's resulted in thick ice upstream. This particular frost lasted from the beginning of December to 5 February. In December John Evelyn recorded that it was 'exceedingly mortal' and 'unsufferably cold'. By 1 January streets of booths were being set up on the ice, scenes so appealingly depicted in paintings. By the third week in January, as the cold became much more severe, the curving Thames looked like one continuous fair.

Fun was combined with business. Sleds and skates made of bone appeared, and on the ice from Westminster to the Temple 'coaches plied as if in the street'. The book *Great Britain's Wonder* of 1684 noted that above the Bridge there was 'bull-baiting, horse and coach races, puppet plays and interludes, cooks and tippling, and lewder places . . . There was a street of booths built from the Temple to Southwark, where were sold all sorts of goods imaginable, namely cloaths, plate, earthenware, meat, drink, brandy, tobacco, and a hundred sorts of commodities not here inserted: it being the wonder of the present age and a great consternation to all the spectators.'

Small printers set up their temporary presses on the ice. On a sheet they printed the customer's name and a message, which might be: 'London; Printed by G. Croom, on the ICE, on the river of Thames, January 31, 1684.' Charles II, Queen Catherine and the

A frost fair on the Thames upstream of the Bridge, winter of 1715–16.

Duke of York were among those who enjoyed this novelty. The event was commemorated in a ballad:

> The Thames is now both fair and market too,
> Where many thousands daily do resort.
> There you may see the coaches swiftly run,
> As if beneath the ice were waters none,
> And shoals of people everywhere there be,
> Just like the herrings in the brackish sea.
>
> There you may also this hard frosty winter
> See on the rocky ice a Working-Printer,
> Who hopes by his own art to reap some gain
> Which he perchance does think he may obtain.
>
> There on a sign you may most plainly see't,
> Here's the first tavern built in Freezeland Street.

Who could resist the explosion of activity on the ice, man joyously seeming to dominate – for a short time – Nature, even if a high price was paid when the ice broke up. And Nature always won. The severe cold instantly made an already hard daily life much more of a struggle. The smoke and pollution from the coal fires didn't rise in the cold air, and it became hard to breathe. Water pipes and engines were frozen, brewers and many other tradesmen were unable to work, and one disastrous slippery accident followed another.

When life returned to normal, the great markets of London – controlled by the Corporation of the City of London – were again supplied by produce coming from the country by river and over the Bridge. Smithfield was for living cattle, with a horse fair on Fridays. Flesh markets were located in Southwark and thirteen other places in an effort to keep the deeply unpleasant business of slaughtering away from the centre. Above the Bridge, the cherry and apple markets were located by the Three Cranes, while malt and corn were sold at Queenhithe.

With the great trade on the river, the Custom House Quays were sited downstream at the loop in the river at Limehouse Basin, where there might be as many as two thousand ships of sail. The wharves extended from Tower Stairs to London Bridge, peopled by porters, watchmen and 'poor working men'. The revenue brought in by these wharves was usually more than £40,000 per year. From these quays wool and grain, hides and salt, silks and spices, barrels of tar and casks of wine were sold.

Billingsgate, a fish market for centuries, by 1699 had been designated a free market for fish six days a week, while, in the days before food could be easily preserved other than by salting, mackerel was allowed to be sold before or after divine service on Sundays. There were strict rules about how fish were caught, including no net with a mesh of squares less than six inches wide and only two casts at low water. Following ancient laws, at least eight species of fish were sized, from salmon (sixteen inches in length) and pike (fourteen inches) to trout (eight inches) and flounder (six inches), as recorded in James S. Ogilvy's *Relics and Memorials of London City*.

In addition to all other activity around the Bridge was the normal business of the watermen. Back in 1676, according to M.P. Ashley in *Life in Stuart England*, there had been over two thousand watermen on the river, although Pepys not so long before had said there were ten thousand licensed watermen and a few hundred lightermen. Their fares were regulated. In 1671 to go 'over the water directly' was fourpence for two men 'with oars' and tuppence for one man with 'skulls'. 'London Bridge to Westminster (all stairs)' was sixpence, but from London to Windsor on the royal river fourteen shillings. Each additional passenger was a penny to a shilling, depending on distance.

Such a dominant, vigorous force as the watermen, the most numerous of the tradesmen, could easily become a nuisance. In 1716 the wherrymen and watermen were accused of using the public stairs and landing places 'to make clean, trim and dress their Boats or Wherries', causing obstruction and annoyance, and damaging the stairs. This was forbidden, and they were warned not to feign ignorance in future.

The great Thames highway was, and still is, used for games and contests of skill. The race on the river for Doggett's Coat and Badge for newly qualified tideway watermen was first held in 1715. A comedian, Thomas Doggett, offered the prize, 'a livery with a badge representing Liberty to be rowed for by six watermen from The Swan, London Bridge to Cadogan Pier, near where the Old Swan in Chelsea stood, annually on the same day, August 1, for ever'. Young men still race for the orange livery and enormous silver arm badge, an event now managed by the Fishmongers Company.

The Thames setting was a magnet for artists, and not just during extraordinary times like frost fairs and fires. There is a tradition that Hans Holbein 'the younger' (1497–1543) had once lived on the Bridge. A story that may be apocryphal was much later told by Horace Walpole, Lord Orford. Holbein reputedly lived with the family of a goldsmith to whom he gave a painting. The father of Lord Treasurer Oxford on crossing London Bridge was caught in a shower, and stepped inside a shop. There he saw a painting by Holbein, who had apparently lived in that house, and offered the goldsmith £100 for it. The goldsmith agreed. Unfortunately, the painting was destroyed in one of the great fires of the 1600s. Holbein did have links with goldsmiths, for even after his genius as a painter was acknowledged, he still drew designs for them, as well as for jewellers and bookbinders.

Peter Monamy, born in about 1670 in Jersey, was apprenticed to a sign- and house-painter, William Clarke, on London Bridge around 1696. By 1710 he had started painting seascapes and became a well-known marine artist, no doubt encouraged by the marvellous vantage point his apprenticeship had offered him, when he had been able to study the vessels below the Bridge and the nuances of light on water. Horace Walpole noted that: 'the shallow waves that rolled under his window, taught young Monamy what his master [the sign-painter] could not teach him, and fitted him to paint the turbulence of the ocean'. Monamy based his style on the Willem van de Veldes, elder and younger, and when the latter died his work filled a gap in the market. Experts considered him accurate on details such as rigging, less good on colour. In 1703 Monamy had been made a Freeman of the Painter-Stainers Company – Sir Peter Lely, Sir James Thornhill and Sir Joshua Reynolds were also Freemen – and in 1726 he presented a large sea-piece to the Painter-

Stainers; it hung in their Hall until destroyed by fire in 1941 during World War II. At some point after 1730 he himself was painted by Hogarth, depicted showing a marine painting to his patron, Mr Walker, a Customs commissioner. It was said that Peter Monamy kept his prices too low, and so did not make as much money as he should have.

Charles II had died in 1685, and his brother, Catholic James II, became king only to be deposed three years later in 1688 and replaced by Protestants William and Mary (1689–1702) – Mary was James's daughter – in the Glorious Revolution. The times were reasonably peaceful for the Bridge. Queen Anne, younger sister of Mary, began her twelve-year reign in 1702, by which time London had largely recovered from the hugely draining effects of the Great Fire.

Interestingly, the rebuilt Waterworks – the noise of which those in St Magnus had to suffer – were required to contribute towards the poor rate of the parish, funds always greatly needed. The church accounts give little insights into life and death on the Bridge, leaving us to imagine the hidden story. The church wardens' accounts record casual payments: 'Pd for a Coffin and Shroud for a Woman yt died on the Bridge 5s. 6d.' In 1713 a poor man named Thomas Dixkens expired in the Three Neats' Tongues on the Bridge, one of the few references to this inn. The church wardens had to pay £1 11s. 8d., and then 15s. 4d. for the doctor, clerk, sexton, gravemaker, bearers and register; in addition, a coffin and shroud and 'Expenses at 3 Tongues' came to £1 1s. 4d.

Even in death, there could be humour. In the churchyard of St Magnus is the tombstone of a Robert Preston, who died in 1730. He worked at the Boar's Head tavern in Great Eastcheap, and had apparently been an abstainer surrounded by temptation. From his tombstone:

> Bacchus, to give the toping world surprize,
> Produced one Sober Son, and here he lies.
> Tho' nurs'd among full Hogheads he defy'd
> The charms of Wine and ev'ry vice beside
> O Reader, if to Justice thou'rt inclin'd

Keep honest PRESTON daily in thy mind.
He drew good Wine, took care to fill his Pots
Had many virtues that outweigh'd his faults.
You that on *Bacchus* have the like dependance
Pray copy *Bob* in Measure and attendance.

In 1714 the Bridge House paid eighteen shillings to the church
wardens to rent rooms built over their cloister. The sum of five
shillings was paid to Robert Pirkins in 1727 at St Magnus 'for
looking after ye bridge to keep it clear of them yt sold things on
the Sabbath Day', for which work he received a shilling a week.

An organ for the church was commissioned and paid for by Sir
Charles Duncombe, an alderman for the ward of Bridge Within
and Lord Mayor in 1709. The work of building the organ went to
a carpenter, Abraham Jordan, who had a shop close to St Magnus.
This instrument was a source of great pride, and an announcement
appeared in *The Spectator* on 8 February 1712: '. . . Messrs. Abraham
Jordan, senior and junior, have with their own hands (joinery
excluded) made and erected a very fine organ for St Magnus Church,
at the foot of London Bridge . . . The above said Abraham Jordan
gives notice that he will attend every day next week at the said
church to accommodate all those gentlemen who shall have a
curiosity to hear it.'

Sir Charles was a most important visitor. Not only the organ,
but the St Magnus clock in its prominent position over the bridge
street had been donated by him, and erected in 1709, the year in
which he attained the highest position in the City. When he was
an apprentice, he had been told to meet his master at a certain place
on the Bridge. There was no clock, he arrived late and so was
dismissed. He vowed that the same fate would not befall another
apprentice, and that when he was rich he would set up a clock,
which he did, and it is still there.

When Sir Charles visited the church in 1712, great care was
taken that he be treated with the deference he deserved: they got
in cakes and pastries for him, and a 'Mr Preston's Maid' was paid
to bring an easy chair for him to sit on.

* * *

Nature remained unpredictable and mysterious. For a brief period in the autumn of 1716 a bridge became unnecessary, as a gale from the west-south-west apparently somehow held back the water. The Thames disappeared and thousands of people had the unique experience of crossing it on foot, both above and below the Bridge, as well as being able to walk through most of the arches.

This extraordinary event was short-lived, and attention remained focused on dealing with the problems of the busy bridge street. In 1722 a landmark decision was made regarding rules of the road: 'keep to the left' became part of everyday life on the Bridge. Those coming into the City were to keep to the west side of the bridge street, those leaving the City to the east side. The Common Council, led by Lord Mayor Sir Gerard Conyers, passed the 'keep to the left' law, which would one day be taken up throughout Britain and in a number of countries around the world, from Australia to Japan.

This order, aimed to ease the 'great inconvenience and Mischiefs by the disorderly Driving of Cars, Carts, Coaches and other Carriages, over *London-Bridge*, whereby the common Passage there is greatly obstructed, doth strictly order and injoin (pursuant to several former Orders made by this Court, for prevention of those Mischiefs)'.

To enforce the new law on the Bridge, three 'sufficient and able Persons' were appointed: one paid by the Governors of Christ's Hospital, one by the inhabitants of the ward of Bridge Within, and the third by the Bridge Wardens. These three were to be present at each end of the Bridge every day 'to hinder and prevent the said inconveniences; and for that purpose, to direct and take Care that all Carts, and Coaches, and other Carriages, going out of this City, do keep all along on the East [left, leaving the City] Side of the said Bridge; and that no cartman be suffered to stand across the said Bridge, to load or unload; and that they shall apprehend all such who shall be refractory, or offend herein, and carry them before some of his Majesty's Justices of the Peace for this City and Liberties, to be dealt with according to Law'.

Additionally the collector of tolls had to ensure that traffic was not held up as he collected the tolls. If a cartman did not have his coins ready he could be charged with obstruction, but in the crush of people, animals and carts it is difficult to see how this was enforced effectively. There were a lot of tolls to be taken:

For every cart or waggon with shod wheels	4d.
For drays with five Barrels	1d.
For each pipe or butt	1d.
For a ton of any goods	2d.
For anything less than a ton	1d.

Unbelievably, only a decade after the Great Fire, another very serious fire broke out in Southwark. This time the authorities acted quickly and decisively by blowing up the densely packed houses in its path to prevent it spreading to the Bridge. Sadly, many of the famous great old inns lining the east side of Borough High Street disappeared in 'The Great and Terrible Fire in Southwark'. The Queens Head, the Talbot, the George, the White Hart, the King's Head and the Green Dragon, together with a prison, a market and about five hundred houses 'were burned down, blown up and wholly destroyed'.

On 8 September 1725 a further fire started in Southwark, due to the carelessness of a servant in a brush-maker's house near St Olave's Street (now Tooley Street). On the first two arches on the east side of the Bridge all the houses were destroyed, and some on the opposite side damaged, as noted in Robert Seymour's *A Survey of the Cities of London and Westminster* of 1734. The Great Stone Gate prevented the spread of the flames, but it too was seriously damaged. Until this very late date – 1727, only about thirty years before all the buildings were removed – the gateway had remained a constricting eleven feet wide. It was rebuilt eighteen feet wide, enough for two coaches to pass, and included an entrance on each side for foot travellers.

There was always rivalry among people trying to get across the Bridge, and among the watermen who bunched together to wait for the tide to change, their craft sometimes dangerously locking together in the race to pass through the Bridge. There was also rivalry among the tradesmen on the Bridge. In the seventeenth and eighteenth centuries it remained a favourite location for booksellers. They sold cheap and cheerful publications, such as ready-reckoners, for people from the country, servant girls and sailors. Henry Tracey robustly defended his sign, the Three Bibles, and along with it one of his sidelines: the sale of a 'Balsam of Chili'. In 1724 he used the publication of a book, *The Mariner's Jewell; or a Pocket Companion for the Ingenious* by James Love, in an attempt to repel a nearby rival and interloper who had a similar sign and was selling something very much like Tracey's medicinal balsam. He took action by inserting a warning advertisement at the end of the book:

> All persons are desired to beware of a pretended Balsam of Chili, which for about these seven years last past hath been sold and continues to be sold by Mr John Stuart at The Old Three Bibles, as he calls his sign, although mine was the sign of The Three Bibles twenty years before his. This pretend Balsam sold by Mr Stuart resembles the true Balsam in colour, and is put up in the same Bottles; but it has been found to differ exceedingly from the true sort by several persons, who, through the carelessness of the buyers entrusted, have gone to the wrong place . . . Therefore all persons who send should give strict order to enquire for the name of Tracy; for Mr Stuart's being the very same sign, it is an easy matter to mistake. All other pretended Balsams of Chili, sold elsewhere, are shams and impositions, which may not only be ineffectual, but prove of worse consequence. The right sort is to be had of H. Tracey, at The Three Bibles on London Bridge, at 1s. 6d. a bottle, where it hath been sold these forty years.

The items on sale on the Bridge reflected what was fashionable. Paper-stainer Edward Butling in 1690 was 'At the Old Knave of Clubs at the Bridge-foot in Southwark', where he 'Maketh and Selleth all sorts of Hangings for Rooms in Lengths or in Sheets,

Frosted or Plain: Also a sort of Paper in Imitation of Irish Stitch, of the newest Fashion, and several other sorts viz.: Flock-work, Wainscot, Marble, Damask, Turkey-work. Also Shop-Books, Pocket Books, Writing Paper, Cards, and all Sorts of Stationery Wares.' Wall hangings were becoming fashionable; Mrs Pepys's closet was hung with 'counterfeit damask', probably a 'flocked' paper.

The shop names were colourfully and usefully memorable: a milliner at the Dolphin and Comb; a leather-seller who also made breeches at the Lamb and Breeches; a scale-maker at the Porrige (sic) Pot. The trades were loosely clustered together: stationery, books and toys were near the City end; more heavy-duty, dirty, smelly trades such as leather, coopering and dyeing, rope, twine and cork were near the Southwark end. Clothing and haberdashery was found anywhere along the Bridge. The traders still thrived in this prosperous location on the Bridge, but not for much longer.

CHAPTER EIGHT

'a public nuisance, long felt, and universally censured'

I'm amused at the signs,
As I pass through the town,
To see the odd mixture –
A Magpie and Crown;
The Whale and the Crow,
The Razon [Razor?] and Hen;
The Leg and Seven Stars;
The Axe and the Bottle;
The Tun and the Lute;
The Eagle and Child;
The Shovel and Boot.
                              British Apollo, 1710

THE SIXTH STAGE OF THE BRIDGE, 1727 to 1758, was the last period in which the colourful shops and buildings remained on it. George Dance the Elder (1700–68) – a Freeman of the Merchant Taylors Company and Master in 1799 – was a man who knew the Bridge well, for he had worked on several projects associated with it. At various times he was Surveyor for the Bridge House Estates, Clerk of the Works to the City of London and City Surveyor. It was Dance who accurately measured the Bridge for the first time in 1799, only thirty-two years before it was demolished. In 1745 it fell to him to design

Detail of a painting by Hogarth, showing the leaning houses of the Bridge.

the last houses to be built on the Bridge, which were at the northern end on the east side.

The construction of new buildings seemed to bode well for the future of the Bridge. At a time when the tenants in the older structures near the Southwark end were mainly pin- or needle-makers, 'oeconomical ladies [who] were wont to drive from the St James's end of town to make cheap purchases' first perhaps admired this colonnaded four-storey block of ten new houses; because of the colonnades this section was named 'the Piazza'. There were twenty-one eight-foot-high colonnades, yet it looked stark and featureless.

The uninteresting façade facing the street was plain, and its neatness jarred with the appearance of the rest of the bridge street, which was irregular in every respect.

Behind the colonnade was an eight-foot-deep walkway, and it was probably the intention to continue this colonnade all the way along the Bridge, whenever new houses were added. The space for the walkway had been created by recessing the ground floor, and it is hard to imagine how everything was accommodated, but it was.

On the ground floor of each of the ten houses was one room with a stairwell in a corner; the floor above had two rooms, each with a fireplace, and the floor above that was similar. The top floor with smaller windows was presumably for staff and servants. Along the roofline was a continuous balustrade. This plan, the only surviving one of houses on Old London Bridge, is preserved at the Guildhall.

The older parts of the Bridge created the opposite kind of view, and an unwelcome one. Where there had once been charm, the view from the wharves and quays on the east side was now 'exceedingly disagreeable', William Harrison's *Description of England* noted. The backs of houses had neither uniformity nor beauty, 'the line being broken by a great number of closets that projected from the buildings, and hung over the sterlings [piers]'. 'This deformity' looked even worse, because the houses extended a considerable distance over the sides of the Bridge, and some further than the others. The tops of all the arches, except the nearest to the viewer, were hidden by these structures. The Bridge appeared 'like a multitude of rude piers, with only an arch or two at the end, and the rest, consisting of beams, extending from the tops of flat piers, without any other arches, quite across the river'.

In contrast, Bristol Bridge of 1739 had been designed so the outer sides pleased the eye. Over the five floors on four arches there were oriel windows, decorative timberwork and ornamental plaster. Alexander Pope described it as being 'built on both sides like London Bridge, and as much crowded'. However, the River Avon was narrow, and there were only seven or eight, not perhaps as many as 138, dwellings to decorate.

The Great Stone Gate, the last gateway on the Bridge, rebuilt 1727.

In about 1750, Welsh writer and naturalist Thomas Pennant, in *Some Account of London*, confirmed that the arches of the Bridge were notably deformed by the piers, and the houses on both sides 'overhung and leaned in a most terrific manner'. His impression of the bridge street: 'I well remember the street on London Bridge, narrow, darksome, and dangerous to passengers from the multitude of carriages: frequent arches of strong timber crossed the street, from the tops of the houses to keep them together, and from falling into the river. Nothing but use could preserve the rest of the inmates, who soon grew deaf to the noise of the falling waters, the clamours of watermen, or the frequent shrieks of drowning wretches.' But at least by this time more space had been created on each side for views of the river, and more importantly to make places of refuge from the life-threatening carts and coaches. Those who regularly crossed the Bridge knew enough to stay close behind a carriage forcing its way through.

Occasionally an exceptional circumstance totally blocked the single crossing. To celebrate the peace treaty at Aix-la-Chapelle which ended the War of the Austrian Succession, George Friederich Handel somewhat unwillingly composed his famous *Music for the Royal Fireworks* for his patron, George II, who requested mainly martial instruments and 'hoped there would be no fidles'. On 21 April 1749 there was a rehearsal of the music in the public Vauxhall Gardens on the south bank, which attracted 12,000 people. After the free show, the huge crowd returning to the City completely blocked the Bridge, stopping all traffic for three hours. Six days later at the actual performance in Green Park, the fireworks, arranged in an ornate display on a specially constructed stage, set themselves – and the music stands – alight. This feature of the royal proceedings was enshrined in an engraving: 'A Grand Whim for Posterity to Laugh at'. A week later the Duke of Richmond produced his own spectacular firework display on the Thames, presumably to demonstrate how it should be done.

But the importance of the river crossing was affirmed for the future by the layout of the roads leading to Old London Bridge, which ensured that it would continue to attract a heavy proportion of the traffic no matter how many other bridges were built. Indeed, there would be plenty of traffic for all the bridges that were to come in a period reflecting the beginning of industrialization, extraordinary economic growth and international competition. The population of London reached about 700,000 in 1750, and according to one estimate, one out of every six adults lived in London at some point in their lives.

But the inevitable finally happened in 1729 when the old structure's 520-year monopoly was broken. Putney Bridge was the first of more than a dozen bridges that would be built over the Thames at London. W. Maitland's *History and Survey of London* records that the City had made great efforts to stop this bridge from being approved, as ever protecting the unique commercial opportunities of their London Bridge. The innkeepers of Southwark, the Borough of Southwark, the West Country bargemen and the Thames watermen – always opposed to any bridge – joined in the opposition, and submitted a petition to Parliament in 1722.

Self-interest, perhaps fear, did not win the day. The new bridge went ahead. Among its supporters was Sir Robert Walpole, a skilled politician. Hanoverian George I (1714–27) spoke no English and therefore could not preside at meetings of the Cabinet, where his place was taken by Walpole, who after 1721 in effect became England's first, and longest-serving, prime minister. Later he became the First Earl of Orford, and in 1749 published *Anecdotes of Painting in England, with some account of the principal artists*, in three volumes, the source for much of the information linking artists to the Bridge.

Soon there would be a much closer and more directly challenging rival: Westminster Bridge. First proposed in 1722, it was begun in 1738 and fully opened in 1750. Self-interest again came to the fore. A petition against this new bridge was supported by the alarmed bridge-dwellers themselves. This spot had always been an important river crossing, for the horse ferry by Lambeth Palace, home of the Archbishop of Canterbury, was almost opposite the power-base of Royal Westminster. For generations it had been used by people with horses and carts going to the west of the City. Now the See of Canterbury was paid compensation for loss of income from the well-used ferry.

Designed by the Swiss engineer Charles Labelye, fourteen-arched Westminster Bridge was elegant and wide. Jealousy of foreign Labelye meant he was deeply resented and denounced. When the bridge was nearly finished in 1749 there was severe subsidence, and the opening was delayed until 1750. The 'INSOLVENT IGNO-RANT ARROGATING SWISS' Labelye was furiously attacked in pamphlets and a ballad: 'The Downfall of Westminster Bridge, or my Lord in the Suds'. The 'lord' was the Earl of Pembroke, who had promoted Labelye. The Common Council responded to the abuse directed at them for the appointment by giving Labelye an honorarium of £2,000. All was put right, and Westminster Bridge (replaced in 1854–62), with its practical approach roads and width for four carriages to pass abreast, was judged to be far superior to Old London Bridge, which was clearly several centuries out of date. Now that the spell had been broken, thoughts turned to more bridges, and even to fully embanking the river.

The arrival in London of Antonio Canaletto (1697–1768) in 1741 coincided with the building of Westminster Bridge, which he painted many times both during and after its construction. Born near the Ponte di Rialto in Venice, his commissions there had melted away with the onset of the War of the Austrian Succession. He remained in the much quieter and more restrained London from 1746 to 1756, but the London he painted was always seen through his Venetian eyes, and he influenced English painters.

Canaletto also painted Old London Bridge, and one view from the west (upriver) in line and wash; William James, possibly one of his students, painted it from the south-east. In Venice Canaletto's main agent, English businessman and collector Joseph Smith, became British Consul. Smith – named 'the merchant of Venice' by Horace Walpole – eventually sold his own art collection to George IV for £20,000 – the foundation of today's almost unrivalled Royal Collection.

Contemporary illustrations of the Bridge include those of Samuel Scott, whose paintings, after the arrival of Canaletto, also took on an appealingly Venetian flavour, and Scott too painted Westminster Bridge. Old London Bridge was one of his favourite subjects, and he painted it eleven times between 1741 and 1771, including five views from the south-east, one from the south-west and a distant view from the west.

The charming Bridewell Footbridge over the Fleet where it joins the Thames was painted by Scott in the Venetian-looking *Entrance to the Fleet River*. There are timber wharves, Blackfriars Stairs and a busy river with West Country barges, lighters, sprit-rigged sailing barges and wherries carrying people and goods. After the Great

Fire of London, Sir Christopher Wren had been determined to beautify the Fleet River – appropriately called the Fleet Ditch – which flowed into the Thames above the Bridge, and was tidal as far as Holborn. A deep, elegant canal fifty feet wide had been constructed, lined with thirty-foot-wide wharves and crossed by four small humpbacked bridges. The painting makes one long for the now hidden river, but not for its deeply unpleasant contents.

Wren's considerable efforts were in vain. The locals continued to throw their rubbish into the Fleet, a problem compounded by both silting up and labour shortages. What was a river remained a 'ditch', as ever more filth flowed down it to be caught up at the bridge weir. Jonathan Swift described it in the *Tatler* in October 1710:

Now from all parts the swelling kennels flow,
And bear their trophies with them as they go:
Filth of all hues and colours seem to tell
What street they sail'd from, by their sight and smell . . .
Sweepings from butchers' stalls, dung, guts and blood,
Drown'd puppies, stinking sprats, all drenched in mud,
Dead cats, and turnip tops, come tumbling down the flood.

But at least one butcher benefited. 'A fatter boar was hardly ever seen than one taken up this day, coming out of Fleet Ditch into the Thames. It proved to be a butcher's near Springfield Bar, who had missed him five month, all which time he had been in the common sewer, and was improved in price from ten shillings to two guineas', as reported in the *Gentleman's Magazine* of 1844. The Fleet Ditch was unhealthy and dangerous. In 1763 a drunken barber from Bromley slipped in, got stuck in the mud and froze to death.

The City's waterways were becoming designated sewers, a process that had started with the Walbrook, which had been covered over even before John Stow's time (1598), and which now became the London Bridge Sewer. As for the Fleet, the solution in 1733 was to remove the bridges and arch it over as far as the Fleet Bridge; the job was completed in 1766. Under New Bridge Street and Farringdon Road the Fleet still flows unseen to the Thames.

Samuel Scott was a close friend of William Hogarth (1697–1764), who so memorably depicted the exuberance and cruelty of London at this time. Scott was with Hogarth in the group in 1732 that went on the famous 'Five Days' Peregrenation' along the Thames, enjoying the river while mocking the idea of the Grand Tour. Hogarth lived, was apprenticed and died in Leicester Fields (now Leicester Square, which his statue surveys). Success had evaded his clever and ambitious father, who was at heart a teacher; he had run a coffee house where only Latin was spoken in a noble attempt to promote Latin among adults, and was also a hack writer, a 'corrector of the press', and finally an engraver of frontispieces for books. In his autobiography Hogarth commented: 'But the tribe of booksellers remained as my father had left them when he died . . . of an illness occasioned partly by the treatment he met with from this set of people . . .'

The son, who reputedly lived on Old London Bridge for a time, had begun by engraving cutlery and tableware, where he worked on 'the monsters' of heraldry, then on plates for book- and print-sellers. In Hogarth's younger days, according to Ephraim Hardcastle in *Wine and Walnuts*, which is the only source, he lived on the first floor on the east side of the Bridge adjoining the Great Stone Gate. Hardcastle described his room, which resembled an alchemist's laboratory. Through the smoke-stained confusion could be seen 'a German-stove, crucibles, pipkins, nests of drawers with rings of twine to pull them out; here a box of asphaltum, there glass-stoppered bottles, varnishes, dabbers, gravers, etching tools, balls of wax, obsolete copper-plates, many engraved on both sides, caricatures and poetry scribbled over the walls; a pallet hung up as an heirloom, the colours dry upon it, hard as stone; an easel; all the multifarious *arcanalia* of engraving, and, lastly, a Printing-press!'

When the successful painter and engraver published his twelve prints in *The Effects of Industry and Idleness* series, he went round the print shops, pleased to see a crowd at each. They were not, however, entranced by Hogarth's moral tale – almost like a strip cartoon – but were trying to identify each person on whom he had based a caricature: the world's largest city was still small enough to have this level of intimacy, and Hogarth was himself a readily recognized figure in the streets of London.

Life on the Bridge with all its characters and ever-varying turmoil would have appealed to his unerring eye for human foibles. Hogarth did paint the Bridge, for a glimpse of it can be seen in *The Death of the Countess*, Plate VI in his great moralistic *Mariage à la Mode* series (1743–5). The dying countess is at her merchant father's house, which has seen better days, confirming the advancing decrepitude of the area on and around the Bridge. The miserly father is seen removing his dying daughter's ring; there is a bare floor, a starving dog, a broken pane in the window. Through one pane there is a tantalizing glimpse of the jumble of tilting houses on the Bridge – about twelve years before they were removed – as a Thames barge, mast lowered, resolutely aims for one of the arches.

Another bridge, a drawbridge, was central to one of Hogarth's most famous works. On a trip to France he was arrested as a spy while sketching a drawbridge in Calais. Even though he demonstrated to the governor that he was an artist by drawing him, he was incarcerated, and eventually escorted on to a ship by soldiers, who left only when the vessel was a league out to sea and after mocking him. He got his revenge in the print *The Gate of Calais, O the Roast Beef of Old England, etc.*, published in March 1749. In it an immense piece of beef has been landed at Calais for a well-known inn there that catered to the English. Before the jaw-like gates of the drawbridge Hogarth drew images of a starving nation. Friars follow the beef, fisherwomen hungrily survey a monkfish, their faces resembling that of the fish. This print was published again during the British beef crisis of the late 1990s.

Another artist connected with the Bridge at this time was John Laguerre, son of the French artist Louis Laguerre who painted allegorical decoration at the Palace of Whitehall, Petworth, Chatsworth and elsewhere. Born in London, young Laguerre lived on the first floor of a house belonging to a book-seller, Crispin Tucker, who owned half a shop. Laguerre's studio – in the rooms that Hogarth had once occupied – was apparently a bow-windowed room projecting out over the water on the east side of the Bridge, which trembled when a heavy tide came in. From his vantage point he would have seen lively, ever-changing views that would have inspired most artists, but, lazy and careless, he gave up art to become an actor and died a pauper in 1748.

A scene similar to that which Laguerre would have seen from his studio is depicted by William Marlow – an apprentice of Scott's and also influenced by Canaletto – in his 1760 *Fresh Wharf, London Bridge*. With the Bridge in view, there are exotically dressed merchants, and a bookkeeper with tri-corner hat sits on a bale checking a list of bales and barrels. Among other paintings by Marlow was the 1788 *London Bridge from Pepper Alley Stairs*.

The Bridge also featured in the eventful life of French artist Dominick Serres. He ran away to sea to avoid entering the Church. From Auch, Gascony, he walked to a Spanish port, sailed for South America as an ordinary seaman, and later became master of a trading vessel. During the Seven Years War (1756–63) he was captured by an English frigate, and brought to London where as a prisoner-of-war he was incarcerated in the Marshalsea prison in Borough High Street, Southwark, in 1758. On his release he set up a shop on the Bridge, where he painted seascapes, influenced by Monamy, and reflecting his own skills and experiences at sea. With the removal of the buildings on the Bridge, he was forced to move to Piccadilly, where he successfully sold his paintings. Knowing there was a market for paintings of events in the American War of Independence, he completed one. In 1792, a year before his death, he became Marine Painter to George III and Librarian to the Royal Academy; large seapieces by him are at Hampton Court Palace and Greenwich. His son, John Thomas Serres, who knew J.M.W. Turner, would also become Marine Painter to the King.

A 1751 drawing by John Boydell – illustrator, engraver and printer – depicted the sad sight of the once brilliant Nonesuch House, from the downstream viewpoint of St Olave's Stairs. It was still there, but almost all its fantastic ornamentation had gone. The windows were reduced in size, and sheds had been built along the roofline as this once magnificent structure deteriorated. But the building so famously held together with wooden pegs proved sound: in spite of severe neglect, it was still standing – used as tenements – until the mid-1700s when all the buildings on Old London Bridge were finally removed.

Boydell was also a successful print publisher on the corner of Old Jewry and Cheapside. He formed the basis of the substantial and important collection now in the Guildhall Art Gallery when in 1789 he presented several paintings to the Corporation. One painting by Richard Paton, the figures painted by Francis Wheatley, depicts the lively scene of the Lord Mayor's Parade on the river in 1789, for among Boydell's high aims – he was an alderman and Lord Mayor 1790–1 – was to show Londoners 'the most likely paths to arrive at Honour and Riches'. Another Lord Mayor's Parade is depicted in a memorable painting by William Logsdail, *The Ninth of November* (1888), the ninth being the traditional date for the parade (now the second Saturday in November); the parade has sadly been held on land since 1857, depriving Londoners of the sight of the magnificent water procession of the barges of the Lord Mayor and the Livery Companies. In yet another painting, in 1827 the waterborne Lord Mayor's Parade is passing under Rennie's half-built bridge, decorated with flags.

Boydell was an exceptional character who created a 'Shakespeare Gallery', in a building in Pall Mall designed by George Dance the Elder, with 162 paintings by well-known artists. He became carried away with his project, and in 1803 he spent huge sums of money on a volume of plates of these paintings to accompany a nine-volume edition of Shakespeare's works. The unfortunate result of his enthusiasm was bankruptcy.

The seventeenth-century tradition of frost fairs continued over the next two hundred years. In 1739 severe weather began on Christmas Day, and another fair soon emerged on the ice. But when on 21 January 1740 it became slightly warmer, the ice started to thaw and the stall-holders abruptly departed for the safety of the riverbank. The ice broke up into large sheets, leaving a jumbled vista. The *Universal Spectator* of 26 January 1740 reported that on the Monday morning 'the inhabitants of the western prospect of the Bridge were presented with a very odd scene, for on the opening of their windows there appeared underneath on the river a parcel of booths, shops and huts of different forms, but without any inhabitants . . . Here stood a booth with trinkets, here a hut with a dram of Old Gold, in another place a skittle frame and pins, and in a fourth "The Noble Art and Mystery of Painting".' No lives were lost when the ice broke up, but it was dangerous, even impossible to retrieve valuables.

The river then refroze in fearsomely jagged chunks of ice. But among the bumps and lumps of ice was one long main 'street' on the river following the City shore, while others at right angles to it crossed to the opposite side. One of these followed along the path where Westminster Bridge was under construction, depicted by Jan Griffier the Younger in *The Thames during the Great Frost of 1739–40*. Small booths sold toys, millinery and souvenirs. Instead of having his own name printed on a souvenir sheet, Hogarth had 'Printed on the Ice' the name of 'Trump', his bull-terrier, whose face, it was truthfully said, resembled his own. Amusements included bear-baiting, cat-throwing – especially distressing to Hogarth, who exposed gross cruelty to animals in his art – and 'flying coaches', being flung around on a roundabout.

'Multitudes' walked over the river, and when the ice again broke up some lives were tragically lost. Although the Bridge survived, according to *The Daily Post* of 14 February 1740, the severe damage to the piers cost Bridge Wardens John Lund and Thomas Hyde several thousand pounds to put right.

The Thames was still fished, and on the bridge street at least one shop appropriately enough sold fishing gear. The Blue Boar had been on the Bridge before 1633, for in a list of the 'Houses that were Burnt upon the Bridge' recorded in the *Gentleman's Magazine* in 1824, the 'Blew Bore' was listed as 'emptie'. This shop on the west side 'by the sixteen-house from the North end' was leased in 1744 to 'Coles Child, haberdasher'. In 1755 Coles Child chiefly sold toys, but among his range of other goods was 'Fishing rods & Lines & all Sorts of Fishing Tackle'.

But toys and fishing gear were an infinitesimal part of his extraordinary and overwhelming range. This included needles of every kind, thimbles, buttons in cane, hazel, horn, leather and Bath metal, shoemakers' tackle, leather ink pots and inkhorns, horn dram cups, drinking horns, writing implements of every kind, scissors, knives and razors, tobacco and snuff items, spurs, corkscrews, whipcord, combs and toothbrushes, curtain rings, hog rings, brass nutmeg graters, steel and whalebone busks and powder boxes. There were 'Fine Knitt & Spring Purses, Necklaces and Pendants, Essence Bottles in pewter, Brass & Bone Curtain Rings Powder Flasks & Shott Baggs Powder Horns & Gun Flints Hunting Horns', dog collars, bells and bellows. For the children there were marbles and trumpets, balls, counters, and toys in brass, pewter, tin, lead and wood. And much more in what must have been a fascinating shop.

Mr Child remained on the Bridge until the house was pulled down in 1760, when he moved close by to Upper Thames Street. In later entries he is described as 'toyman', by then in houses facing St Magnus. Coles Child, born in 1702, was buried at St Magnus in 1771, where there is a 1798 memorial tablet to his nephew of the same name.

A unique account remains of work and life in a shop on the Bridge. Even at this late date, London Bridge was still making history. On the most commercial site in London a shop named Flint and Palmers was the first to have fixed prices – a landmark in the retail world. One day when they opened their doors each item among the variety of goods had a price tag. Robert Owen (1771–1858), the social reformer, worked there as a boy, receiving his board and lodgings and £25 per year. He recalled the experience in *The Life of Robert Owen by Himself*: 'Not much time was allowed for bargaining, a price being fixed for everything and, compared with other houses, cheap. If any demur was made or much hesitation, the article asked for was withdrawn, and as the shop was generally full from morning till late in the evening, another customer was attended to.'

The large shop was crowded from eight a.m. until eleven p.m. And each night the 'innumerable items of haberdashery' had to be tidied up and restocked, which usually took until two a.m. The boy Owen was 'scarcely able with the aid of the bannister to go upstairs to bed'. Nevertheless, by eight a.m. every morning all the assistants were up and ready for the customers, who Owen considered to be of an inferior class, based on his previous shop experience, which had started at the age of ten. After just a few hours' sleep, considerable effort was required by the staff to be correctly presented each morning. The boy had to wait his turn for the hairdresser 'to powder and pomatum and curl my hair'. His hair was tied in a stiff pigtail, with a large curl on each side.

Business at Flint and Palmers was brisk due to the low prices and the elimination of time wasted on bargaining, and Mr Flint became wealthy. When other shopkeepers observed his success and growing fortune, they too began pricing their goods. It was another landmark for the Bridge.

At the Bridge, a supremely logical step for a trader was to link the selling of life-saving equipment to the famously dangerous waters. The bridgefoot at Southwark was the chosen location in about 1760 of John Ward, a cork merchant, who was the 'Inventor and Proprietor of the Cork Jacket, as approv'd by the Society of Arts. At his Warehouse, the Sign of the Cork Jacket the foot of London Bridge, Southwark.' He also sold cork, 'and cuts all sorts of corks, Where Merchants (for Exportation), Brewers, Vintners, Shopkeepers &c. may be supplyed with any Quantity, at Reasonable Rates'. Ward's life-saving contrivance of the sleeved and buttoned cork life jacket must have been one of the earliest inventions to gain the approval of the new 'Society for the Encouragement of Arts Manufactures and Commerce'.

Later, in 1806, a Mr F.C. Daniels of the Gun Dock at Wapping produced an advertisement in caricature demonstrating his 'Life Preserver in Case of Shipwreck' on seven individuals, also wearing swimming caps and playing musical instruments, while passing through Old London Bridge to the cheers of both commons and nobility, who watched from nearby craft.

The shop and tavern signs added interest to an already lively scene, as they had done for centuries. In so vividly appealing for trade they colourfully guided the illiterate to the right address. But as competition increased, the poles on which they hung became dangerously longer, and the equally larger and insecure signs themselves sometimes fell fatally on people's heads or blew away in a high wind. This tradition would come to an end in 1762, when street numbering was required by law. Until then, each well-known image indicated the trade beneath. A cupid and torch was the symbol for a glazier; an elephant represented combs of ivory and other items and so on.

Personal decoration and beautification was another theme among the shops on the Bridge – from goldsmiths and necklace-sellers to hair merchants. The few goldsmiths recorded included John Buck at the Black Boy in 1710. In 1750 goldsmith and jeweller Basil Denn Junior, at 'Ye Gold Ring on London Bridge near Southwark', sold 'all sorts of Plate, Rings & Jewels in the best & Newest fashion', as well as second-hand plate, jewels and watches '& Gives ye most Mony for the Same'. On his tradesman's card a rich rococo frame is hung with various specimens of his art and craft; at the foot of the design are emblems of Freemasonry. Although records of others may have been lost – and Cheapside was famed throughout Europe as the location for gold and jewellery – it seems odd that there were so few jewellers on Old London Bridge, for inhabited bridges were often deemed the most suitable places for luxury goods, as can still be seen on the Ponte Vecchio in Florence.

Necklace-maker James Howard was in 1735 at the Hand & Beads selling 'stone necklaces 5s., undress earrings at 2s. 3d., drops at 4s. and so on'; he occupied a tenement at the north end on the west side, paying an annual rent of £6 13s. 4d. up until Lady Day 1760, after which, no doubt, his house was pulled down. The business then relocated nearby at another Hand & Beads, that of similarly named John Howard, on Fish Street Hill. The latter, about 1763, was 'Necklace-maker from London Bridge at Ye Hand & Beads, next the Monument Yard, Fish Street Hill, London'. His wares included 'Stomachers, Sleeve Knotts, Caps and Agretts, of every Quality and Degree' of English or French design, 'Wax, Garnet-Jett, Paste-Stones, or other Compositions, for Dress and

Undress'. In a contemporary engraved view of Fish Street Hill John Howard's sign, the Hand & Beads, can be seen projecting from the house 'next ye Monument Yard'.

Hair merchant John Allan in about 1755 was at the Locks of Hair, stocked with 'all sorts of Hair, Curled or Uncurled, Bags, roses, Cauks, Ribbons, Weaving, Sewing Silk, Cards and Blocks. With all goods made by Peruke Makers at the Lowest Prices.' He was granted a seven-year lease of his shop on the west side near the middle of the Bridge, from 1750, at a rental of £36 per annum, but paid a reduced rent from the expiration of his lease until the house was demolished.

Right to the very end the Bridge remained popular with stationers and book-sellers. There was John Benskin, a stationer 'at Ye Bible and Star on Ye Bridge London'. His card comprised an allegorical design of two figures, representing Genius and Prudence, above books and articles of stationery.

A prominent stationer and book-seller was James Brooke at Ye Anchor & Crown near the Square on the west side from 1702 to his death in 1750. In 1718 Baskett, the King's Printer, mortgaged his letterpress and other stock at Oxford to Brooke for £4,000. In 1738 Brooke was made sheriff of the City of London, and on his death he bequeathed a sum of £50 to the Poor of the Stationers Company.

But what was to be done about popular, crumbling, dangerous, inadequate Old London Bridge? Although some members of the Common Council favoured rebuilding, the majority wanted the old structure to remain but with drastic changes.

Implementing the plans of George Dance the Elder for a new bridge would cost £185,950, much more than the Bridge House Estates could afford. This prompted an alternative suggestion: widening the existing bridge after removing all of its superstructure. A committee formed to examine the matter announced that they were 'humbly of opinion that the houses upon London Bridge are a public nuisance, long felt, and universally censured and complained of'. All houses were to be be taken down, but first Mr

Dance, the City Surveyor, was to make a survey of the piers and their foundations.

By about 1750 most of the houses were leaning in a worrying way, and a number of the older houses on the downriver east side towards Southwark sagged by as much as eighteen inches. In 1755 a correspondent in one of the London newspapers asked why the new houses on the east side at the City end ('the Piazza'), built only ten years before, were 'already declined about half a yard'. The houses on the west side were built to the same plan and of the same materials. Were the foundations at fault? Was it due to shoddy workmanship? One comment: 'Yet, it is obvious to every person who passes over the Bridge that those on the west side do not lean any more now than the new ones . . . at the north end of the Bridge; for about the middle, the houses on both sides are so bad, that I cannot justly say which are the worst . . .' The conclusion: the foundations were bad.

But Dance's report maintained that the foundations were good, and with the usual annual repairs were likely to stand for some time to come.

His plan and elevation for the alterations, costing £30,000, were accepted. The houses – including the Piazza built between 1745 and 1747 – were to be removed, along with the former Chapel, Nonesuch House and the Great Stone Gate (rebuilt as recently as 1727–8). Additionally, two of the arches near the centre were to be made into one – the Great Arch – by removing a pier, and the roadway widened to forty-six feet, leaving space for footways. And there was to be a balustraded stone parapet on each side.

Time was – albeit very slowly – running out for the Bridge. On 25 June 1756 the London Bridge Act was passed giving the Common Council of the Corporation the authority to buy and demolish all the houses on or near the Bridge, which would allow the widening for the speedier flow of traffic. Measurements were specified: width thirty-one feet; footways seven feet. Lamps were to be kept burning from sunset to sunrise, and a watch was to be maintained. The cost of all this work was to be defrayed out of the funds of Bridge House Estates.

The Act dealt at length with mortgaged premises, tithes, rates and land tax, preserved the rights and privileges of the Waterworks, authorized the erection of toll-gates and toll-houses, and detailed numerous additions to the tolls already charged, on the credit of which the Mayor and the Corporation were empowered to raise £30,000 per annum until the estimated cost of £160,000 had been reached.

The tolls imposed to help defray the cost were considered high by those going over the Bridge: coaches drawn by six horses 2s.; by four horses 1s. 6d.; 1s. for fewer than that. Horses, mules and asses used as pack animals were a penny each and pedestrians a half-penny (on Sundays raised to a penny).

The watermen were still on the river, still vigorously plying their trade along it:

> Two-pence to London Bridge, threepence to the Strand,
> Fourpence, Sir, to Whitehall, or else you'll go by land.

Tolls were also to be imposed on those passing under the Bridge. The watermen as usual vociferously defended their interests. They kept their argument simple: they didn't want any bridge, and to charge a toll for what was an obstruction, a danger to life and harmful to business was contradictory and objectionable. But the tolls went ahead:

> For every hoy, barge, vessel, lighter or other craft having any goods on board not exceeding five tons burthen, for every time any such craft shall pass through any of the arches of the Bridge – two pence.
> Not exceeding ten tons – threepence.
> Not exceeding twenty-five tons – sixpence.
> And above the burthen of twenty-five tons – one shilling.

Exempt were all craft loaded with straw, manure, dung, compost or lime to be used for cultivating the soil. But the tolls were diffi-cult to enforce, and the actual collection of them hindered both

The burning of the temporary wooden bridge, 11 April 1758.

traffic and navigation. However, in 1765 the farm or lease to collect the tolls for going through the Bridge was re-let for 2,000 guineas and a yearly rent of £735 for twenty-one years.

With funding organized, the next move was to make the work of removing the houses much easier and safer by erecting a temporary wooden bridge on the west side of the stone bridge. It was built of oak above the piers, entered at each end via the stone bridge and opened in October 1757.

But all these irreversible – even unthinkable – changes were alarming to many people. Perhaps because of this, only about six months after the wooden bridge was opened for use, late in the evening of 11 April 1758, fire broke out – suspiciously, in two places at the same time. The dry oak meant that the whole bridge was soon on fire. Sir Charles Asgill, Lord Mayor, led the efforts to stop it spreading, but it '. . . continued to burn till noon the next day, when the ruins fell into the river', as recorded in the *Annual Register*.

Oddly – was it planned? – none of the houses on the stone Bridge was burned, but the 'troughs' that took the water from the Waterworks to Southwark were gone. Now there was no usable bridge of either wood or stone, and the way under was obstructed by fallen debris, except in the arches close to the shores, and those were the places blocked by the waterwheels. There was no direct run through.

Just before the fire erupted, some strange goings-on had caught the attention of several people. A Mrs John Dennis, the *London Chronicle* reported, was in the watch house of the Dyers Hall near the Bridge when she happened to notice the light of a lantern near the Chapel pier, then between the timbers of the great pier. It disappeared, then there were three more near the Chapel pier where the fire actually started. A small flame came and went, and shortly there was a fierce blaze. She rushed to the wharf to raise the alarm. Watchmen at the Custom House Quays and others reported that they saw someone in a boat carrying a candle in a lantern 'who was busy about the wood opposite the stone pier, which is to be taken down to lay two arches into one [the Great Arch]'. They saw him extinguish the candle and go off, and a few minutes later the bridge burst into flames.

The cause of the fire was never proven, although the Court of Common Council offered a reward, but everyone believed that the wooden bridge had been torched and they would never be convinced otherwise.

The Common Council of the Corporation of the City of London now demonstrated their great capability in dealing with such a devastating emergency. On 13 April – less than two days after the fire – they brought together George Dance the Elder, Sir Robert Taylor, Architect of the Bank of England, and Thomas Philips, who were to be jointly responsible for the construction of a new temporary bridge. These men concluded that if enough workmen were available and could work on Sundays, the bridge could be repaired by 1 May, to be usable for coaches and carriages. The City responded robustly: five hundred men were immediately employed to work day and night to make a passageway over the Bridge itself, and another five hundred were engaged in building another temporary bridge alongside.

Six days later Old London Bridge was ready for foot-passengers, and it was opened for carriages in less than a month. The second temporary wooden bridge was in use by 18 October 1758.

The Common Council also ensured there would be no repeat performance. A watch was kept every night, amid rumours that someone intended to set fire to the bridge again. For the first fortnight a boat containing five watermen armed with blunderbusses and cutlasses was stationed under the Great Arch from ten p.m. to five a.m. After that two armed men patrolled in a special wooden gallery built on the bridge just below the line of the road.

The City appealed to Parliament for financial help, and were awarded a grant of £15,000 towards the extra expenditure. At the same time the tolls for passing over and under the Bridge were abolished, presumably to ease the agitation stirred up by the changes. But John Noorthouck's *A New History of London* noted the unequivocal new law to protect the Bridge. No quarter would be given if any part of the structure or the works belonging to it was wilfully harmed. The penalty was death without benefit of clergy.

The tradesmen on the Bridge had a well-honed instinct for what would sell. After the 1758 fire William Herbert at the sign of the Golden Globe under the Piazza – within yards of the fire – quickly responded to the sensational event by publishing a print: *An Exact View of London Bridge since the conflagration of the Temporary Bridge*.

The fate of St Magnus was still linked to the Bridge in what was the last of centuries of fires. On 18 April 1760 fire broke out at the 'Oyl Shop' adjoining the church. So momentous was this disaster to the church that the tale is hugely inscribed in gold on the north-east wall of the vestibule. The fire quickly burned down the vestry room, destroyed most of the roof and 'consumed the organ'. As if that weren't enough, the parish of St Magnus was charged £2 3s. 9d. for the fire engines. But by 1762 the organ was 're-inflated and made good again', and a new vestry room and an 'engine house' were built on the south side.

Mishaps continued to be recorded in the church accounts. There were payments to a man hurt at the church corner, 'to get Anne Tully into the Hospital having broke her leg on the Bridge', and 'for carrying the Woman home that went to drown herself'. In 1758 a woman and child were crushed to death between two carts. Sometimes there was a happy result: in 1758 a boat with six passengers coming through the bridge weir overturned, but several boats set off to assist, and no one was lost.

Thefts occurred in the Chapel itself as well as in the shops on the Bridge. In the confined space and compressed turmoil people, especially country-folk, were an easy target. There were always gangs waiting for them on both Old London Bridge and Westminster Bridge. But the danger started far back on the approach roads to the Bridge. At St George's Fields in 1754 a group of villains passed themselves off as a press gang to a visitor from the country. When they promised to let him go if he handed over all his money, he gave them his two guineas, and went on his way. But at the bridge-foot he encountered a real press gang and was seized a second time. He told them what had already happened to him, and showed them the way to the tavern where the gang had gone, and where the bold imposters were arrested.

*   *   *

But great and final changes were coming for the Bridge. The intense pressure of people and traffic was finally overcoming fear, hesitation and lethargy. In 1763 – very late in the day – the tower of St Magnus was opened up at street level so the footpath on to the Bridge at the City end could go right through it. Wren must have anticipated this, for the tower was built so strongly that the side arches could be opened up without any weakening of the whole structure.

Two arches of the Bridge had been knocked into one to create the Great Arch in 1759, but this created serious problems only a few months later. The power of the waterwheels was lessened because most water flowed through the Great Arch and with much more force, also scouring the base of the piers and causing erosion. The actual excavations during the construction of the Great Arch had weakened both the new arch and the adjoining piers. The situation looked so alarming that people began to avoid going either over or under the Great Arch. Bridge and canal expert John Smeaton was called to come from Yorkshire at once. He recommended that the City buy back the stone from the City gateways that had just been demolished and throw it around the piers. Once again the City acted decisively. The work started immediately, even though it was a Sunday. The cost was £100,000. But the problems were mounting: the iron water pipes laid across the Bridge in 1762 leaked and the water percolated into the stone, the expensive damage thus caused resulting in an enquiry, reported in the *Public Advertiser* of 7 June 1762.

The section of houses between the Drawbridge and the Square was removed. In a section appropriately called Middle West, the last tenant was the wonderfully named Clement Corderoy of Nonesuch House, who had sublet to William West; they gave up possession at Christmas 1756, and in February 1757 work began on taking down these houses. The *Gentleman's Magazine* reported that workmen soon found three pots of gold and silver from the reign of Elizabeth in one of the houses – probably in Nonesuch House, the only Elizabethan building to be demolished at this time – and one imagines that the find gave the workmen a considerable burst of energy. The next section to go sat north of the Square on the City end of the Bridge, and included the new block of ten houses designed by Dance in 1745. In 1760 two more sections were vacated. Thomas Wright and William Gill, who occupied the former Chapel, were the final tenants on the eastern, downriver, side. The sad progression of demolition continued. On the north-west section twenty-two leases terminated simultaneously.

Newspapers had recorded the all-too-usual deaths during work on such a large project: in 1758 a workman fell from a ladder and was drowned, as was a carpenter demolishing one of the houses; and in 1762 a man crossing the Bridge was killed instantly when hit by a piece of broken brick from one of the houses.

South of the Drawbridge Lock all the tenants had gone by 1758. In June 1761 the leases of Elizabeth Smith and Alice Court expired together, and on 25 March 1762 the very last tenancy ended. This tenement on the east side had been held by Mary Russell and let to John Evans, who seems to have had the distinction of being the last dweller on the medieval Bridge that had been so colourfully inhabited for the previous 550 years.

The Great Stone Gate, the last vestige of what had been a great barbican of the City – never taken in battle – had been removed in 1760. The royal coat of arms was purchased by a publican who built it into his tavern in King Street (now Newcomen Street); he then named it the King's Arms. When this pub was rebuilt in 1890 the coat of arms most fortunately was retained, and is still there on a modern front.

So much a part of the vitality of the Bridge for four and a half centuries, the sign of the chained and muzzled bear no longer swung at the bridgefoot in Southwark. The Bear, built about 1319, was demolished in 1761 as part of the alterations. Here too Elizabethan gold and silver coins were found 'and other monies to a considerable value'.

All the houses were down by 1762. The rent books of the Bridge House Estates, following the final entry for each section of the houses, noted in their usual meticulous way: 'All the houses on this part of the Bridge have been taken down in pursuance of the late

Act of Parliament (Geo. II. 29, 1755) made to improve, &c., London Bridge.' The twenty-foot-wide Bridge now became a safer forty-six feet wide.

The appearance of Old London Bridge was changed for ever: now it looked much the same as many other bridges. But a shiver of romance still clung to the stone structure in its historic setting, and artists continued to be attracted to it.

CHAPTER NINE

'a remedy for this evil'

The Bravest sight that I e'er ken
Was London Bridge with its gay shopmen:
Where all might find what they did lack,
From an ABC to a pin's pack;
But now the shops are clear'd away,
Heigh-ho! Alas! and a well-a-day!

Anon.

I T HAD TAKEN ABOUT FOUR YEARS TO REMOVE ALL THE HOUSES AND GATEWAYS ON OLD LONDON BRIDGE, and to create what was a more practical, but vastly different-looking structure in its seventh and final stage, 1762–1831. The *British Chronicle* reported that Old London Bridge was now 'finished in the Gothic taste'.

The square buttresses were ornamented with pairs of lancet-shaped panels with an elongated quatrefoil between them. At somewhat irregular intervals, due to the original structure of the Bridge, the piers were built out in pentagonal form at street level to make recesses for pedestrians. Dickens mentioned them in *David Copperfield*: 'I was often up at six o'clock, and my favourite lounging place was old London Bridge, where I was wont to sit in one of the stone recesses, watching the people go by, or to look over the balustrades at the sun shining in the water, and lighting up the golden flame on the Monument.' Spaced out along the Bridge, some of the recesses had handsome half-domes of solid stone – seven on each side – in which to shelter.

The northern arches in the seventh stage, and St Magnus the Martyr.

There were stone balustrades on the river side of the walkways, which, it was triumphally noted, were wider than those on Westminster Bridge. On the inner side – the roadway side – pedestrians were protected by chain-linked posts 'to secure foot passengers from any injuries which might otherwise happen from cattle'. In 1787 Thomas Rowlandson produced a vigorous aquatint, *The*

Overdrove Ox, a chaotic scene as a bolting ox is being chased across the altered Bridge by a rabble of people and dogs, and a coach is overturned. This is one of several views by the London-born caricaturist that included the Bridge in its final stage.

No sooner were the alterations completed than events took a slight backward step when a 250-ton ship broke from her moorings to be carried by the tide and ice up against the Bridge: the bowsprit demolished twenty feet of the new stone balustrading, and came to rest reaching halfway across the bridge street; the crew of

One of the stone alcoves, erected 1758–62.

men and boys clambered along the pointed spar to make a unique ascent on to the old structure.

Artists and romance were never far from Bridge and river. Lord Byron, so famously and notoriously 'mad, bad and dangerous to know', once swam from Lambeth to Old London Bridge, a distance of about two and a half miles, no doubt at an ebbing tide. It was challenging, but not as challenging as this gentleman-athlete's later famous swim across the Hellespont, re-enacting Leander's legendary nightly adventure.

A glamorous figure, Byron was the most renowned English traveller of the time, but the extent of his European wanderings was exceeded by those of J.M.W. Turner. Dissimilar in both background and appearance, they did however share an appreciation of the natural beauty of the world. Plain Turner was an admirer of elegant Byron's poetry, whose words seemed to echo the scenes painted by the great watercolourist and landscape painter. Turner in the 1820s would illustrate *Byron's Life and Works*.

Of all artists, the Thames was Turner's touchstone, and he never lived far from it. He was born in the bustling City in 1775, but it was the serenity of the river and of nature that appealed. With his love of nostalgic retrospection, he depicted Old London Bridge several times, and the Thames, fishermen and shipping on numerous occasions. Turner's sketch *Old London Bridge, with the Monument and the Church of St Magnus King and Martyr* shows the Bridge in its final stage after all the buildings had been removed. The view looks north from the mid-arch, upstream to dominating St Magnus. From the sketch he painted a finished watercolour dated about 1795, in which two boats attempt to negotiate the rapids at the bridge weir as the river flowing to the sea dangerously meets the force of the incoming tide, making it look as if the river is flowing backwards.

Early in his career, Turner moved to a house in George Street, Hanover Square. He was not pleased to learn that artist John Thomas Serres (1759–1825), son of Dominick, would have the use of two rooms in the house for part of the day. He feared he would be disturbed because, although the Serres family lived elsewhere, Mrs Serres, also an artist, was violent. This may have reminded Turner of home life with his unstable mother. Serres also painted Old London Bridge in *River Thames, Old Fishmongers Hall and Billingsgate.* Due to extravagant spending, blamed on his wife, Serres ended up in a debtors' prison.

Throughout his life Turner studied the Old Masters, including Canaletto and the Venetian school, and his own first painting of Venice was of the Bridge of Sighs. Bridges appeared in the whole range of Turner's paintings, with themes from classical antiquity to contemporary life, including the two upriver bridges at Walton-on-Thames, which also had been painted by Canaletto, as Old London Bridge had been in the mid-1700s.

Various strands in the story of the Bridge somehow come together at this time and in Turner. There was a mood of confidence and change in Hanoverian London, the hypocrisy of which Hogarth was so unrelenting and uncompromising in depicting. Turner saw around him the unsettling beginnings of social and industrial change, and he also observed his patron Lord Egremont's work for social change at Petworth, his Surrey estate.

From 1809 Turner regularly visited Petworth, described by Constable as 'that house of art', where he painted and studied Van Dyck's paintings. As it happened, this was where the portrait hung of Mrs Kirke, who had drowned at the Bridge in 1641 (the only known image of the thousands who perished there); Turner painted pastiches of some of these Van Dycks. Elsewhere, he made large coloured drawings, including one of the habitable Pulteney Bridge at Bath, and a pencil and watercolour of St George's, Bloomsbury, which had been designed by the architect Nicholas Hawksmoor, who had assisted Wren and was interested in Old London Bridge.

In this period after the French Revolution in 1789, paintings poured into London, and one very fine collection – so extensive it took two huge sales to disperse it – was that of the Duke of Orléans. This recalls the captivity in London of the Duke's ancestor, which led to the creation of the first precious illustration of the Bridge, dating from about 1500.

*   *   *

Old London Bridge in its final stage – after 550 years – was no longer inhabited, but passing through the Bridge was still avoided by the sensible among those who actually had a choice. Dr Samuel Johnson and his biographer, James Boswell, went to Greenwich by water on 30 July 1763: 'We landed at the "Old Swan" and walked to Billingsgate where we took oars and moved along silver Thames.' Boswell noted that if the distinguished writer and lexicographer received any verbal abuse from the watermen, he gave as good as he got.

But for those who worked on the river there was no way to escape the bridge weir. In 1763 when two lightermen, one in a boat loaded with coals, the other in one loaded with stone, were competing to be the first through the Bridge, both sank; but the men were saved by boats which put off to help. In such races to get through, boats could become locked together with disastrous results. One barge, heavily loaded with timber, ran against a pier, taking part of it away, and with the bump one of the bargemen fell overboard and was drowned. In 1767, a boat with three women and two men over-turned in the darkness, and all perished, although several boats with lanterns had tried to rescue them.

Drownings occurred in every possible way, and the cause could be something as light-hearted as a wager. In 1803 *The Times* reported: 'The man, who sometime ago leaped from London, Blackfriars and Westminster Bridges in three quarters of an hour, undertook for a wager to perform the same exploit yesterday. Having leaped from London Bridge in the water, he sank and rose no more.'

Even after all the buildings were removed, many traders who had been on the Bridge stayed close by it. The firm of stationer Richard Walkden is the longest traceable example of a firm on the Bridge and round about it. The business of the stationer and ink-maker had been founded on London Bridge in 1735 at the Bell on the west side, opposite and five or six doors from St Magnus. He aimed his tradesman's card at country shopkeepers, merchants and sea captains, who could make their own ink from his 'Fine British Ink-

Powder for making Black Writing Ink'. Traders were proud to advertise a wide range of wares, and Walkden's tradesman's card outlined a long alphabetical list of ninety items, including 'Blue papers Purple and Sky', 'Burial Prints for Tickets', 'Fish Skin Ink Cases', 'Fountain Brass Pens', 'Horn Books, Primers &c', 'Ink Horns', 'King's Tax Printed Rects', 'Lottery Pictures' and 'New Fashioned Paper Hangings for Rooms'.

Richard Walkden (died 1780) had remained on the Bridge until 1760, when the houses were being taken down. References to this or a very similar business occur round about the Bridge for a number of years afterwards. A tradesman's card shows a move from the Bell, No. 7, just off the bridgefoot in Southwark, to 113 Lower Thames Street in the City, and Walkden's son John carried on in Fleet Street.

Richard's grandson, also John, was a notable London eccentric. He acquired a large fortune which enabled him to indulge in his passion for Handel's music. At his house in Highbury he built a spacious music room with a bust of the composer over the organ, on which he himself played competently. On his death in 1808 his collection was disposed of in a six-day sale.

The stationery business continued down through the family and in partnership with others. In the City Directories of 1832 appeared 'Charles Terry, quill merchant and manufacturer of Walkden's British Ink Powder'. The business passed in 1882 to Terry's great-nephew Philip Cooper, who was still the head of the business in 1930. In 1892 it became Cooper, Dennison & Walkden, at Nos. 7 and 9, St Bride Street, widely known as the sole British concessionaries of 'Dennison's Tags'. The unbroken, detailed descent from one of the shops on Old London Bridge can be traced for nearly two hundred years.

Did the Walkdens and others who lived on or near the Bridge ever become hardened to the screams of the drowning? Those screams were only part of a cacophony to which they did become deaf. A Mr Baldwin, a haberdasher located in the upper part of the former Chapel in the eighteenth century, who had been born there amid the noise, found that he was unable to sleep when, aged seventy-one, he was sent to Chislehurst in Kent for a change of air.

The noise at the ancient river crossing did not lessen with the years, as noted by Dickens in *David Copperfield*: 'We went on through a great noise and an uproar that confused my weary head beyond description and over a bridge which, no doubt was London Bridge . . .' St Magnus – with four waterwheels on one side and the ear-splitting fishmongers' calls and noise of Billingsgate on the other – in 1762 argued for a reduction in the noise penetrating the church made by the iron-rimmed carts working in Billingsgate.

The clamouring waterwheels were the main provider of water for much of London. The Waterworks could raise two thousand gallons of water a minute, and had the power to force the water up to the second floor. The business was extremely profitable because each subscriber paid a fee. When the owners petitioned the Corporation in 1765 for a lease on a fifth arch, there was an enquiry. Among those consulted was John Smeaton, who won a medal for his research into the mechanics of waterwheels and windmills. They eventually took Smeaton's advice, which was in favour of the fifth waterwheel. He also recommended that wheels be placed in the two arches at the Southwark end, so the leaking water pipe over the Bridge to Southwark could be removed. The other consultants were, however, opposed to wheels at the southern end, and most advised removing all the wheels.

Opposition to the noise and obstruction of the waterwheels increased. An interesting legal point was raised in the *Gazetteer* of 28 December 1767: did the Corporation of the City of London actually have the right to impede passage on a navigable river? This question was ignored, and the plan was carried forward. At the City end the fifth waterwheel was put in place, interfering with the water flow there and causing more damaging eddies. By December 1767 two arches at the Southwark end were blocked so the wheels could be placed upstream of them, and three years later a steam engine was added to these waterworks.

Scenes on the riverbanks at this time had some similarities to Victorian photographs of the unembanked river. On the Southwark riverside an array of tilting ladders, movable with the tide, extended from the rickety houses down to the muddy, stinking banks where tied-up rowing boats rose and fell. The activities of working vessels were watched by those in Southwark who paused to lean out of misshapen windows, for the riverside tenements tilted as much as or more than had those on the Bridge.

Dickens knew the old Bridge during the first nineteen years of his life, that is in the period after all the buildings had been removed. As a boy, he lived at Lant Street in Southwark on the west side of Borough High Street, visited his father in the nearby Marshalsea prison on the east side, and worked in Warren's rat-infested boot-blacking factory, near Hungerford Stairs on the City side of the Thames. Of Southwark he wrote in *Pickwick Papers*: 'The population is migratory, usually disappearing on the verges of the quarter-day and generally by night. His majesty's revenues are seldom collected in this happy valley, the rents are dubious and the water communication is very frequently cut off.'

Southwark was changing. To ease the congestion, the ancient High Street market had already been moved to a different site. There was more poverty, while at the same time more industry was being attracted to an already varied and curious conglomeration located so close to the prosperous City. John Timbs, in *Curiosities of London*, recorded 'rope-walks, tan-pits [tanneries], barge and boat-builders, sawyers and timber merchants; hat-making, breweries, vinegar-yards and distilleries, glass houses, potteries and soap and candle works'.

Hop warehouses were located near both ends of the Bridge, for Southwark was the centre of the English hop trade, and the Hop Exchange building is still there. The hops were stored in the warehouses then sold on to the brewers. For centuries hops from Kent, brewing and Southwark went together; according to the Miller in Chaucer's *Canterbury Tales*:

> If the words get muddled in my tale,
> Just put it down to too much Southwark ale.

The hop warehouse of Messrs Judd and Sanderson at the City end caught fire on 31 October 1779, which quickly spread to the

Waterworks and '. . . in less than an hour reduced them nearly even with the river. Whilst the outside woodworks were blazing to an astonishing height, the water was thrown from the pipes with inconceivable velocity, and afforded an awful spectacle, as if the two elements had been contending for the masonry.' This disaster was recorded in the *Gentleman's Magazine* of 31 October 1779 and in a dramatic painting by William Marlow: *Waterworks at London Bridge on Fire*.

The fire may have been linked to the mounting agitation in the build-up to the Gordon Riots of 1780, which were named after the unfortunate, unstable Lord George Gordon. He aimed to provoke anti-Catholic feeling, but at various times supported the Catholics, led an anti-Catholic mob of 50,000, and, finally, became a Jew. The riots were the greatest breakdown in public order in the eighteenth century. This period of radicalism had multiple causes, including the war in America, agitation for reform of the House of Commons and elsewhere, and anti-Catholic feeling reinforced by a threat of invasion from Catholic France and Spain.

In the riots, chapels and prisons were sacked, and the toll-gates on Blackfriars Bridge were broken down and the account books destroyed. Nine-arched Blackfriars Bridge had been opened in stages and was finally completed in 1769, when the watermen argued for and received compensation for loss of business. Turner painted it in watercolour in about 1795, and as is so often the case in the complicated stories of bridges, it was replaced in stone between 1860 and 1869, then widened during 1907–9.

While George III was losing America, in London more rivals to Old London Bridge were appearing. In 1772 the first Battersea Bridge, of wood, was opened where there had been a ferry. Miles away in Shropshire, the first iron bridge in the world was built in 1779 over the Severn; such a single-span erection would later be considered for a new London bridge, but the idea was rejected. In 1782 all tolls on London Bridge were removed for the last time, with the instant result that the traffic over it increased accordingly.

* * *

Social reform was urgently needed, as revealed by Hogarth and others, including Captain Thomas Coram (whose Foundling Hospital had been established 1742–52, acknowledging the truly desperate plight of poor or unmarried mothers). Hogarth depicted the conditions in which many Londoners lived, never concealing the coarseness and rawness of life, in etchings like *A Harlot's Progress*, *Gin Lane* and *Beer Street*; he and other artists donated their paintings to the Foundling Hospital, thus creating the country's first national collection.

St Magnus cooperated with the Bridge House in providing poor relief for those who worked on the Bridge and for their families. The 'Record of poor Persons chargeable to London Bridge, 1788–1814' gives a glimpse into the existence of one family connected to the Bridge. Jane Holloway (1735–89) was the widow of a Samuel Holloway who had been an apprentice to William Edward, a printer on the Bridge. She applied for poor relief from the church wardens at St Magnus. In the close examination of her case, it was reported that following the death of Samuel she had been a housekeeper in Rochester, Kent, for ten years, but paid no taxes. There were five children living, one lame girl who resided with her mother, and one who was made a ward of the Charity School. The church wardens '. . . were desired not to allow the said Jane Holloway no more than four shillings a week in future', as noted in the Bridge House Records. There were three bastard children, the father being Mr John Loveland of His Majesty's ship, *Queen Charlotte*. In 1795 unsuccessful efforts were made to apprehend him. Finally, the youngest child was placed under the care of the parish of St Magnus.

The bridge weir was increasingly dangerous, with five arches blocked at the City end, and two at the Southwark end, but the place still attracted thrill-seekers. George Borrow, in his semi-autobiographical *Lavengro* (1851), wrote: 'As I stood on the bridge gazing into the jaws of the pool, a small boat shot suddenly through the arch beneath my feet. There were three persons in it: an oarsman in the middle whilst a man and a woman sat in the stern. I shall never forget the thrill of horror which went through me at this sudden apparition.'

Only the foolish approached it incautiously. Author John Wilson Croker unwillingly shot the Bridge when he was among a river party attending the Duke of York (brother of George IV) and his Duchess. As the boat was being steered for a landing place above the Bridge the perverse Duchess asked why. On being told of the danger, she refused to get out of the boat. The rest of the party reluctantly agreed to shoot the rapids, where they took on a lot of water and all got very wet, but the Duchess showed no regret.

In the busy scene around the Bridge, by 1798 the lower part of the former Chapel – all that remained – was used as a paper warehouse by Wright and Gill (partners for more than fifty years and both aldermen), even though at high tide the black-and-white marble floor was ten to twelve feet below water level. Such was the construction of the Bridge, the paper remained 'as safe and dry as it would have been in a garret', as reported in the *Morning Advertiser* of 26 April 1798. The paper was brought into and out of the warehouse via a crane at the side of the Chapel Lock to a doorway above high-water mark. An engraving of the former Chapel in the *Gentleman's Magazine* in 1753 shows a doorway for taking in goods from boats or barges, possibly the doorway through which the fishermen once went for their daily prayers. The barges, of course, timed their arrival for still water.

On the flat surface of Chapel Pier there was a hollowed-out square fish pond covered with a wire net, which effortlessly trapped fish as the tide flowed and ebbed. In 1827 'an ancient servant of London Bridge, now verging upon his hundredth summer' recalled descending through what had been the Chapel to fish in this unusual pond.

Fishing vessels abounded – in an engraving of one of Turner's works, depicting the north side of the river near the Bridge, there is a crush of fishing boats, some unloading their catch – for as late as 1828 fishing was still important on the Thames and there were about four hundred fishermen between Deptford and London. A mere twenty-five years later there would be far fewer, due to pollution and sewage, for by then lavatories had been introduced in an overcrowded city. The river was busy with spritsail sailing barges, 'stackies' bringing in hay to feed the horses and taking out the horse manure to the gardens of Kent and Essex, and lighters. Now there were steam packets and steam tugs as well.

After so many harsh winters with the ensuing major repairs, the long controversy then began over the construction of a new London Bridge. This time the discussion remained in focus because of the constant worry about the weakening of the foundations. Much of its character had gone and with it some of the emotional attachment – and now there were rival bridges. The only good reason for keeping the old Bridge seemed to be to justify the large amount recently spent widening it. In this respect little had changed since Shakespeare's day, when Ben Jonson wrote:

> A curtesie no more than London-bridge
> What arch was mended last.

William Gifford, editor of the *Quarterly Review,* referring to the Jonson quote, complained with sarcasm in 1789:

Two hundred years have nearly elapsed since this was written, and the observation still holds. This pernicious structure has wasted more money in perpetual repairs than would have sufficed to build a dozen safe and commodious bridges, and cost the lives, perhaps, of as many as a thousand people. This may seem little to those whom it concerns – but there is blood on the city, and a heavy account is before them. Had an alderman or turtle been lost there, the nuisance would have been long removed.

But the Bridge had been there for so long, there was a deep-seated fear about the effect on the river if it were removed, and wild predictions abounded about what would happen. Arguments for and against were published. A defence of the Bridge in the *Morning Herald* of 6 October 1789 stated: 'The rebuilding of this edifice has frequently been recommended; but it will not be improved, if erected on any other plan than the present.' The argument illogically continued that a bridge with wider arches would make the ebb and the flow equal in time, instead of eight hours to run out and four to return, and equally surprising that navigation to the sea would be impaired because the river would flow too easily.

A reply to the above in the *Public Advertiser* argued that the wider arches would not mean loss of water above the Bridge, for the two hours' additional flow would have to return and could only do so as fast as the sea would permit. 'The accursed abuse of the Bridge is in stopping the shipping two hours every flood.' Another writer predicted in 1831, when demolition was imminent, that 'startling and alarming' effects would result from the construction of Rennie's bridge, for the conditions would be much altered.

Even Sir H.C. Englefield, a distinguished scientist and Linnaean, robustly presented an overwhelming range of confusing and frightening possibilities in *Observations on the Probable Consequences of the Demolition of London Bridge*: the tide would run about three miles higher up the river; the Bridge had been a weir for so long it had in effect become part of the river, performing an important service by checking the quantity and speed of the flood tides; any increase in depth at high water would be useless to navigation; the increased speed of the water would add to the existing dangers and the difficulties faced by the watermen; a quicker outfall would leave the bed of the river nearly dry at the spring ebb tides, and the silt from the sewers would therefore have much more shore on which to deposit itself. Finally, he said that the stronger flood would cause the upper parts of the river to be choked with the mud carried up from London and less mud would be carried downstream. It was all too much, and too worrying, to think about for very long.

Tampering with the old Bridge by creating the Great Arch had led to unanticipated, frightening and expensive-to-put-right results. Now there was the fear that if the Bridge were removed completely, the increased current would deepen the stream, cause the undermining of wharves and embankments and the foundations of the other bridges now on the river, besides causing harm to the low-lying lands between Rotherhithe and Battersea. Typical of the extreme views, it was even said that St George's Fields, Vauxhall and Lambeth might be rendered unhealthy, even uninhabitable, 'from damps and stagnant waters'.

Progress towards a decision was inevitably hindered by the fact that the Bridge was of vital importance to everyone, so everyone naturally involved themselves in what would happen to it. But in 1801 *The Third Report from the Select Committee upon the Improvement of the Port of London* made it clear that the end of Old London Bridge was in sight. The expense of maintenance was too great, combined with the dangers to navigation. Designs fulfilling certain conditions were to be prepared for an entirely new structure: a new bridge must allow for passage under the central arch of vessels up to two hundred tons with the top-masts struck, requiring an arch of sixty-five feet above high-water mark; there must be the greatest convenience and low acclivity for crossing; it must provide access to important streets while causing as little disturbance to private property as possible; and the new bridge had to be an ornament to the metropolis.

Competition designs by a distinguished group of bridge-builders – Ralph Dodd, Samuel Wyatt, Thomas Telford, James Douglas and George Dance the Younger – fell into three groups:

1. A bridge with a high central arch with approaches ascending from important streets.
2. A bridge with a similar central arch, but approached by an easier gradient from embankments built in front of the wharves.
3. Twin bridges giving a continual communication between the two banks, one of the drawbridges always being down.

Unbelievably, in spite of all this activity, inertia prevailed for many more years to come.

All the while, competiton was hotting up, and loyalties were rapidly shifting. More rival bridges appeared one after another, but, in such a burgeoning urban agglomeration, they still did not relieve the congestion. Vauxhall Bridge was opened in 1816. Then, in 1817, came civil engineer John Rennie senior's Waterloo Bridge, owned by a joint-stock company and described by the Venetian sculptor Antonio Canova as 'the noblest bridge in the world'.

It was the age of iron, and Old London Bridge did not entirely escape, for an iron waterwheel replaced one of the wooden ones in 1817. In 1819 Rennie's three-arched Southwark Bridge, the iron bridge of Dickens's *Little Dorrit*, was opened as a commercial venture with tolls. But it attracted only one-fortieth the traffic of nearby London Bridge.

The Corporation of the City of London had continued to oppose new bridges. The Corporation had so strongly argued against Southwark Bridge, insisting that it would hinder traffic on the Thames, that it was built with only two piers and three spans; the central one was the longest at 262½ feet, a feat achieved through the use of cast iron. When the project went bankrupt in 1868, the Corporation acquired it, and the bridge was replaced between 1912 and 1921.

The fun of the frost fairs was more than equalled by the damage to the Bridge caused by the ice. In 1763 a severe frost had blocked all the arches except the central one. The water poured through it with such force that the torn-up bed of the river exposed the foundations of the piers. The repairs for this episode alone had cost the Bridge Wardens a considerable £6,800. The next harsh winter soon followed in 1766–7, although no damage was done, nor in 1785 after a frost lasting 115 days.

Frostiana: or a History of the River Thames in a Frozen State (1814) described the freeze-up of 1789. To keep the waterwheels moving, workers and volunteers poured boiling water over them – a laborious process for the water had to be heated over coal fires – and each day twenty-five horses were used to pull the floating chunks of ice away from the wheels. So extreme were the conditions, with the river entirely blocked by ice between London and Woolwich, that the East Indiamen were moved to Greenwich for safety. By the 1790s the East India Company had built bonded warehouses at London – essential to protect the spices and goods from the

Two boys and a dog are rescued at the Bridge during the frost of 1814.

thievery that prevailed in the port. After 1800 the enclosed docks downriver from the Tower comprised the West India Docks, the London Dock, the East India Dock, the Surrey Docks, and in 1820 St Katharine's Dock.

Since the frost fairs on the Thames at London were linked to the damming effect of Old London Bridge, the end was coming for them too. The last one marked the very hard winter of 1813–14. The severe weather began on 27 December with a thick fog that lasted for eight days. Then for forty-eight hours snow fell in vast quantities. Communication with western and northern parts of the country ceased. The Thames was frozen for five days at the beginning of February.

With the thaw came the violent destruction of people and property. Several people drowned, and craft on the river between the

Bridge and Westminster were damaged at an estimated cost of £20,000. In a famous incident, a boat carrying two boys and a dog was wrecked on one of the piers, and they were hoisted up to safety.

There were immediate consequences for the Bridge. Damage to it resulted in new proposals in November 1814 and a fresh determination to do something about it. George Dance the Younger, with three others, sent a report to a committee of the Corporation proposing that four of the medieval piers be removed, converting eight arches into four. One pier was opened for examination – but again no decision was made.

Then, in 1822, after almost 250 years, the thudding of the Waterworks was heard no more, finally removing a great danger to navigation. The London Bridge Waterworks – an enterprise that had created a precedent for supplying water to the public for profit – had remained in the Morris family for almost 120 years. When an additional asset, the lease for a fourth arch, had been obtained in 1701, Peter Morris's grandson sold the enterprise for £36,000 to a London goldsmith, Richard Soames. Soames wisely had the transaction confirmed by the City authorities, and they renewed the lease for the unexpired portion of the original period for twenty shillings per year and a payment of £300. Soames turned it into a company of three hundred shares at £500 per share, giving him the funds to have the pumping machinery redesigned. By 1749 the wheels were twenty feet in diameter, and, rotating six times a minute, drove the pumps to raise 123,120 gallons per hour to 120 feet. The river water was stored in a tall cistern at the north-west end of the Bridge from where it was conducted via nine main pipes to houses in the City. When there was a fire, all the pipes except the one nearest the fire could be turned off, creating one powerful source of water.

The Corporation paid the proprietors of the Waterworks £10,000 (the loan raised with the Bridge House Estates as security) in compensation for the removal of the wheels. The shares and the machinery were transferred to the New River Company, which was given six months to remove the wheels, work that was done after the tide tables had been carefully consulted. In 1904 the Metropolitan Water Board took over the New River Company and with it the shares. The original lease to Peter Morris for five hundred years would have expired in 2082.

The Committee of the House of Commons appointed to deal with the Bridge, having finally had enough of the ongoing expense and unpredictable results of tampering with the old Bridge by removing arches, finally proposed an entirely new bridge.

Time for the Bridge had run out. A newspaper compared it to 'a thick wall, pierced with small uneven holes, through which the water, dammed up by this clumsy fabric, rushes or rather leaps, with a velocity extremely dangerous to boats and barges'. No one could deny the continuing unacceptable number of deaths both under the Bridge and on it. And commerce both on the river and in the City was being harmed by the congestion.

On the Thames the larger barges, heavily loaded, went through the Great Arch, but it was passable for only six hours in twenty-four or for the three hours after high tide. And with so many boats striving to use this one arch, there were more accidents than ever, and the piers – still being repaired and so still increasing in size – often damaged, beached or sank the vessels.

An astonishing statistic remains regarding traffic on the bridge street in 1811. Every day 90,000 people on foot, 800 wagons, 2,000 carts and drays, 1,300 coaches, 500 gigs and 'tax carts' and 800 people on horseback crossed over it.

The authorities finally mustered the will to move ahead, now that the nation was more prosperous and the finances of the Corporation had improved. *The Times* noted that 'the present bridge is a nuisance which deserved to be abated'. Final decisions were made. Another competition was held in 1821, but the outcome was again ignored: a committee of the House of Commons decided to adopt a design by famed bridge-builder John Rennie senior. On 4 July 1823 Royal Assent was given to 'An Act for the Rebuilding London Bridge and for the improving and making suitable Approaches thereto'. Fear and concern for loss of income continued. Petitions against a new bridge were presented by ship-owners, the affected parishes, wharfingers (the owners and managers of wharfs) and warehousemen.

Still the old Bridge lived on. To avoid total chaos and loss of business, it was to continue in use until the new bridge was open. To help cover the cost, the national exchequer assisted with £150,000; the balance was provided on the credit of the Bridge House Estates. The site, design and finances settled, on 15 March 1824 the first pile was driven in opposite the fourth arch of the old Bridge at the Southwark end and about 180 feet to the west of it. With the first blow of the pile-driver, the watching crowd cheered.

After the first wooden coffer dam – opposite the fourth arch from the Southwark end of Old London Bridge – had been completed, a ceremony to lay 'The First Stone of the New London Bridge' was held on 15 June 1825, the tenth anniversary of the Battle of Waterloo. However, the hero of Waterloo, the Duke of Wellington – who had been actively involved in pushing ahead preparations for the new bridge – did not take part in the ceremony, because it was feared that his well-known anti-reform stance would lead to a disturbance.

On the route of the Lord Mayor's procession – which the City was ever adept at organizing – from the Guildhall to the old Bridge, all buildings, public and private, 'were literally roofed and walled with human beings, clinging to them in all sorts of possible and impossible attitudes'. The river was full of craft loaded with people. Southwark Bridge, free of tolls for the day, was 'clustered over like a bee-hive'. Old London Bridge was closed at eleven a.m., and there was a feeling of 'awful solemnity' among the spectators on seeing the great thoroughfare for once free of people, traffic and noise; perhaps there was a thought for the approaching demise of their old companion.

Newspapers luxuriated in the 'grandeur of purpose' and 'splendid effect' of the procession and ceremony. Every detail was considered fascinating, from the silence that finally fell among those who had waited for hours for the event to begin, to the difficulties the watermen experienced in carrying their colours into the narrow entrance of the coffer dam. Finally the procession arrived, led by a division of the Artillery Company with their field pieces. The Junior City Marshal on horseback and the Water Bailiff were followed by barge masters and City watermen bearing their elaborate colours; the Bridge Wardens, Lewis Lewis and William Gillman, and the Clerk of the Bridge House preceded the two contractors, the Reverend William J. Jolliffe (who was to preserve stone from the old Bridge) and Sir Edward Banks. Labourers carried before them a model of Rennie's bridge.

John Rennie senior had died in 1821, his place taken by his second son, also John, who adhered to his father's design and was the only engineer and superintendent during the construction of the bridge. Richard Thomson's *Chronicles of London Bridge* of 1827 records how Rennie (knighted on completion of the bridge in 1831) processed with members of the New Bridge Committee, followed by the Comptroller of the Bridge House, members of the Committee of the Royal Society, the High Bailiff of Southwark, the Under Sheriffs, the Clerk of the Peace of the City of London, the City Solicitor, and so on. Finally the Lord Mayor in his gold state carriage arrived with Frederick Augustus, Duke of York, the brother of George IV.

It was only a month before the once handsome George IV (1820–30) would be crowned at Westminster Abbey – a ceremony from which he barred his wife, Queen Caroline – yet surprisingly he sent his younger brother to represent him on this important occasion. After nine years as a dissolute Prince of Wales, indulging his extravagant taste in wine, women and the arts, George IV was largely responsible for the extent and quality of the Royal Collection today. The collection includes the world's largest number of paintings by Canaletto, the famed Venetian artist who was also entranced by the Thames and its bridges.

On this occasion, Old London Bridge was reduced in status to providing access to the ceremony for the new bridge. For this, it was further disfigured when a length of its parapet was cut away to allow for an entranceway and flight of stairs to a long wooden passage to the coffer dam. Forty-five feet below high-water mark, the floor of the dam accommodated four hundred of the two thousand ticketed guests. Erected over all was a vast marquee raised on a little forest of scaffolding poles, itself almost dwarfed by enormous flags: the Union Jack, the Red Ensign and the Royal Standard.

Even now, the City felt it had to explain to those present and to posterity why the venerable old structure was being replaced. An engraved copper plaque – Latin on one side, English on the other – was read out before being placed under the foundation stone of the new bridge:

> The free course of the river being obstructed by the numerous piles of the ancient bridge, and the passage of boats and vessels through its narrow channels being often attended with danger and loss of life by reason of the force and the rapidity of the current, the city of London, desirous of providing a remedy for this evil, and at the same time consulting the convenience of commerce in this vast emporium of all nations, under the sanction and with the liberal aid of Parliament, resolved to erect a new bridge upon a foundation altogether new, with arches of a wider span, and of a character corresponding to the dignity and importance of this royal city: nor does any other time seem to be more suitable for such an undertaking than when, in a period of universal peace, the British Empire flourishing in glory, wealth, population, and domestic union, is governed by a prince, the patron and encourager of the arts, under whose auspices the metropolis has been daily advancing in elegance and splendour.

The focus of attention at the centre of the coffer dam was a massive block of Aberdeen granite. The four-ton stone was suspended by a tackle ready to be swung into the place 'that it is destined to occupy for centuries'. The Lord Mayor, the Rt. Hon. John Garratt, wearing his furred scarlet robes and his great chain of office, spread the mortar and the stone was lowered into place by two men at a windlass, the ceremony witnessed by the Duke of York, who wore a plain blue coat with the Garter round his knee, the Star of that order on his breast. (This was the Duke whose foolish Duchess had once insisted on shooting Old London Bridge, and whose own ill-considered expeditions inspired the rhyme 'The Grand Old Duke of York'.)

The ceremony concluded with 'God Save the King' and 'three series of huzzas for the Duke of York, Old England and Mr Rennie'. Carriages waited on the old Bridge to convey guests to the Mansion House for a banquet in the Egyptian Hall, where 376 people dined on turtle and venison, champagne and claret. Back at the coffer dam people moved closer to examine the foundation stone, some even climbing up and walking on it, including the editor of the *Every-Day Book*, who, 'toeing it and heeling it, With ball-room grace, and merry face, kept lively quadriling it', a performance 'unprecedented, unimitated, and unimitable'.

At this time of great civic pride, the Court of Common Council presented Lord Mayor Garratt with a gold medallion commemorating the laying of the first stone, and twenty silver medals were struck to be presented to the engineers and their assistants. Tea-dealer John Garratt had previously been alderman of the ward of Bridge Within, and it was to him that Richard Thomson dedicated his *Chronicles of London Bridge*.

Surprisingly, work continued on both bridges at the same time, for the intense pressure of use forced more alterations to the old Bridge, even as the new one was being built alongside it. And every time changes were made, more details of its construction were revealed. The road surface had been opened up in 1826 when two arches were converted into one: the surface had been considerably made up over time, and at least five separate strata were visible, raising the bridge street eight and a half feet above the crown of the arch. First there was gravel twenty inches thick, then a layer of chalk and gravel, followed by a stratum of mixed materials and then the thickest layer, a mixture of burnt wood, 'ruins' and black earth. The top layer was of mixed materials on which was laid the granite cobblestone paving (perhaps added after the buildings were removed 1757–62). Now the Bridge looked different again, and not for the better: there were three large openings in the old structure, and the two new ones were supported only by unattractive timber arches.

Contractors Jolliffe and Banks undertook to build the new bridge in six years from 2 March 1824, but it did not actually open to the public until 1 August 1831, almost a year and a half late. The new bridge, including land arches, abutments and paving, would cost £680,232. Although steam power was available, it was used only to pump water out of the coffer dams. There were trucks and rails for carrying the stone to the crane, but in many ways the builders had much in common with their medieval predecessors more than six hundred years earlier – and shared similar hazards. Building work and the river remained as dangerous as ever. Of more than eight hundred workmen, forty were drowned or killed during construction.

Fortunately illustrations remain depicting stages in the demolition of the old Bridge and the construction of the new one, for on the spot was Edward William Cooke. Edward was only fifteen years old in 1826 when he began his series of over forty most beautiful pencil drawings. From these he engraved twelve etchings, which were published in 1833 as *Views of Old and New London Bridges* with text by John Rennie junior. They show the great granite blocks lifted by handworked derricks and cranes, among innumerable valuable and informative details.

New approach roads were obviously required for Rennie's bridge, and they proved to be more costly, at nearly £2 million, than the new bridge itself, although work on some of the approach roads was not completed until thirty years later. At the City end, St Michael, Crooked Lane, was removed. This was the seventeenth-century church, rebuilt after the Great Fire, to which John and Charles Wesley had come numerous times; the decision was strongly opposed by the vestry, who addressed the Committee for the New London Bridge. But there was no choice. Even Bishop Andrew's Chapel at the medieval St Saviour's (Southwark Cathedral) went, later regretted as an unnecesary demolition. Houses and streets like Pepper Alley Stairs in Southwark disappeared, and with it all much of the character around both ends of the Bridge vanished for ever.

Old Fishmongers Hall had been painted many times by Canaletto and others, but much more space was required for the new bridge, and a strip twenty feet wide was needed from the Hall itself. In the event Fishmongers Hall was demolished and compensation paid by the City, and the Hall was rebuilt from 1831 to 1835, as it stands today.

Seventy years earlier, the 'gay shopmen' and bridge-dwellers had been dislodged from the once-acclaimed wonder of the world. But businesses that had been on the Bridge still clung to a mention of it. Randall Aldersey was at 'Ye Brig House Gate'; Joseph Brocket at the Sign of the Talbot (hunting-dog with chain), 'Bridge foot, Southwark'; and Henry Phillips at the Sign of the Sugar Loaf, 'Bridg Foot, Southwark'.

Rennie's bridge was officially opened on 1 August 1831 by blunt, affable William IV (1830–7) – who had acceded to the throne just over a year before – and Queen Adelaide. They embarked at Somerset House, and all the way to London Bridge the royal barge was surrounded by other heavily gilded barges in a magnificent water pageant on a river that was deeply lined with festively decorated vessels of every kind. To cheers, doffed hats and military music, the royal pair disembarked on steps at the north-west side at the City end of the new bridge. An enormous marquee stretched almost halfway along the length of Rennie's bridge, decorated in 'the colours of all nations', and where an elaborate reception and banquet was held. First, those lining the riverbanks, the rooftops and the tower of St Magnus rejoiced as the royal pair performed the opening ceremony by walking across the structure of blue and white granite. As they reached the Southwark end, Mr Charles Green, a famous balloonist on his 192nd voyage in the air, 'ascended in his celebrated balloon'. Of all the extraordinary events – the bloody battles, the famed joust, the richly splendid ceremonies – that the old Bridge had witnessed over more than six hundred years, this one was the most significant: it marked its own end.

Old London Bridge had been at the centre of life and commerce, fire and plague, revolt and civil war for over six centuries. It was there astride the Thames when the Magna Carta was signed, at the time of Agincourt and the Field of the Cloth of Gold, the Reformation and the Restoration, the Hundred Years War and the Battle of Waterloo. It stood while the Plantagenets, Lancastrians and Yorks, Tudors, Stuarts and Hanoverians ruled. Three kings had watched it being built, thirty English kings and queens had passed over it, and Queen Victoria saw it as a child. But Old London

Bridge entered folklore because this characterful organic structure was part of the everyday fabric of life for countless thousands of ordinary people – and they would never forget it.

At the time of the laying of the foundation stone of Rennie's London Bridge, when the determination had been to look confidently ahead, one newspaper looked back. There was a thought for the thousands who had 'passed to the bottom' at this turbulent place, and equally 'Let us remember the bridge that has carried us safe over.'

What came after

Londoners had – for a time – the bridge they wanted. As a news-paper declaimed: it 'is the symbol of an honourable British merchant: it unites plainness with strength and capacity. . .' Rennie's new bridge was a very different kind of structure, in place 180 feet west of the old Bridge. In contrast to the twenty disarmingly irregular arches of Kentish ragstone, five semi-elliptical arches in smooth granite, unrivalled in 'the perfection of proportion', spanned 1,005 feet: the longest spans of any stone bridge in Europe at the time. Within a year, the new bridge had settled unevenly, giving it a downstream tilt, but it was declared safe by Thomas Telford, the son of a shep-herd who became a bridge-builder extraordinaire.

By the end, remarkably little of Old London Bridge actually dated back to its earliest years, because so much had been rebuilt over the centuries following collapse, fire, natural disasters and alter-ations. Of the twenty arches, seven had been rebuilt entirely. Three piers and six arches had been removed, the rest patched and repatched, reinforced with stone ribs and widened to more than double their original width. Nearly two-thirds of the stone in the Bridge was no older than the latter half of the eighteenth century, although the foundations dating from the twelfth century were still encased within the later alterations.

The final destruction of the ancient Bridge began as soon as Rennie's bridge had been opened by the King. By January 1832 the arches had been stripped to the extent that Edward Cooke was able to draw them

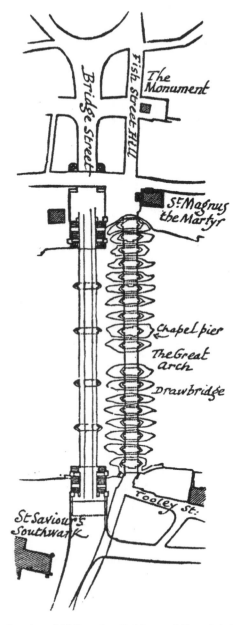

A plan showing Old London Bridge and Rennie's bridge.

with the filling of the spandrels removed. By the end of July the massive boat-like piers were being taken apart, but the southernmost arch was still intact, the piers still defiantly forming a weir on the upstream side at the incoming tide. The foundations were revealed, as shown in a dramatic painting by James Holland dated 1832. The removed materials were lightered down the Thames, but people with imagination and energy preserved some portions of the Bridge.

Then, what had been the undercroft of the lower Chapel was unexpectedly opened up on the west side, the place where the remains of the priest-architect Peter de Colechurch had been placed more than half a millennium earlier. The enclosure was found to be built up in small courses of firestone 'to contain a person of the middle stature'. At the Museum of London is a very small casket – presumably made from the wood of the Bridge – containing a few bones reputed to be those of Peter de Colechurch. The *Gentleman's Magazine* in 1832 reported that when the bones were analysed they were found to be part of 'a human arm bone, a cow bone and three goose bones'.

All too soon it was the turn of Rennie's bridge to be deemed inadequate in the capital of the British Empire. Between 1902 and 1904 it was widened by ten feet to sixty-five feet to help accommodate the ever-increasing traffic in what was the largest city and port in the world.

Life was changing: the first Parliamentary Reform Bill had been passed in 1832. Problems in the 'Great Smoke' were finally being addressed in this period of vigorous development. If the essence of civilization is 'drains and discipline', London was advancing. The Metropolitan Commissioners of Sewers was set up in 1843, but the new sewers flowed untreated into the Thames. In 1864–5, the Metropolitan Board of Works finally constructed a new sewage and waterworks system, which worked to a degree, but it was to be many years before sewage was treated. And after 1868 Londoners could boast of a contained Thames with the completion of the Victoria, Albert and Chelsea Embankments. They usefully eased traffic, beautified the Thames – and the Victoria Embankment also concealed the main sewer.

An Edward Cooke view of the demolition in progress, 1832.

There was a revolution in transport, as the horse-drawn coaches that had displaced the watermen were now themselves pushed aside by the railways being built between the 1830s and 1860s. In 1836, the terminus of the first railway coming to London was at London Bridge. The first underground railway opened in 1863, and an early tube line went from Stockwell to King William Street at the City end of London Bridge. In the mid-nineteenth century the number of passengers at London Bridge railway station in Southwark increased to ten million annually, almost all of whom walked over the bridge to work in the City.

And bridges in London were multiplying at a rapid rate: Chelsea Bridge, between Battersea and Vauxhall bridges, was opened in 1858; Albert Bridge, between Chelsea and Battersea bridges, in 1873; and Lambeth Bridge in 1879.

Then, in 1894, majestic Tower Bridge was completed: 11,000 tons of steel faced with stone and in neo-Gothic style, so as not to visually jar with the Tower of London. Tower Bridge with its draw-bridge was clearly inspired by the fortified bridges of the past, and it comes very close to being a habitable bridge: large rooms contain machinery and now a museum. The Prince of Wales, later Edward

VII, formally opened Tower Bridge, within sight of London Bridge. On the latter, in 1863, his bride of that year, Princess Alexandra of Denmark, had been magnificently welcomed by the Lord Mayor and sheriffs; the splendid procession passed under a seventy-foot-high triumphal arch, echoing the ceremonies centuries earlier on Old London Bridge. At the opening ceremony for Tower Bridge, the Prince acknowledged the debt of the new bridge to Old London Bridge. The famous Bridge, through the Bridge House Estates, had paid for it in full.

In December 1884 there was an unsuccessful attempt attributed to the Irish-American Fenians to blow up Rennie's London Bridge. Earlier, in 1857, Rochester Bridge, after four and a half centuries of use, had been replaced by a new one built alongside. This was considered an unmissable opportunity for the Royal Artillery – who in 1855 had been so successful at destroying the docks at Sebastopol in the Crimea – to blow up the substantive fourteenth-century foundations of the old bridge in a series of great explosions, watched by an appreciative crowd.

In the world wars of the twentieth century, bombs fell around Rennie's London Bridge. In World War I the Fishmongers Hall was used as a military hospital, and outside straw was strewn on London Bridge to suppress the noise of the traffic. In World War II the main Hall was used as a 'British Restaurant', as such places providing cheap food were called, and the building suffered extensive bomb damage in 1940.

By the mid-twentieth century Rennie's bridge was showing signs of instability, cracks were appearing and it was obviously too narrow for the increasing traffic, which was by then approaching 20,000 pedestrians and 3,000 cars per hour at peak periods. The decision was made to replace the 1831 bridge less than 140 years after it had been built to last for centuries.

Today's three-arched London Bridge, on the site of Rennie's London Bridge, was constructed by building and civil engineering contractors John Mowlem & Co. Ltd. Costing the Bridge House Estates £4.5 million, it was officially opened in 1973. At one and two-thirds the width of Rennie's bridge, it weighs only half as much, for it was built of pre-stressed concrete, not granite. For icy weather, there is under-heating on the wide footways for the thousands of foot passengers, many arriving at London Bridge station, and on the carriageways for the 40,000 cars a day that pass over it.

But part of Rennie's structure remains in place: bankside portions in Southwark form huge supports for the roadway on to today's bridge, creating a large enclosed area within which remain the original granite staircases. This section can be seen from the western end of Tooley Street, along with the tunnel and stone arch joining Tooley Street and the Clink. Extraordinarily, Rennie's bridge was to go on to a new life.

In a bizarre footnote to the history of Rennie's London Bridge, in April 1968 it was sold by the Corporation of London to the McCulloch Oil Corporation for US$2,460,000, part of the eventual US$7 million it would cost to get the bridge to its new home at Lake Havasu City in western Arizona. American entrepreneur Robert McCulloch senior had founded his self-supporting city on the site of a World War II Army Air Corps rest camp, all 16,630 acres of land reclaimed from the desert. A London bridge was to be the star attraction.

Thirty-three thousand tons of granite, including 10,000 tons of numbered facing stone, was imported duty-free into the USA as 'a genuine large antique'. The stone, some pieces weighing as much as eight tons, was transported more than 10,000 miles, first by sea to Long Beach, California, then trucked overland to Lake Havasu City, about two hundred miles south of Las Vegas. A place on Earth more unlike London cannot be imagined.

The Lord Mayor of London, Sir Gilbert Inglefield, was there to lay the foundation stone on 23 September 1968, and reconstruction began. Under the direction of Robert Beresford, a civil engineer from Nottingham in England, forty men worked on the project for a year and a half. The granite was affixed to the steel-reinforced concrete superstructure of a bridge that would span a specially built mile-long scenic waterway, for which over two million cubic yards of earth had been excavated, the water to fill it coming from the Lower Colorado River. An 'island' was created in Lake Havasu (Native American for 'blue water') by severing the neck of the existing peninsula; the bridge was to link island and mainland.

British pageantry and American razzamatazz merged flamboyantly on 10 October 1971. Before 100,000 people in a dedication spectacle that reputedly cost Robert McCulloch US$500,000, Rennie's London Bridge was formally rededicated by the Lord Mayor of London. The Rt. Hon. Sir Peter M. Studd arrived at the bridge in a bunting-draped paddle-steamer, escorted by a fleet of canoes paddled by Native Americans to the drum-beat of the Lord Mayor's bodyguard – the Honourable Artillery Company of Pikemen and Musketeers – in full woollen ceremonial livery, while a band played 'London Bridge is Falling Down'. There were rockets, thousands of balloons, hundreds of white pigeons, sky-divers trailing coloured smoke, and a seventy-foot-high hot-air balloon in red, white and blue, the latter echoing the ascent of the balloon 140 years earlier at the bridge's first opening before King William and Queen Adelaide in old London Town. Nothing was omitted: a parade and a barbecue followed.

Today, Rennie's London Bridge is primarily a tourist attraction, with an 'English' village, an international resort and hotel complex adjacent to the north end of the bridge, a thousand businesses, two newspapers and a college. Looking surprisingly comfortable in its unlikely setting, the landscaped bridge is seen by hundreds of thousands of tourists each year. Such is the enduring allure of a London bridge.

The cumulative history and romance absorbed by the original Old London Bridge was transferred to an odd assortment of intriguing relics and mementoes that were preserved through the foresight of individuals.

Enormous amounts of the stonework were sold off, because the romance of the stone appealed to the rich to build their houses. At the Museum of London a miniature book in Purbeck marble is inscribed 'From Alderman Harmer who bought the Old Bridge'.

He purchased large quantities of the stonework, and used it to build Ingress Abbey near Greenhithe, Kent.

Three of the large, handsome domed stone alcoves from the final stage of the Bridge were saved for the public. Two were resited in Victoria Park in Hackney, east London, while another migrated a short distance south of where Old London Bridge once stood to a courtyard of Guy's Hospital.

A sculptured stone shield from the Bridge, bearing three leopards with angels on either side, forms the inside keystone of the tower arch of St Katharine, Merstham, near Reigate, Surrey, in the Diocese of Southwark. The Reverend William Jolliffe, one of the contractors for Rennie's bridge, lived nearby. Some of the stone for the Bridge probably came from the Chaldon and Merstham area, only about eighteen miles from Southwark, and thanks to Jolliffe a small heraldic piece made the return journey.

Sometimes what was initially preserved was ultimately lost. Granite pillars from Dance's 1745 colonnaded Piazza were presented to dramatist David Garrick who erected them in front of his villa on the Thames at Hampton, which he had bought in 1754, five years before all the buildings were removed from the Bridge. When the road at Hampton was widened for a tramway, the pillars were removed to a storage yard, and two were set up at the entrance to a dry dock, where they were damaged by trucks. They were then placed in the grounds of Hampton Grammar School, near the river, but seemingly disappeared when the school moved in the 1940s and the original building was demolished.

Archaeological relics include an oak pile with iron points, dated between 1300 and 1500, which was dredged up from the river bed; a stone tablet of 1509, presumably recording repairs to the Bridge; and other stones brought up by dredgers in 1930. A few stones are preserved at St Magnus the Martyr.

Now-valuable artefacts were made from the materials of Old London Bridge. At Fishmongers Hall in pride of place is an armchair made from the once-submerged piles, the raw materials having been rescued by a churchman; the open back is formed of four splats on which are carved four bridges: Old London Bridge,

Westminster Bridge, Rennie's London Bridge and the first Blackfriars Bridge; within the seat is a piece of Purbeck marble, believed to be from the foundation stone of the old Bridge. There also exists a canteen of superior cutlery bearing the initials of Nathan Meyer Rothschild, which was created by John Weiss of 62, The Strand, from wood and iron from the Bridge; he bought fifteen tons of iron from the tips of the wooden piles, a wise investment, for he found that the iron made fine steel.

There was a wish for the old Bridge to bless the new one. A level made in 1826 from wood from Old London Bridge was used by William Thompson, Lord Mayor, to align the last keystone of Rennie's London Bridge. *The Times* reported that '. . . his Lordship dashing a glass of Champagne on the keystone, drank "Success to the Bridge"'.

The ancient Bridge of the nursery rhyme made the leap into another millennium and into the electronic age. When the BBC set up its 3-D section on its website one of the first images it produced was that of the medieval Old London Bridge, as it appeared in 1540, at the peak of its interest and beauty.

On a human level, Old London Bridge was the most successful bridge ever built over the Thames, perhaps anywhere. It is no more, but Dickens's 'giant-wardens of the ancient bridge' – the Church of St Magnus the Martyr on the north side and Southwark Cathedral on the south – still watch over today's bridge, over the people of the City and of Southwark, and over an irrepressible, elemental river. This river is like another river, T.S. Eliot's '. . . strong brown god – sullen, untamed and intractable . . . reminder/Of what men choose to forget. Unhonoured, unpropitiated/By worshippers of the machine, but waiting, watching and waiting.'*

---

*T.S. Eliot, *Four Quartets*.

Sources and Notes

Many books have been consulted from the enormous range published on London, including *The Oxford Illustrated History of Britain* edited by Kenneth O. Morgan (Oxford, 1984); *London, A History* by Francis Sheppard (Oxford, 1999); *The English, A Social History 1066–1945* by Christopher Hibbert (London, 1987); and *Studies in London History* edited by A.E.J. Hollaender and William Kellaway (London, 1969). For food, *Londoners' Larder, English Cuisine from Chaucer to the Present* by Annette Hope (Edinburgh, 1990); for dress, *The Visual History of Costume* by Aileen Ribeiro and Valerie Cumming (London, 1989); *Old London Cries* by A.W. Tuer (London, 1885); and *The Dictionary of National Biography* revised edition (Oxford, 1973).

SOURCES ON OLD LONDON BRIDGE

The Corporation of the City of London's Guildhall Library, Guildhall Art Gallery and Guildhall Records Office hold a treasure trove of information and images of London and Old London Bridge.

The Guildhall Records Office has much original material relating to the Bridge. The Bridge House Records are mainly concerned with land, houses and rents, faithfully recorded by the Bridge Wardens for hundreds of years, and initially written on vellum rolls. They include: muniments of title (title deeds) twelfth to eighteenth centuries; rentals 1358–1359, 1404–1953; Bridge Masters' account rolls 1381–1405 (with gaps); Bridge House Estates Committee 1622–1968; legal case books 1786–1833; granaries records 1568–81, 1673–1714; other financial records 1568–1936 (with gaps); grants and contract books 1570–1923; and weekly payments 1404–45, 1505–38, 1552–1741.

The original Letter Books, 1275–1689, are from the early years of Edward I to the close of the reign of James II, in fifty volumes. They are the registers of bonds and recognizances, arranged alphabetically and subsequently used as minute books by the Court of Aldermen and Court of Common Council, also in part in published form: *Calendar of Letter Books preserved among the Archives of the Corporation of the City of London at the Guildhall*, eleven volumes, 'A' to 'L', edited by Reginald R. Sharpe (London, 1899–1912).

Here also is the Remembrancia, 1579–1640, 1660–4, correspondence between the sovereign, ministers, the Privy Council, the Lord Mayor, aldermen and so on, and much more, some of the material published in: *Remembrancia* by W.H. and H.C. Overall, two volumes (London, 1898), where, for example, Lord Burghley's letters are found (Chapter Five).

BOOKS

The primary reference throughout is *Old London Bridge* by Gordon Home (London, 1931). It is the standard work, and in it more detailed sources for specific facts and events can be found.

Other important sources:

London Bridge: Selected Accounts and Rentals, 1381–1538 by Laura Wright, edited by Vanessa Harding (London Record Society, Vol. 31, 1995), and 'Supplying London Bridge, 1380–1540' by Vanessa Harding (*Franco British Studies, Journal of the British Institute in Paris*, Autumn 1995); *Sources of London English: Medieval Thames Vocabulary* by Laura Wright (Oxford, 1996).

Rochester Bridge: 1357–1856, A History of Its Early Years, compiled from the Wardens' Accounts, by M. Janet Becker (London, Cambridge, Calcutta; Oxford, Madras, Leipzig, Toronto, 1930). This book includes references to Old London Bridge and details of bridge construction as they applied to Rochester Bridge, and likely to London's Bridge. These Bridge Wardens' accounts are the only existing ones other than those for Old London Bridge.

London Bridge by Peter Jackson (London, 1971) is illustrated mainly with his own drawings, in which he depicts the Bridge at various stages and the notable events that occurred on it. In 1998 in the Print Room, Guildhall Library, there was an exhibition of Peter Jackson's work, 'Old London Reconstructed', that included a number of his drawings of the Bridge.

The History of the Tower Bridge and other Bridges over the Thames by Charles Welch (London, 1894). An important source often referring back to the Bridge House Records.

The Story of Three Bridges: The History of London Bridge by the City of London, City Engineers Department (London, 1973).

The Story of the Bridge by Frederick William Robins (Birmingham, 1948).

A Thousand Years of London Bridge by C.W. Shepherd (London, New York, 1971). This contains a description of John Stow by Edward Howes, his literary executor.

Bridge, Church and Palace in Old London by John E.N. Hearsey (London, 1961).

The Lost Rivers of London by Nicholas Barton (London, 1992), a valuable source for the many now hidden rivers and streams in London, which were important in its founding and development, and which still flow under the city.

A Survey of London and Westminster by John Stow (1598, 1603), introduction and notes by C.L. Kingsford, two volumes (Oxford, 1908). This was the first attempt at recording London's history.

Annals, or A Generall Chronicle of England by John Stow (1580, 1615); continued by Richard Meighan (1631); also for Stow, a pamphlet 'printed on the Bridge by T. Harris at the Looking Glass on London Bridge, and sold by C. Corbet at Addison's Head in Fleet Street, 1744. Price 6d.' (British Museum).

The Chronicles of England, Scotland and Ireland of 1577 by Raphael Holinshed, two volumes (London, 1807). Stow assisted with the second edition.

Chronicles of London Bridge by Richard Thomson (London, 1827) is a main reference.

Bede's Ecclesiastical History of the English People edited by Bertram Colgrave and R.A.B. Mynors (Oxford, 1969). In 894–5 King Alfred (871–99) had it translated into Anglo-Saxon. Written in the early eighth century, it is the most important single source for Anglo-Saxon history.

English Social History: A Survey of Six Centuries, Chaucer to Queen Victoria by G.M. Trevelyan (London, New York, Toronto, 1946).

London in Paintings, Guildhall Art Gallery by Ralph Hyde (London, 1999).

By Chapter

Following are sources and notes by chapter, entries in no specific order within a chapter, the references in each chapter in addition to those listed above and to the entries in previous chapters.

What came before
For the Celts:

'Bridging History, A celebration of London's bridges', exhibition at the Museum of London, Spring 2000, for information so far revealed about the remains of the 3,500-year-old Celtic bridge at Vauxhall.

For the Romans:

Caesar's Gallic War translated by Rev. F.P. Long (Oxford, 1911); *Dio's Roman History* translated by E. Cary (London, 1961); *The Works of Tacitus*, Oxford translation, Book 14 (London, 1872–4); Strabo, *The Geography of Strabo*, translated by Horace Leonard Jones (London, 1917–23); 'Traders' Signs on Old London Bridge' by H. Syer Cuming, in *The Journal of the British Archaeological Association*, Vol. 43 (London, 1887); *London Museum Guide: Roman London*, preface by R.E.M. Wheeler (London, 1930); *Roman London* by Jenny Hall and Ralph Merrifield (London, 2000); *The Port of Roman London* by Gustav Milne (London, 1985); *Roman London: Urban archaeology in the nation's capital* by Gustav Milne (London, 1995); *Londonium: London in the Roman Empire* by John Morris, revised by Sarah Macready (London, 1999).

For the Anglo-Saxons:

The Anglo-Saxon Chronicle translated by G.N. Garmonsway (London, revised edition, 1953) (this chronicle of social, political and economic events in England was ordered to be compiled by King Alfred in 891; it was written in Anglo-Saxon rather than Latin, and continuously updated to the twelfth century); 'The Anglo-Saxon Period' by John Blair in *The Oxford Illustrated History of Britain* by Kenneth O. Morgan (Oxford, 1984).

For the Vikings:

Heimskringla, '*The Olaf Sagas*', by Snorri Sturluson, edited by Ernest Rhys, translated by Samuel Laing, introduction and notes by John Beveridge (London, Toronto, New York, 1922) (Chapter XII for the wonderful account of the Viking battle at the Bridge); *The Penguin Historical Atlas of the Vikings* by J. Haywood (London, 1995); *The Vikings* by J.D. Roesdahl (London, 1991).

Chapter One: 'to the Queen . . . the custody of the Bridge'

Her Majesty's Tower, four volumes, by William Hepworth Dixon (London, 1901); *Norman London, with a Translation of William Fitz Stephen's Description* by F.M. Stenton (London, 1934) (FitzStephen was Becket's biographer; for insights and descriptions of London); *Annales monastici* (Annals of Waverley Abbey) edited by H.R. Luard (London, 1864–9); *A Short, Historical Account of London Bridge with a Proposition for a New Stone-Bridge at Westminster, 1736, Tracts of London and Westminster Bridges by Nicholas Hawksmoor* (Hawksmoor was interested in the Bridge, and designed some of the City's churches; he was Wren's assistant and recorded the latter's views on whether the river had been 'turned' during construction of the Bridge); *Chronicles of the Mayors and Sheriffs of London*, A.D. *1188 to* A.D. *1274* (from the original Latin and Anglo-Norman of the *Liber de Antiquis Legibus*, attributed to Arnald Fitz-Thedmar) translated by Henry Thomas Riley (London, 1863); *Liber Albus: the White book of the City of London* of 1419 (compiled by the town clerk, John Carpenter, codifying the City's customs and regulations, some from much earlier) translated by H.T. Riley (London, 1861); *Memorials of London and London Life, 13th, 14th and 15th centuries* edited by H.T. Riley (London, 1868); *Calendar of Pleas and Memoranda Rolls*, 1323–1437, six volumes, edited by A.H. Thomas; 1437-82, edited by P.E. Jones (London, 1926–61); *Calendar of Wills proved and enrolled in the Court of Hustings*, 1258–1688, two volumes, edited by Reginald R. Sharpe (London, 1889–90); *London and the Kingdom, a history derived mainly from the archives at Guildhall*, three volumes, by Reginald R. Sharpe (London, 1894–5); *Calendar of Coroners Rolls of the City of London: AD 1300–1378* edited by Reginald R. Sharpe (London, 1913); *Calendar of Early Mayor's Court Rolls, AD 1298–1307, Roll B*, edited by A.H. Thomas (London, 1924); *A Chronicle of London*, 1089–1483, by Charles Wriothesley, edited by W.D. Hamilton (London, 1875); *The Early Modern City, 1450–1750* by Christopher R. Friedrichs (London, 1995); *London 800–1216: the Shaping of a City* by Christopher N.L. Brooke Dee and Gillian Keir (London, 1927, 1975); *Tavern Anecdotes, Sayings, and Reminiscences* by Charles Hindley (London, 1875); *Inns and Taverns of London* by Henry C. Shelle (London, 1909); *Chronicles of London* edited by Charles Lethbridge Kingsford (London, 1827, 1905).

Chapter Two: 'with speares sharpe groond for life and death'

The New Chronicles of England and France of 1516, 2nd edition 1533, by Robert Fabyan, two parts, edited by Henry Ellis (London, 1811) (of most value as a chronicle of London which begins with the accession of Richard I); *Chronicles of England, France and Spain*, two volumes, by Jean Froissart (*c.* 1333–*c.* 1404), edited by Thomas Johnes (London, 1862); *Relics and Memorials of London City* by James S. Ogilvy (London, Toronto, New York, 1910); *The Itinerary of John Leland in or about the years 1535-1543* by Lucy Toulmin Smith (London, 1909); *A Chronicle of London, 1089–1483: written in the fifteenth century* edited by H.N. Nicholls (London, 1827); *Original Chronicle* by Andrew of Wyntoun, edited by F.J. Amours (Edinburgh, 1903–14); *Calendar of MSS relating to Scotland* edited by J. Bain (Edinburgh, 1888); *Henry Yevele, c. 1320 to 1400: the Life of an English Architect* by John Hooper Harvey (London, 1944).

For the joust:

The Tournament in England, 1100–1400 (Woodbridge, 1986); *Tournaments, Jousts, Chivalry and Pageants in the Middle Ages* by Richard Barber and Juliet R.V. Barker (Woodbridge, 1989).

Chapter Three: 'Jack Cade hath gotten London Bridge'

Three Fifteenth Century Chronicles, 1437, edited by James Gairdner (Camden Society, 1880); *The Paston Letters, 1422–1509 A.D.*, six volumes, edited by James Gairdner, reprint of 1872–5 edition (Edinburgh, 1910; reprinted 1983); 'Gregory's Chronicle', in *Historical Collections of a Citizen of London*, 1428–9, edited by James Gairdner (Camden Society, 1876).

Chapter Four: 'this confusion of wives, so many . . . great personages . . . beheaded'

Letters and Papers illustrative of the Reigns of Richard III and Henry VII edited by James Gairdner (London, 1861); *Wolsey* by A.F. Pollard (London, New York, 1953); *The Life and Death of Cardinal Wolsey* by George Cavendish (first printed in 1641, 1667, 1706), edited by Richard S. Sylvester (London, New York, 1959); *The Earlier Tudors, 1485–1558, The Oxford History of England* by J.D. Mackie (Oxford, 1952, 1983); *The Life of Fisher* by Richard Hall (1539–1604), transcribed from Harleian MS. 6382 by the Rev. Ronald Bayne (London, 1921); *The Life and Death of Sir Thomas More, Lord High Chancellor of England* by his great-grandson Cresacre More, 1631, edited by J. Hunter (London, 1828); *Thomas Cromwell* by B.B. Merriman (London, 1902); *The Book of Martyrs (Actes and Monuments of these latter and perillous dayes ...*) by John Fox (1563); *A Chronicle of England during the Reigns of the Tudors, From AD 1485 to 1559* by Charles Wriothesley, two volumes, edited by William Douglas Hamilton (Camden Society, 1875); *The Diary of Henry Machyn 1550–1563* edited by J.G. Nichols (Camden Society, 1848);

Anecdotes of Painting in England, with some account of the principal artists, 1798–1822, by Horace Walpole, Lord Orford (London 1849), and Edward Edward's continuation (London, 1888); *Street Life in Medieval England* by G.T. Salusbury (Oxford, 1939, 1948); *A Century of the English Book Trade*, 1457–1557, by E. Gordon Duff (London, 1905); *Hall's Chronicle*, R. Grafton (ed.) (London, 1809).

Chapter Five: '. . . one of the wonders of the world'

Londinopolis; an Historicall Discourse or Perlustration of the City of London. The Imperial Chamber, and chief Emporium of Great Britain by James Howell (London, 1657); *Neighbourhood and Society: A London Suburb in the Seventeenth Century* by Jeremy Boulton (Cambridge, 1987); *Southwark and the City* by David J. Johnson (Oxford, 1969); *Old and New London* by W. Thornbury and E. Walford (London, 1873); *The Ash Wednesday Supper* by Giordano Bruno, edited by Edward A. Gosselin and Lawrence S. Lerner (London, 1977); 'Notes upon Norden and His Map of London, 1593', *London Topographical Record* by H.B. Wheatley (London, 1868); *English Warfaring Life in the Middle Ages (XIVth Century)* by J.J. Jusserand, translated by Lucy Toulmin Smith (London, 2nd edition, 1920); *Elizabethan England* by Alison Plowden (London, 1982); *Henry VIII and his Court* by Neville Williams (London, 1971); *The England of Elizabeth: The Structure of Society* by A.L. Rowse (London, 1950); *Thomas Platter's Travels in England, 1599* translated from the German by Clare Williams (London, 1937); *The London Spy, the Varieties and Vices of the Town Exposed to View* by Edward (Ned) Ward (first published 1698–1703; London, 1927).

Chapter Six: 'the late terrible fire on London Bridge'

For Charles I, Civil War and Commonwealth, and Restoration:

Calendar of State Papers, Domestic, 1641–3 edited by W.D. Hamilton (London, 1887); *Memorials of English Affairs during the Reign of Charles I* by Bulstrode Whitelock (London, 1686; Oxford, 1853); *The Army Lists of the Roundheads and Cavaliers, containing the names of the officers in the Royal and Parliamentary Armies of 1642* edited by Edward

Peacock (London, 1863), at the Public Record Office, Kew; 'The Original Officers List of the New Model Army (1645)', by R.R. Temple, in *Bulletin of the Institute of Historical Research* 59, 1986; *Clarendon's History of the Great Rebellion* edited by Roger Lockyer (London, 1967); *New Model Army in England, Ireland, Scotland* by I. Gentles (Oxford, 1992); *The Cities Loyalty Display'd* (London, 1661).

Travels of Cosmo the Third Grand Duke of Tuscany Through England during the Reign of King Charles II 1669 by Count Lorenzo Magalotti (London, 1821).

For Evelyn and Pepys:

Fumifugium, or the Inconvenience if the Aer and Smoake of London Dissipated by John Evelyn (1661); *Correspondence of John Evelyn, F.R.S.*, two volumes, edited by William Bray (London, 1898); Samuel Pepys, *The Diary of Samuel Pepys*, deciphered by the Rev. J. Smith, edited by Lord Braybrooke (London, New York, 1906).

For the plague and the 1633 and 1666 fires:

A Record of the Mercies of God; or, a Thoughtful Remembrance by Nehemiah Wallington; *A Tour Through the Whole Island of Great Britain* by Daniel Defoe, edited and with an introduction and notes by Pat Rogers (Exeter, 1986); *A Journal of the Plague Year* by Daniel Defoe, 1722, edited by A. Burgess (Harmondsworth, 1966); *God's Terrible Voice in the City* by Rev. Thomas Vincent (London, 1667); *The Plague Pamphlets of Thomas Dekker* edited by F.P. Wilson (Oxford, 1925); *The Great Plague in London in 1665* by Walter George Bell (London, 1924, 1951, 1994); *The Story of London's Great Fire* by W.G. Bell (London, 1929); *The Great Fire of London* by Gustav Milne (London, 1986).

For Wenceslaus Hollar:

A Bohemian Artist in England by R. Godfrey (New Haven, 1994); *Hollar's Journey on the Rhine* translated by Milos V. Kratochvil and Roberta Finlayson Samsour (Prague, 1965); *Wenceslaus Hollar, Delineator of His Time* by Katherine S. Van Eerde (Charlottesville, Virginia, 1970); *Brief Lives* by John Aubrey (1669–96), two volumes, edited by A. Clark (Oxford, 1898).

Chapter Seven: 'keep to the left'

The History and Survey of London, two volumes, by W. Maitland (London, 1756); *New View of London*, two volumes, by Edward Hatton (London, 1708); *London Coffee Houses* by Bryant Lillywhite (London, 1963); *The History of Coffee Houses in England* by Edward Forbes Robinson (London, 1893); *Memorials of Temple Bar with some account of Fleet Street and the parishes* by T.C. Noble (London, 1869); *Sign Boards of Old London Shops* by Ambrose Heal (London, 1957).

For Charles II:

Life in Stuart England by M.P. Ashley (London, 1964); *Charles II* by Ronald Hutton (Oxford, 1989); *Restoration London* by Liza Picard (London, 1997).

Chapter Eight: 'a public nuisance, long felt, and universally censured'

Wine and Walnuts by William Henry Pyne (pseudonym Ephraim Hardcastle) (London, 1824); *Some Account of London* by Thomas Pennant (London, 4th edition, 1805); *The Life of Robert Owen written by Himself with some selections from his writings* by Robert Owen (1857, 1858; London, 1967) (a rare description of life in a shop on the Bridge); *Harrison's Description of England in Shakespeare's Youth* by William Harrison (1534–93) (London, 1877; New York, 1994); *A New History of London: including Westminster and Southwark* by John Noorthouck (London, 1773); *Canaletto* by Katherine Baxter and J.G. Links (New York, 1989); *European Urbanization, 1500–1800* by Jan De Vries (London, 1984).

Chapter Nine: 'a remedy for this evil'

For Hogarth:

Hogarth's London by H.B. Wheatley (London, 1909); *Hogarth and Commercial Britain* by David Dabydeen (London, 1987); *Hogarth* by Jenny Uglow (London, 1997).

For Turner:

Turner on the Thames, River Journeys in the year 1805 by David Hill

(New Haven, London, 1993); *The Art of J.M.W. Turner* by David Blayney Brown (London, 1990); *Landscape & Memory* by Simon Schama (London, 1995).

Literary Anecdotes of the Eighteenth Century by John Nichols, edited by Colin Clair (London, 1867); *Life of Johnson* by James Boswell, introduction by Pat Rogers (Oxford, 1904, 1980); *The Borough at London Bridge, An Urban Study* by Kim Wilkies Associates (London, 1999).

Exhibitions

'London Bridge in Art', Guildhall Art Gallery, 10 June–5 July 1969, with an introduction on the history of the Bridge.

'To God and the Bridge: The story of the City's bridge', catalogue of the exhibition held at the Guildhall Art Gallery, 1 June–28 September 1972.

'Living Bridges: The Inhabited bridge, past, present and future', Royal Academy of Arts, London, 26 September–18 December 1996.

'Old London Reconstructed', drawings by Peter Jackson, 12 May–25 September 1998, Print Room, Guildhall Library.

'Bridging History' exhibition, Museum of London, April–May 2000.

Websites

Guildhall Art Gallery: www.guildhall-art-gallery.org.uk

The Corporation of London ('Collage' image database): http://collage.nhil.com

The Corporation of London (information on the City and the Guildhall Library): www.corpoflondon.gov.uk

The Corporation of London (manuscripts): http://ihr.sas.ac.uk/gh

Museum of London: www.museumoflondon.org.uk

Tate Britain (paintings by Turner): www.tate.org.uk

Fishmongers Company: www.fishhall.co.uk

Mercers Company (The Whittington Charity): www.mercers.co

Millennium Footbridge: www.mbridge.ft.com

Lake Havasu City, Arizona (Rennie's London Bridge): www.lakehavasucity.com

Acknowledgements

Extracts from *Four Quartets*, 'The Dry Salvages' by T.S. Eliot (Faber & Faber, London, 1944), and *The Waste Land* by T.S. Eliot (first published by Faber & Faber in *Collected Poems, 1909-62*, London, 1963) used by permission. Quote by Gustav Milne in 'What came before' is from his *The Port of Roman London* (Batsford, London, 1985).

I wish to thank Heather Holden-Brown, Non-fiction Publishing Director, and Lorraine Jerram, Non-fiction Senior Editor, at Headline; my agent, Sara Menguc; Clive Priddle; Marion Dent; Sandy Ransford; clergy and guides at Southwark Cathedral and the Church of St Magnus the Martyr; Prints and Drawings Department at Tate Britain; the Archivist, Fishmongers Hall. Also the staff at the Museum of London and at the Guildhall Library for their unfailing helpfulness and courtesy.

Where to see Old London Bridge

Websites

London Bridge Museum Trust (history and plans for a London Bridge Museum): www.oldlondonbridge.com
www.bbb.education.history (BBC website for a 3-D walk across the medieval Bridge)

Models

St Magnus the Martyr
Lower Thames Street
London EC3R 6DN
Tel: (020) 7623 8022

A fine detailed model about fourteen feet long sits in the lobby of Church of England Anglo-Catholic St Magnus. It depicts the Bridge in the 1400s, and even on a specific day, for in the abundance of people coming and going on the Bridge is King Henry V's procession leaving for Agincourt. It was modelled in 1987 by David T. Aggett, who is a Liveryman of the Plumbers Company, one of the Livery Companies whose Guild church this is. Mr Aggett was also a London policeman, and St Magnus fell within his beat; you can find him in his uniform among the crowd above the fifth arch from the City end.

Open Tue–Fri (10am–3.30pm), Sun (10am–2pm)
Mass: Tue–Thur 12.30pm; Benediction: Fri 1.05pm;
Solemn Sung Mass: Sun 11am

MUSEUM OF LONDON
London Wall
London EC2Y 5HN
Tel: (020) 7600 3699
Model of the Roman bridge; partial model of Old London Bridge.

Paintings

GUILDHALL ART GALLERY
Guildhall Yard
London EC2P 2EJ
Tel: (020) 7332 3700

Make this your first stop. For images of Old London Bridge see the 'Collage' computer program at the Guildhall Library and Art Gallery, which holds almost 600 pictures of the Bridge, among 30,000 of London.

The many paintings of interest include: William Marlow's (1740–1813) dramatic oil painting, *The Waterworks at London Bridge on Fire*, 1779 and his *Fresh Wharf, London Bridge*; an oil on canvas attributed to 'Waggoner', *The Great Fire of London 1666*; Daniel Turner's (1782–1817) oil of a view from the south-west, showing the Bridge during the great frost of 1817; Clarkson Stanfield's (1793–1867) oil, *The Opening of London Bridge*; anon., *Demolition of Old London Bridge*; a line and wash dated 18 April 1627, possibly by Alexander Keirrinckx (1600–c. 1652); George Scharf senior's (1788–1860) two watercolours of old and new London bridges from the east; Edward W. Cooke's (1811–80) series of pencil drawings, later engraved on copper and published in 1833, among sixty-nine images by him in the collection; Claude de Jongh's *Three Cranes at Low Water; The View of Old London Bridge*, 1630, and two drawings, dated 1627; Samuel Scott's (1710–72) oil painting of a view of the Bridge from the south-east, and his Venetian-looking *Entrance to the Fleet River*; Jan Griffier the Younger's (active 1738–73) oil, *The Thames during the Great Frost of 1739–40*.

GUILDHALL LIBRARY
Prints and Maps Collection
Aldermansbury
London EC2P 2EJ
Tel: (020) 7606 3030

The 'Collage' computer program is also accessible here. The large
collection includes Wenceslaus Hollar's (1607–77) map showing the
devastation of the Great Fire; and much other original material
relating to the Bridge. The Guildhall Records Office holds George
Dance the Younger's (1741–1825) plan and elevation for ten new
houses, dated 1745, and the Bridge House Records.

MUSEUM OF LONDON

Much of interest for adults and children, including *London from
Southwark, c.* 1650, the first painted view before the Great Fire in
1666 (Anglo-Dutch school); *Great Fire of London 1666*, view from
Tower Wharf (Dutch school oil); Hollar's view, enlarged, in 1644;
anon. oil painting of Sir William Hewett in sheriff's robes; artefacts relating to the Bridge. Not to be missed.

BRITISH MUSEUM
Great Russell Street
London WC1B 3DG
Tel: (020) 7636 1555

Claus Jansz Visscher's (1580–?) line engraving from the south-west
with the Great Stone Gate in the foreground, 1616; John Norden's
(*c.* 1546–*c.* 1626) line engraving from the south-west, *c.* 1600, in
the Crace Collection; Antonio Canaletto's (1697–1768) line and
wash of the Bridge from the west, *c.* 1750; Sutton Nicholls (active
1680–1740) line engraving from the west, *c.* 1710; a watercolour
from the south-west attributed to R.P. Bonnington (1802–28); also
Roman and other relics and coins, found in the Thames near the
Bridge site during excavations, as well as traders' tokens (illegal
currency used during the Civil War).

BRITISH LIBRARY
96 Euston Road
London NW1 2DB
Tel: (020) 7412 7000

Anon. illuminated volume of poems by Charles, Duke of Orléans (Royal MSS, 16 F.II. 15), with the northern half of the Bridge in the background, the first time it was depicted; Claus Jansz Visscher's famous 1616 engraving, *Long Prospect of London*, an accurate and detailed long view of the Bridge from the south-west (in the King's Library).

TATE BRITAIN
Millbank
London SW1P 4RG
Tel: (020) 7887 8000

In the Prints and Drawings Room in the Clore Gallery: J.M.W. Turner's (1775–1851) pencil and watercolour *Old London Bridge, with the Monument and the Church of St Magnus King and Martyr*, 1794–5, and pencil studies for it; Turner's three small sketchbooks in which Old London Bridge appears, too fragile to handle, but can be viewed on microfilm.

In the Collection of Tate: two of Turner's pastiches of the Van Dycks that were once at Petworth; Samuel Scott's oil *A View of London Bridge before the late alterations* (in storage; can be seen on website); Daniel Turner's (active 1782–1801) oil, *Old London Bridge* (after Samuel Scott) (in storage; can be seen on website).

FISHMONGERS HALL
London Bridge
London EC4R 9EL
Tel: (020) 7626 3531

The elegant Hall holds a fascinating collection of paintings and artefacts, including: Samuel Scott's oil, *London Bridge*, from the southeast, before the mid-eighteenth-century alterations; John Thomas

Serres' (1759–1825) *River Thames, Old Fishmongers Hall and Billingsgate*; James Holland's (1800–70) wonderful oil, *The Demolition of Old London Bridge*, 1832; the chair made from the underwater wood of the piers and stone from the foundation stone of Old London Bridge; images of this and other bridges are carved on the back slats. Tours of the Hall can be arranged by appointment.

NATIONAL GALLERY
Trafalgar Square
London WC2N 5DN
Tel: (020) 7747 2885

William Hogarth's (1697–1764) *The Death of the Countess*, from his *Mariage à la Mode* series, in which a glimpse of the Bridge can be seen through a window.

SHAKESPEARE'S GLOBE
21 New Globe Walk
London SE1 9DT
Tel: (020) 7902 1400

The tour of the exhibition and the thatched theatre evokes the atmosphere of life in Shakespeare's London, Southwark and around the Bridge.

THE IVEAGH BEQUEST
Kenwood House
Hampstead Lane
London NW3 7JR
Tel: (020) 8348 1286

Claude de Jongh's (*c.* 1600–63) oil painting, *Old London Bridge*, from the west, signed and dated 'C. de Jongh 1630'.

VICTORIA AND ALBERT MUSEUM
Cromwell Road
South Kensington
London SW7 2RL
Tel: (020) 7942 2000

The Prints, Drawings and Paintings Department houses Claude de Jongh's (*c.* 1600–63) oil, *View of Old London Bridge from the West*, dated 1650 on the frame, but certainly before the 1633 fire. It is broadly accurate, but there are some discrepancies; for example, the Drawbridge is over the ninth arch instead of the seventh from the Southwark end. The department is also home to an anonymous watercolour, *Old and New London Bridges from the Surrey Shore*, that is from the west, *c.* 1831; and, from a 1749 engraving by Samuel Buck (1696–1779) and Nathaniel Buck (active first half eighteenth century), a lithograph by R. Martin, *London Bridge: West Side with the Waterworks*, from the south-west. The Bucks' work was used as a reference for the sixth stage of Old London Bridge (although it incorrectly depicted the Drawbridge over the sixth arch instead of the seventh).

LONDON BRIDGE MUSEUM TRUST

A London Bridge Museum Trust, under the guidance of founder, Peter Lennard, has in hand plans for a Museum of London Bridge to be opened around 2005. It will be located under the Southwark end of today's London Bridge, where a surprisingly substantial portion of Rennie's London Bridge remains, including 'Nancy's steps' from Dickens' *Oliver Twist*. The sixteen distinguished trustees include President Sir Peter Studd, who as Lord Mayor of the City of London officially opened Rennie's reconstructed London Bridge at Lake Havasu City in 1971; Chairman Sir Peter Gadsden, Lord Mayor of the City of London (1979–80); the Very Reverend Colin Slee, Dean of Southwark Cathedral; Peter Jackson, artist/historian and Chairman of the London Topographical Society; and Linda Binder, Lake Havasu City Representative in the Arizona State Assembly.

NOTE: This is a selected list. There may be more works within a collection. Always check on opening times, and whether the item of interest is on display or if an appointment is necessary. Some rare items have limited access, or may be viewed only on the website of the institution concerned.

Chronology

1500 BC	Bronze Age Celtic bridge built over the Thames at Vauxhall.
54 BC	Caesar's second expedition to Britain.
AD **43**	Romans invade and conquer Britain.
AD **50**	The Romans found Londinium where no settlement existed.
AD **60**	In a revolt led by Boudicca, Queen of the Iceni, London is burned to the ground; no bridge could have survived.
AD **80**	The Romans make a decision to rebuild Londinium with the features of a principal Roman city.
AD **80–90**	The first Roman wooden bridge is built.
AD **100**	Londinium becomes capital of the Roman province of Britain, with a bridge or sequence of wooden bridges built over the Thames on the spot where Old London Bridge would one day stand.
c. AD **407**	The Romans abandon London.
c. **490–1066**	The Anglo-Saxon period begins when West German Saxons invade and conquer.
c. **730**	Bede reports that London has become 'a mart of many peoples coming by land and sea'.
793–1042	The Viking Age in England.
842	The Anglo-Saxon settlement is known as Lundenwic.
886	King Alfred recaptures London from the Danes.
979	During the reign of the Saxon King Aethelred II there is a reference to a bridge at London in a list of tolls taken at Billingsgate below London bridge. London is frequently attacked by the Norsemen.

c. 984	Early reference to a London bridge when a widow and her son are found guilty of witchcraft; the woman is thrown into the Thames from London Bridge.
994	For the first time a Viking battle is recorded at the bridge; the attackers are led by the Danish king, Svein I Haraldsson, and Olaf Tryggvason.
1009	London appears in *The Anglo-Saxon Chronicle* for the first time in fifteen years; this is a year in which 'they [the Norsemen] often fought against the town of London'.
1013	The King of Denmark, Svein 'Fork-Beard', and his son Cnut invade; all the kingdoms submit to Svein, and Aethelred flees to Normandy.
1014	Svein dies early in the year, and Cnut succeeds his father; in an all-out attempt to regain his capital from the Danes, Aethelred returns, aided by King Olaf II Haraldsson of Norway; King Olaf leads the attack in the famously described battle at London Bridge which is the basis of the nursery rhyme.
1016	Aethelred dies. His son Edmund Ironside is chosen by the southern Anglo-Saxon nobles to be king – but the Danes choose Cnut. Cnut digs a ditch to get past London Bridge and defeats Edmund, but they agree to each rule part of the country. Edmund dies, and Cnut becomes King of England.
1052	Banished Earl Godwin returns with a fleet, leading to a confrontation at the bridge.
1066	The Battle of Hastings results in the Norman Conquest.
1087–1100	William II (Rufus), son of 'the Conqueror', is credited with rebuilding the wooden London Bridge, probably financed by levies on land in Surrey and Middlesex.
1100–35	Henry I exempts a manor belonging to the monks of Battle Abbey from the work of London Bridge.
1097	Districts near London are required to provide forced labour for London Bridge.
1122	The London Bridge of wood already possesses revenue-producing lands.

1131   First mention of an individual associated with working on the bridge: Geoffrey, 'Ingeniator', is paid £25 for rebuilding two arches.

1135   Major fire burns London and the wooden bridge; the bridge is rebuilt.

c. 1163   The last wooden bridge is built of elm under the direction of Peter de Colechurch, Chaplain of St Mary Colechurch.

1176   Peter de Colechurch begins to build Old London Bridge, the first one of stone anywhere in the British Isles since the Romans left 800 years earlier.

Henry II imposes a tax on wool to support the building of the Bridge.

1189–99   Richard I, 'the Lionheart', depletes the country of vast sums of money, probably delaying the construction of the Bridge.

1192   Henry Fitz-Ailwin becomes the first Mayor of London; later the position is called 'Lord Mayor'.

1199–1216   King John supports the Bridge by giving the City some 'void places' for 'building upon', the rents from which help to pay for construction and repairs. Also, the half-pence taken from foreign merchants is given to the work of the Bridge.

The King attempts to appoint a successor to Peter: Isembert, Master of the Schools of Xainctes (Saintes), but there is no record that he ever arrived.

1201   King John decrees that the rents and profits of the houses to be erected on the Bridge be used for its repair and upkeep, confirming that the Bridge was built as a habitable structure.

1205   Peter de Colechurch dies, and is buried in the undercroft of the Chapel of St Thomas à Becket on Old London Bridge.

King John appoints 'Brother Wasce' and some others 'for the custody of London Bridge'.

1209–1384: First of the Seven Stages of Old London Bridge

c. **1209**　Old London Bridge is complete with houses on it.

1212　On 11 July a major fire starts in Southwark, destroys St Mary Overie, many houses on the Bridge and damages the Chapel; there are numerous casualties.

1215　King John meets the barons and signs Magna Carta.

1216　Louis, Dauphin of France, crosses the Bridge, invited by the Barons who deposed King John.

　　　　John dies a few months later; the child-king Henry III is crowned and Louis is paid to leave.

1243　The Bridge House, the administrative centre of the Bridge, is first mentioned.

1249　Henry III (1216–72) takes over the revenues of London Bridge to pay for his wars.

1252　Henry gives a grant of protection to the Brethren of the Bridge, allowing them to beg for funds.

1257　First mention of the Drawbridge.

1258　City establishes its control of the entire length of the Bridge.

　　　　There is agitation against Henry III's misgovernment. He signs the Provisions of Oxford in 1258 limiting royal power, but repudiates the document in 1261.

1261　The civil war known as the Barons' War begins.

1263　Unpopular Queen Eleanor, who withheld vital funds for repairs, is pelted by citizens as her barge tries to pass under the Bridge, forcing her to return to the Tower.

1264　The leader of the barons, Simon de Montfort, and his forces occupy Southwark; he is opposed by some in the City and the Drawbridge is raised against him, but the commons side with him and lower it.

1265　By now Bridge funds are administered by 'the Brethren and Chaplains of the Chapel of St Thomas'.

　　　　De Montfort summons the first English parliament; in the same year he is killed at the Battle of Evesham.

1267　Earl of Gloucester, leader of the barons, occupies Southwark; the Drawbridge is raised but Gloucester gets control of the City and its gates.

1269	King Henry again grants Queen Eleanor custody of the Bridge.
1270	The Bridge is in danger of collapse from lack of repair. Queen Eleanor resigns custody of the Bridge, but two weeks later takes it back, continuing to divert funds.
1281	In the reign of Edward I (1272–1307), control of the Bridge finally returns to the City.
	King Edward commands that alms be collected throughout the country to raise money for the Bridge.
1281–2	In a severe winter roads appear on the ice between Westminster and Lambeth; when five arches are destroyed by the ice, the rhyme of the *Olaf Sagas* is adapted to become the nursery rhyme 'London Bridge is Falling Down'.
1282	King Edward establishes the regular appointment of Bridge Wardens. He also imposes what amounts to a charter for the Bridge: pontage or bridge tax. Sources of income are arranged: tolls are introduced, and the King gives portions of wasteland and the Stocks Market to the Bridge, the rents to provide funds.
1305	The head of William Wallace, Scottish patriot, is exhibited on the Bridge, the first recorded instance of this practice.
1309–10	In a harsh winter, there is the first recorded occasion of festive activities taking place on the river near the Bridge; the Bridge is damaged by ice.
1319	The Bear tavern at the bridgefoot in Southwark is first mentioned.
1337–60	Hundred Years War (first phase).
1348–9	The Black Death is in London.
1357	Edward, the Black Prince, eldest son of Edward III, returns to London after his victory at Poitiers; he crosses the decorated Bridge in triumph with his captive, John II, King of France.
	King John is allowed to return to France to raise his own enormous ransom, leaving his son Louis, Duke of Anjou, in his place.

1358	The Bridge Wardens' accounts record 138 shops on the Bridge, bringing in £160 4s in rents.
1363	Louis escapes, and 'John the Good' of France honourably returns to captivity, only to die shortly after.
1377–99	Richard II reigns.
1377–80	A series of ever higher poll taxes is imposed.
1381	Wat Tyler leads the Peasants' Revolt. The young King meets Tyler, who is slain by Walworth; the heads of Tyler and others go to the Bridge.
1384–97	The entire structure of London Bridge is rebuilt, when master mason and architect Henry Yevele is a Bridge Warden; this includes a new chapel in the Perpendicular Gothic style.
1388	A new drawbridge is constructed.
1390	On 23 April the Champion of England and the Champion of Scotland joust on the Bridge.
1392	Angry King Richard, refused money by the City, replaces the Mayor and sheriffs, transfers the courts to York and imposes a huge fine on the City; peace is made when King Richard and Queen Anne (d. 1394) are received at the Bridge with lavish gifts and money, part of a great reception.
1395	King Richard and Charles VI of France meet at Arls in Picardy; a peace treaty is drawn up.
1396	King Richard marries Charles's eight-year-old daughter Isabel; she is greeted on Old London Bridge.
1397	King Richard's four knights murder his uncle, the Duke of Gloucester, in Calais; the knights are beheaded, their heads exhibited on the Bridge.
1399	Richard is deposed and dies in 1400.
1403	During the reign of the Lancastrian Henry IV (1399–1413), Kent is the centre of a rising led by Henry Percy, Earl of Northumberland, and his son 'Hotspur'.
1411–30	The Guildhall is constructed in stone.
1413	The Hundred Years War is reopened by Henry V (1413–22) (second phase).
1415	Henry V, victorious at Agincourt, is welcomed home in

a reception more magnificent than anything preceding it; he brings back the captured French commander, Charles, Duke of Orléans, who will be held captive in the Tower for twenty-five years. This leads to the first illustration of London Bridge.

1421   Henry V is received on the Bridge with his new Queen, Catherine, daughter of Charles VI of France.
Prince Henry is born, and Henry V returns to France.

1422   Henry V dies at Vincennes, from where his funeral procession returns over the Bridge. The infant Henry VI soon becomes King of France as well.

1424   One of the arches cracks; iron-shod carts are banned from the Bridge for the first of many times.

1426–8   A new Drawbridge Gate is built.

1437   On 14 January, the Great Stone Gate collapses, bringing down two arches with it; this falls in one piece into the river where it remains for so long it is believed to be a natural rock formation, and the passageway under the third arch is now called 'Rock Lock'.

1438   Extensive repairs to the Bridge begin, supervised by Richard Beck of Canterbury; the result is a strong and beautiful piece of work.

1442   A new drawbridge is begun.

1445   There is a reception on the Bridge for the bride of Henry VI (1422–61/1470–1), Margaret of Anjou; the marriage aims to make peace between England and France.

1450   William de la Pole, Earl of Suffolk, who arranged the royal marriage and was a leading figure in Henry's bankrupt and disastrous government, is murdered. Jack Cade and his rebels reach London. On 5 July fighting begins on the Bridge between Cade's followers and Londoners. In the worst violence ever seen on the Bridge, part of it is burned and many bridge-dwellers are killed. After both sides fight to exhaustion, the rebels retreat; the head of Jack Cade is placed on the Drawbridge Gate.

1453   By the end of the Hundred Years War, Lancastrian Henry VI has lost all of the vast English territories in south-west France; only Calais remains.

1455–85	Wars of the Roses.
1461	Another spectacular and colourful occasion on the Bridge and in the City occurs when Yorkist Edward IV (1461–70/1471–83) comes from Sheen (Richmond) Palace to the Tower to prepare for his coronation.
1463	On 5 May, the Common Council orders that the Drawbridge should be raised for all ships wishing to pass through.
1471	Another uprising starts in Kent, this time led by Thomas 'the Bastard' Fauconbridge. He supports the Lancastrian Henry VI, whom he intends to restore to the throne. They unsuccessfully attack the Bridge and set fire to the newly built Great Stone Gate and thirteen houses; the head of Fauconbridge goes to the Bridge.
1476	Caxton sets up his printing press at Westminster; his apprentice Wynkyn de Worde takes over in 1491.
1481	When a house on the Bridge falls into the Thames, five men are killed. On 27 July, the Bridge Wardens petition the Common Council once again to ban laden carts with iron-shod wheels from passing over the Bridge.
1485–1509	The accession of the first Tudor king, Lancastrian Henry VII, marks the end of the Middle Ages.
1497	The Common Council orders that the decayed Drawbridge be raised only as a defensive measure.

c. 1500: Second Stage of Old London Bridge

c. **1500**	The first illustration of the Bridge appears: the image in the Duke of Orléans' manuscript.
1501	A magnificent reception is held for Catherine of Aragon, bride-to-be of Arthur, Prince of Wales, and later of his brother Henry VIII; she is the last princess to be so welcomed on Old London Bridge.
1504	On 21 November, a serious fire starts at St Magnus and destroys six houses at the northern (City) end of the Bridge.
1506–7	In a severe winter carriages cross the ice on the Thames for most of January.

1509	The funeral procession of Henry VII goes along the bridge street. Henry VIII (1509–47) becomes king.
1515	Wolsey's greatly anticipated cardinal's hat arrives at Dover, and is conveyed to London in triumph.
1518	Wolsey is made papal legate.
1520	Henry VIII and François I meet at the Field of the Cloth of Gold near Calais.
1522	London welcomes the Holy Roman Emperor Charles V, the most powerful ruler to visit to date.
1529	Cardinal Campeggio arrives to hear (with Wolsey) Henry's divorce from Catherine of Aragon. Wolsey is stripped of honours; he dies in 1530.
1530	The Statute of Bridges is introduced to protect and repair bridges throughout the kingdom.
1533	Henry VIII marries Anne Boleyn. King Henry is excommunicated by the Pope. Elizabeth Barton, the 'Maid of Kent', makes treasonable prophecies, especially against the King's recent marriage; her head goes to the Bridge.
1534	The Act of Supremacy makes Henry head of the English Church.
1535	Bishop Fisher's head is sent to the Bridge, followed by that of Sir Thomas More, who did not accept Henry VIII as supreme head of the Church of England.
1535–7	The suppression and the Dissolution of the Monasteries.
1536	Anne Boleyn is beheaded. King Henry marries Jane Seymour.
1537	Prince Edward is born to Jane Seymour, who dies shortly after.
1538	Henry VIII orders that the dedication of the Chapel on the Bridge be changed from that of St Thomas of Canterbury, and all representations of the saint be defaced. It became St Thomas the Apostle, then Our Lady Chapel.
1539–40	A painter alters or paints over the images of Becket in the Chapel.

1540	King Henry marries unattractive Anne of Cleves, blaming Thomas Cromwell, his principal adviser; Cromwell's head goes to the Bridge.
	Henry marries Catherine Howard, who is executed in 1542.
	In the Chapel, only one priest and a clerk remain.
1543	King Henry marries Catherine Parr.
1547	Henry VIII dies. The boy Edward VI (1547–53) becomes king.
1549	A decree is issued ordering the defacing of the Chapel, formerly of St Thomas à Becket, inside and out.
1550	Southwark is sold to the City for £642 2s. 1d.
1553	Edward dies and Mary I (1553–8) becomes queen.
	The Chapel is turned into a shop and a residence, later a warehouse.
1554	Queen Mary's betrothal to Philip of Spain sparks the rebellion led by Sir Thomas Wyatt in which the Bridge is strongly defended; Wyatt is executed.
	The Queen marries Philip.
1558	Mary dies. Elizabeth I becomes queen.
1565	A frost fair is held on the river.
1577	The demolition of the brutal Drawbridge Gate begins, to be replaced by the incomparable Nonesuch House. The Foundation Stone of Nonesuch House is laid on 28 August; it is completed in 1579.
	Heads are now placed on the Great Stone Gate at the Southwark end.
c. **1577**	Near the Southwark end 'the house with many windows' is built.
1580	The City agrees that Dutchman Peter Morris can establish his Waterworks to pump water into the City. Morris is given a lease for the first waterwheel.
1580	Francis Drake returns having circumnavigated the world.
1582	A regular supply of water to the City begins when Morris's first waterwheel is operational; it is not under an arch at the City end of the Bridge, but sits upstream on the west side. A lease is granted for a wheel in the second arch.

A law is passed decreeing that shop counters on the Bridge project no more than four inches beyond the shop front (compared with two and a half feet in the City).

1587	Mary, Queen of Scots, is executed.
1588	After the defeat of the Spanish Armada, eleven captured banners are exhibited on the Great Stone Gate, having being exhibited in St Paul's the previous day.
1591	Corn mills are erected at the Southwark end of the Bridge.

c. 1600: Third Stage of Old London Bridge

c. **1600**	Van den Wyngaerde's view from the south-east (1594), and John Norden's view of the east side (1624) of the Bridge appear, as does the view from the west side now in the Pepysian Collection, Magdalene College, Cambridge.
1603	Queen Elizabeth dies. James VI of Scotland also becomes James I of England.
1605	After the Gunpowder Plot is exposed, the heads of Guy Fawkes and others end up on the Bridge.
1609–13	Sir Hugh Myddelton constructs the New River to bring fresh water to London.
1616	Claes Jansz Visscher's famous *Long Prospect of London*, including the Bridge from the south-west, is published.
1620	Boatmen are not allowed to tie their boats to the piers or to harm any part of the structure, hinder the passageway or remove any of the filling of the piers.
1625	Charles I (1625–49) becomes king, and brings his bride, Henrietta Maria, to London in a water procession.
c. **1631**	Hackney carriages are introduced, increasing traffic on the Bridge.
1633	On 11 February, fire at the City end destroys a third of the forty-three houses on the Bridge. Afterwards, the street is widened and fencing is placed along each side for safety.
1637	Artist Wenceslaus Hollar arrives in England.
1639	One house on the east side at the City end is rebuilt.

1641	On 6 July, the royal barge of Queen Henrietta Maria overturns while 'shooting the Bridge', and Mrs Kirke, the Queen's Lady of the Bedchamber, drowns.
1642	Charles fails to evict five members of Parliament from the council chamber. Alarmed by the crowds, he abandons London. Civil War begins.
1642–9	Civil War.
1645–51	A new block is built at the City end to replace the houses destroyed by the fire of 1633.
1647	The gates of London Bridge are opened to Fairfax and the New Model Army; they march over the Bridge into London, and peacefully back out.
	Wenceslaus Hollar's *Panorama of London*, depicting City and Bridge after the 1633 fire and before the 1666 fire, is published.
1648–1762	Illegal tradesmen's tokens are used in place of currency, a source of information about tradesmen.
1649	Charles I is tried and executed.

1651–66: Fourth Stage of Old London Bridge

1649-60	Rule of Cromwell (d. 1658) and the Commonwealth.
1651	Houses on the Bridge finally completed, replacing those destroyed in the fire of 1633.
1653–8	The period of the Protectorate when Oliver Cromwell holds the title of Lord Protector.
1660	In May there is a great reception for Charles II on the Restoration of the monarchy.
	Samuel Pepys begins his Diary (1660–9).
1665	The plague is in London; by September deaths peak at 10,000 a week.
1666	The Great Fire of London breaks out on 1–2 September, consuming the new block on the Bridge at the City end, as well as the waterwheels. One-third of the buildings are gone. The City is devastated. Within three months Hollar produces *London Before and After the Great Fire*.
1667	Act empowers rebuilding of the City, including waterwheels in two arches at the Bridge.

1676	Serious fire in Southwark.
1678	The last head, that of William Stayley, appears on the Bridge.
1683	Houses are rebuilt at the City end, replacing those burned down in the Great Fire.
1683–4	A famous frost fair is held on the frozen Thames by the Bridge. The fair is visited by Charles II.
1689–1702	Protestants William and Mary rule jointly.
1696	Peter Monamy is apprenticed to a sign- and house-painter on the Bridge; by 1710 he becomes a well-known marine artist.
1701	The Waterworks are granted a lease on a fourth arch from the City end for another wheel. Morris's descendants sell the business and the leases to Richard Soame, a goldsmith, who sells shares and has the pumping machinery redesigned.
1709	St Magnus clock erected.

c. 1710: Fifth Stage of Old London Bridge

c. 1710	Sutton Nicholls' engraving is published depicting two views: the west and east sides of the Bridge; almost all of the buildings are in the new Restoration style. The width of the bridge street is increased to twenty feet.
1722	In a landmark attempt to regulate the traffic on the Bridge, the Lord Mayor orders all vehicles to 'keep to the left'. Drawbridge repaired.
1725	On 8 September, fire destroys all the houses over the first two arches on the east side at the Southwark end; the Great Stone Gate and some houses are burned.

1727–58: Sixth Stage of Old London Bridge

1727–8	The Great Stone Gate, damaged by the fire of 1725, is demolished. New Gate is built eighteen feet wide.
1729	Putney Bridge opens.
1733–66:	The Fleet River is covered over.
1739–40	On 25 December, severe frost sets in, lasting until

February. A frost fair is held, but in January when the ice suddenly begins to thaw people flee, leaving their 'shops' and belongings on the ice; the river refreezes and thaws again: Bridge damaged.

1745–7   A severe-looking block of ten houses, the Piazza, designed by George Dance the Elder is erected on the east side at the northern (City) end of the Bridge.

1749   An engraving of the Bridge by Samuel and Nathaniel Buck is published.

1750   Westminster Bridge is fully open, and is a serious rival to Old London Bridge.

1751–9   Stationers Wright & Gill occupy what remains of the Chapel, now called the Chapel House; the paper stored in the undercroft, below high-water level, remains as dry as if it were in a garret.

1756   On 25 June an Act of Parliament is passed authorizing the removal of all the houses and the widening of the Bridge. Tolls are imposed to defray the demolition costs.

1757–61   The demolition of the houses on the Bridge takes place.

1757   To assist the workmen, a temporary wooden bridge is constructed alongside the stone Bridge on the west side. Access is from each end of the stone Bridge.

1758   On 11 April, the temporary wooden bridge burns down, probably due to arson. A way over the Bridge is constructed by 19 April, and by 18 October the temporary wooden bridge is fully open again for pedestrians and vehicles, the structure guarded by watchmen.

1759   In July, the Great Arch is formed by removing a pier near the centre of the Bridge. The platform of the Bridge is widened to forty-six feet with a balustraded parapet and domed stone alcoves. But the arch lessens the power of the Waterworks, and changes the water flow, undermining the structure. Stone from the just demolished gateways of the City is bought back and dumped around the piers.

c. 1760   Tradesmen's cards or handbills are introduced, advertising shopkeepers' wares and so giving detailed information about shops on the Bridge.

1760	The Great Stone Gate is demolished.
	The Great Arch is found by Smeaton to have been weakened, as a result of the altered river currents.
	St Magnus is damaged by fire.
1761	The third arch from the City end is leased to London Bridge Waterworks to carry water through wooden pipes on the Bridge to Southwark.
	By law, all hanging shop signs are removed from the remaining shops on the Bridge. The Bear tavern is demolished.

1762–1831: Seventh and Final Stage of Old London Bridge

1762	The last tenancy on the Bridge expires. All the remaining houses and shops have been pulled down, and the Bridge widened. Projecting shop signs are banned; street numbering is introduced by law.
1763	A footway on to the Bridge at the City end is created by opening up the archways in the tower of St Magnus.
	All work is completed on the Bridge, which now has a vastly different appearance.
	In a severe frost, all arches are blocked with ice except the Great Arch; the force of the water through it damages the Bridge.
1765	The Waterworks lease the fifth arch at the City end. Smeaton recommends two waterwheels at the Southwark end; the two arches are blocked and the waterwheels installed upstream under a huge shed.
1767	The first and second arches at the Southwark end are blocked and prepared to receive waterwheels to supply water to Southwark.
1769	Blackfriars Bridge opens.
1772	Battersea Bridge opens.
1775–83	American War of Independence.
1779	The Waterworks at the City end burn to the ground.
1780	Gordon Riots occur.
1782	On 27 March, tolls on the Bridge are abolished, and traffic increases accordingly.
1785	In a severe winter, the frost lasts 115 days.

1789	In a hard winter boiling water is poured over the water-wheels to keep them working; each day twenty-five horses pull the ice away from the Bridge.
1799	Old London Bridge is accurately measured for the first time by George Dance the Younger.
1800	Proposals for a new bridge are put forward, but no progress is made.
1801	*The Third Report from the Select Committee upon the Improvement of the Port of London* is published.
1813–14	The last frost fair is held on the Thames at London; the Bridge is damaged by the ice.
1816	Vauxhall Bridge, between Chelsea and Lambeth bridges, opens.
1817	One wooden wheel of the Waterworks is removed, and an iron wheel substituted.
	Rennie's Waterloo Bridge, between Westminster and Blackfriars bridges, opens.
1819	Rennie's three-arched cast-iron Southwark Bridge, between Blackfriars and London bridges, opens.
1820–30	George IV reigns.
1821	A Committee for a new bridge is set up, and prizes are offered for best design. The results of the competition are ignored and a committee of the House of Commons selects John Rennie senior's design.
1822	An act is passed ordering the removal of the water-wheels, which are a danger to navigation.
1823	On 4 July, Royal Assent is given to 'An Act for the Rebuilding London Bridge and for the improving and making suitable Approaches thereto'.
1824	On 15 March, the first pile of new London Bridge (Rennie's bridge) is driven in.
1825	On 15 June, following a grand procession, the foundation stone of Rennie's bridge is laid in the presence of the Duke of York, brother of George IV.
1826	To ease the water traffic and dangerous currents around the pier, two more arches (the fifth pier) of the old Bridge are made into one with a temporary wooden arch.

1827	On 4 August, the first arch (land arch on the Southwark side) of Rennie's London Bridge is completed.
	The eighth pier of the old Bridge is removed and a temporary wooden arch inserted.
1829	An Act of Parliament is passed for the necessary demolition and the construction of the approach roads to Rennie's London Bridge.
1830–7	William IV is on the throne.
1831	On 1 August Rennie's London Bridge is officially opened by William IV and Queen Adelaide.
	The demolition of Old London Bridge begins.
1832	The tomb of priest-architect Peter de Colechurch is discovered within the foundations of Old London Bridge as it is being deconstructed; there is no record of what happened to his remains.
	The Common Council awards £3,000 to tradesmen whose businesses have been harmed by the altered approaches to the old Bridge.
	Evidence of the Roman London Bridge emerges during deconstruction.
1858	Chelsea Bridge, between Battersea and Vauxhall bridges, opens.
1873	Albert Bridge, between Battersea and Chelsea bridges, opens.
1879	Lambeth Bridge, between Vauxhall and Westminster bridges, opens.
1894	Tower Bridge, downstream from London Bridge, opens.
1902–4	Rennie's London Bridge is widened.
1921	On the north bank, workmen uncover the second arch of Old London Bridge, comprising one of Peter de Colechurch's original Gothic arches, flanked by arches added in 1758; it is demolished in spite of a campaign to save it.
1967	The London Bridge Act empowers the Corporation of the City of London to demolish Rennie's bridge and build a new London Bridge.
1967–73	The present London Bridge is built.
1968	Rennie's London Bridge is sold by the Corporation of

London to the McCulloch Oil Corporation. It is dismantled, thousands of stones numbered, and shipped to Lake Havasu City in western Arizona; the foundation stone is ceremoniously laid.

1971   Rennie's bridge is officially opened for the second time in its life at Lake Havasu City, where it is a tourist attraction.

1973   Today's London Bridge is officially dedicated by Queen Elizabeth II.

Index

Index